STANDING ON THE SHOULDERS OF GIANTS

STANDING ON THE SHOULDERS OF GIANTS

SØREN FRANK

B L O O M S B U R Y

LONDON • NEW DELHI • NEW YORK • SYDNEY

Published by Bloomsbury Publishing Plc
50 Bedford Square
London WC1B 3DP
www.bloomsbury.com

First published in Danish in 2008 by People'sPress/ArtPeople

ISBN (print): 978 1 408 1 87425
ISBN (e-pub): 978 1 408 1 87432

Acknowledgements
Cover photograph © Getty Images
Inside photographs © All images © Getty Images with the exception of the following:
pp 156–157, 186–187 and 237 © Press Association Images
Illustrations by Saxon Graphics Ltd
Commissioned by Kirsty Schaper
Edited by Sarah Cole
Translated by Grahame Anderson
Designed by James Watson
Typeset by Saxon Graphics Ltd, Derby

Typeset in 11.5 on 13 Tibrere by Saxon Graphics Ltd, Derby
Printed and bound in Great Britain by CPI Group (UK) Ltd, Croydon, CR0 4YY

10 9 8 7 6 5 4 3 2 1

FOR SEPP

'He knew how to be so generously encouraging
as to make a scrupulous man hesitate on the brink of confidence;
but if I did hesitate it was not for long.'
Joseph Conrad: *Lord Jim*

Contents

Introduction

The year is 1999. Millions of Europeans, except the English and the Danish, decide the time has come to convert their national currency units into the pan-European euro. NATO is bombing targets in Yugoslavia and thereby bringing an end to the war in Kosovo. The American director Stanley Kubrick dies this year and in Stockholm, Günter Grass receives the Nobel Prize for literature. The whole world is impressed by the Wachowskis' movie *The Matrix* and in Russia, on the last day of the year, Boris Yeltsin is replaced by Vladimir Putin.

But 1999 is first and foremost the year of earthquakes. It is a year during which the earth is hit by a series of massive, yet independent, earthquakes. I experience one myself in Puebla, Mexico, when 'El Popo', the volcano Popocatepetl, on an otherwise calm and unassuming night, makes the surrounding region tremble. The earth is saying goodbye to the old millennium, and the doom merchants interpret the tremors as signs indicating it has no intention of saying hello to a new one. As we all know, the apocalypse never materialised, but the fact remains that 1999 was marked by powerful seismic trembling – also in the world of football.

On the evening of 14 April, Arsenal's Patrick Vieira passes the ball across the pitch. We are at Villa Park in Birmingham, and the match is an FA Cup semi-final replay. The opposition are their arch-rivals from Manchester United, who are chasing a historical Treble. The score is 1–1, and the match has gone into extra time. Manchester United are down to ten men as their captain, Roy Keane, has been dismissed after an hour's play because of a characteristically ruthless tackle, some would say assault, on Marc Overmars. That the Red Devils have made it into extra time at all is thanks to Peter Schmeichel. In the dying seconds of regular time the big Dane phenomenally saved a powerful and well-placed penalty from Arsenal's Dennis Bergkamp.

But let us return to Vieira's lateral pass. I don't think he has forgotten it because it doesn't reach one of the red-shirted players from Arsenal. Instead, it ends up at the feet of the white-dressed Ryan Giggs. This proves to be fatal for Arsenal. But it is a gift to Manchester United and their millions of fans. Also millions of 'colour blind' football enthusiasts are grateful to Vieira. Ryan Giggs's goal – this evening at Villa Park in Birmingham, and after a fantastic solo run – becomes the epicentre of a seismic tremor, the strength of which the world of football has never seen before. When Ryan Giggs unexpectedly receives the ball from Patrick Vieira he is ten metres into his own half. Together with Dwight

Yorke he is leading the attacking line of a Manchester United team concentrating solely on surviving until the penalty shoot-out. However, the young Welsh king of dribbling doesn't give a damn about risk minimisation and cynical catenaccio. He is, on the contrary, possessed by the devil of opportunism. It is red, by the way.

In his trademark sliding run Ryan Giggs makes for David Seaman's goal sixty-five metres further up the field. However, his intention is only grasped slowly by the spectators as the distance becomes shorter and shorter. Maybe Giggs only realises it little by little, too. In fact, it is doubtful if we can even use the word 'intention' in relation to Giggs's run. More likely, it is as if his consciousness is forced to retreat in order for his instinct to take control. This is also what seems to be the essence of Alex Ferguson's assessment of the goal in the *Sunday Times* four days after the match: 'The part of Ryan Giggs that made that goal is something I could never have put into him. It is uncoachable. What we saw was the ultimate expression of the incredible natural gifts he has always had since the day he came to us as a thirteen-year-old.'

The first player who attempts to act as an obstacle to the sliding Giggs is the same Vieira who, seconds before, had given away the ball to the Welshman. His attempt seems only half-hearted, though, because Giggs slides past him rather easily. The physically imposing Frenchman quite simply never gets close enough to the evasive Welsh winger. It is like watching two positive magnetic poles drawing closer to each other: at one point they are repelled by one another and thus never touch. In the following moment Giggs, with his slalom movements, paralyses Lee Dixon and once again Vieira, only to subsequently wedge himself in between Dixon, who has temporarily returned, and Martin Keown, who is left wriggling on the ground. Suddenly, Giggs is face to face with David Seaman, Arsenal's d'Artagnan-looking keeper. Maybe Giggs himself is a little surprised at being there. If he is, he certainly doesn't show it. Giggs's instinct coolly finishes the job as he, from his position a little to the left of the goal area and six metres from the goal, cannons the ball diagonally into the top of the net in spectacular fashion. This gives no chance to either Seaman or Tony Adams, who in a last and desperate attempt throws himself on the ground in order to block the shot. Arsenal's players are flabbergasted while United's are ecstatic. Against all odds, Giggs has turned the game around.

And yes, the world of football suddenly changes its course. From that moment, the moment when the ball makes the back of the net bulge, it is as if Manchester United are predestined to fulfil the dream of the Treble. From then on nothing can stop the Red Devils. The tremors emanating from Giggs's stunning goal this April evening in Birmingham spread to Manchester United's team in Barcelona six weeks later. With the clock showing ninety minutes and thirty-five seconds, and Bayern Munich leading one goal to nil, they score two goals in stoppage time. This wins them the most prestigious European club tournament for the first time since 1968.

There are those who believe Giggs's goal against Arsenal is the best goal ever in the history of Manchester United. The goal is without question symptomatic of a season in which Ryan Giggs's brilliant solo run sends seismic shock waves through the world of football, but in which Manchester United also make the world tremble because of their fantasy football, their goals galore, and their historical Treble triumph.

*   *   *

As the description of Ryan Giggs's earthquake-catalysing deed suggests, this book is written by two writers: one has seized control of my left hand and is writing with the driving force of a fan's fascination. The other has seized control of my right hand and is writing with the analytical gaze of the intellectual. I welcome this duality as it is my hope they will jointly contribute to the story of Manchester United in such a way that fascination and comprehension complement each other. Hence, I do not in any way pretend this book is a neutral, 'objective' narrative of a football club's triumphs and tragedies. Rather, the book should be considered a tribute to the game of football in general, but especially a tribute to the football philosophy and symbolic values we have come to associate with Manchester United.

This dimension of praise is then complemented by a more critical (understood as analytical) endeavour designed to situate the club in a broader cultural-historical and football aesthetic context and to nuance and problematise some of the symbolic values the club exploits in the aggressive marketing of itself as an exclusive, global mega-brand.

How can we explain Manchester United's global magnetism? On a general level, it is a result of a precarious balance between tradition, myth, and continuity on the one hand, and renewal, transformation, and rupture on the other (cf. Wagg). In other words, Manchester United have maintained a sort of core identity despite the club's extensive growth and several close-to-annihilation incidents during its 135-year history. In a globalised world, where everything solid seems to dissolve into liquid and metamorphic form, and where traditional markers of identity such as 'the near', 'the local', and 'historical consciousness' are undergoing considerable changes, Manchester United seem to have satisfied both their multinational business partners and their fans. And the club also seems to have found a balance between local and global fans, and between older and younger fans. Admittedly we do hear critical voices from certain fan factions from time to time, especially concerning the club's commercial strategies and the ensuing mutations of the club's 'soul' and its fan base. This book does not attempt to silence this criticism with praise. The point is, however, that at the end of the day Manchester United continues to expand their fan base and win trophies, and they do it in a way that, essentially, remains faithful to the club's traditions.

As an overall explanation of Manchester United's magnetic force, the idea of balance also applies to the club's football philosophy as it unites the prosaic and the poetic. Historically speaking, Manchester United's style is a hybrid between classic English components (realism, hard work, speed, linearity) and Celtic virtues (romance, passion, virtuosity). In recent years this mixture has been infused with impulses from the Brazilian–Portuguese style (passing style, explosions, play, digressions). If Manchester United were a movie, they would be a cross between the social realism of Tony Richardson's *A Taste of Honey* (1961), the post-modernism of Danny Boyle's *Trainspotting* (1996), and the poetry of Marcel Camus's *Orfeu Negro* (1959) – with a touch of James Bond.

Apart from balance as an overall reason for the club's power of attraction, there are four specific reasons behind its magnetism. These four reasons simultaneously represent the four columns making up the Manchester United brand (cf. Rosaaen and Amis). First, it is a club tradition to be committed to free-flowing and attack-oriented football. It is Matt Busby who introduces this philosophy when he is appointed as manager in 1945, and it constitutes a red thread in the club's self-image up until today. Tommy Docherty, Ron Atkinson, and Alex Ferguson all commit themselves to this philosophical heritage from Busby. But in a way, this tradition was already anticipated successfully by Ernest Mangnall between 1903 and 1912, and less successfully by Herbert Bamlett in the late 1920s. Winning is important, but Manchester United are obliged to win in style. In other words, the ends and the means are both essential.

With concepts from Ancient Greece we can characterise Manchester United's footballing philosophy as a mixture of *agon* (rivalry) and *arête* (excellence). The agonistic element is what we traditionally associate with sport. It is the element of competition where it is all about winning within institutionally determined frameworks. With *arête* and its connotations of skill, excellence, courage, and beauty, the agonistic element is supplemented with an aesthetic dimension. *Arête* implies the individual's or the collective's efforts to perfect its skills, and the consequence is one becomes capable of lifting one's performance to its highest limits. It is possible to imagine *agon* without *arête* (two amateur teams that only meet once a week for a match is an example of this), but it is impossible to imagine *arête* without *agon* (the very striving to improve one's skills is always either a competition against oneself or against others whether these others are physically present or absent). When *agon* and *arête* coexist, the player is urged 'to go further, to go where nobody has ever gone before,' claims Hans Ulrich Gumbrecht in his classical book on sport, *In Praise of Athletic Beauty* (2006). We do not know if Alex Ferguson has read Gumbrecht's book, but the Scot nonetheless tellingly repeats Gumbrecht's idea in an interview in the *Sun* on 25 October 2007 in which he emphasises Manchester United's aretic ambitions: 'That's the United way. Never standing still, always striving for higher and higher standards.'

It is precisely because of the fundamentally noble intention of beauty and improvement of skills, which *arête* implies, that I can shamelessly admit this book is a tribute. Like many other of the world's great football clubs, Manchester United have had teams that have lifted the game of football into yet unknown spheres of beauty and players who have demonstrated skills (technical and physical, offensive and defensive) on an artistic–athletic level, which no one had ever seen before. As Pat Crerand, one of the legends from 1968, once remarked about Manchester United's championship drought of 1967–1993: 'We played twenty-six years without winning the title, but still we were the most famous club in the country – by far . . . There exists an aura surrounding United because of the way we play the game.' Crerand's words about aura and style point back to *arête* and the courage demanded by the players who represent Manchester United.

The second reason behind Manchester United's magnetism is that one associates the club with youthful energy and radiance in that it consistently rates young players, many of whom are home-grown and of British heritage. This image can also be traced back to Matt Busby and his legendary Busby Babes in the 1950s. But the tradition continued with players like George Best, Nobby Stiles, Brian Kidd, Sammy McIlroy, Norman Whiteside, Ryan Giggs, Gary Neville, Wayne Rooney and Danny Welbeck. No other British club has managed to develop so many young British players with such great football skills.

In regard to the focus on youth, the concept and phenomenon of continuity have a double relevance. First, the youth policy is a tradition that stretches itself as a red thread throughout the club's history. Second, the commitment to young players means many of these players often achieve long careers and thus – like red micro threads – make up part of the main red thread. Moreover, continuity does not merely relate to players, but also to managers. Matt Busby was manager of Manchester United for twenty-five years, and Alex Ferguson, who was appointed in 1986, has overtaken his record. This is quite simply unique among European mega clubs.

The third fascination factor has to do with the club's close connection to glamour and pop culture. As early as the beginning of the twentieth century, the legendary Billy Meredith was a media star, but it is not until the Busby Babes in the mid-1950s Manchester United's pop-culture image begins to consolidate itself. It is a tragic event that truly catapults the club into the realm of mythology and mass media, though: the Munich air crash in 1958, in which eight of the Babes die. The accident is inscribed in the long series of world historical events in which the combination of youth, unresolved potential and death generates mythology. 'Munich' quite simply transforms Manchester United from a local to a global phenomenon, and ever since the Munich air crash the club has been surrounded by a special mystique that distinguishes it from all other clubs.

Later on, it is players like George Best, Eric Cantona, David Beckham and Cristiano Ronaldo, but also managers like Tommy Docherty and Ron Atkinson, who keep the bonfire of glamour burning. If the first two components in the club's image (attacking football and youth) by and large represent continuity and tradition, the third component (pop culture) represents continuity as well as a massive transformation in the history of Manchester United. The media attention and the link to popular culture may be a constant component in the club's history, but with the transition from the down-to-earth Babes of the 1950s to the pop-iconic Best in the 1960s a small revolution takes place regarding the extent and volume of media attention. This also includes the symbolic meanings of players and club. During the 1990s we witness yet another alteration with the emergence of a player like David Beckham, whose off-field value exceeds his on-field value. Some critics claim that Beckham's image is, in fact, more valuable to the club that owns him than is his performance on the field.

The last and fourth element contributing to Manchester United's global magnetism consists of the club's aggressive marketing of itself as an exclusive transnational brand. This happens through commercial deals with, for example, Nike, Audi and Pepsi, the creation of the club's own TV channel, the launching of the concept of the 'Theatre of Dreams', and the opening of restaurants and mega-stores around the world. Obviously, the marketing of the club incorporates the three previous components of the attacking football philosophy, the commitment to young players, and the pop cultural glamour. These are all crucial parts in the construction of Manchester United as a unique and global mega-brand. The aggressive marketing is a relatively new phenomenon in the history of the club that is only launched for real in the 1990s, but since the PR strategy both exploits and consolidates the myths and traditions as symbolic values with the sole purpose of branding the club as unique, the marketing is not just a sign of the club's transformation from its humble working-class origins to the world's richest club. Through aggressive marketing, transformation and tradition are united: the strategy is new, but the message is old. The effort to contain new fan territory and expand on the global scene happens through the media's comprehensive and the PR machine's determined mythologising of and emphasis on the club's traditions.

* * *

The remaining part of the introduction is about why the book is organised as it is. Readers who are not interested in the book's formal and compositional aspects can proceed to the next chapter. Those readers who take pleasure in meta-reflective thoughts on the relationship between form, meaning and content can read on.

The book is built around three stylistically different tracks: (1) A cultural-historical track, which outlines the club's development from humble working-class club to global mega-brand, and also discusses the symbolic and mythological values linked to the club. (2) An aesthetic track, which closes in on some of the legendary matches and players in the club's history, with the purpose of describing seductive playing patterns and moments of joyful beauty. (3) An informative cataloguing track, where more factual information, such as results, records and the number of trophies are communicated. The three tracks seldom exist in pure form, but cross each other's paths and mix in each of the book's chapters.

But in addition to these three tracks, how else is the book organised? The Romanian poet Paul Celan, once said every poem is '*datierbar*' (i.e. it is possible to date). This idea also lies behind this book's structuring principle in that I have chosen to organise the book as a series of chapters that all bear a date as their title. The reason behind this structure is the idea that a story of Manchester United must be historical in a radical sense. This means Manchester United's story is told by taking as starting points a series of dateable (and thus singular and unique) events on and off the pitch around which a network of interesting meanings and connections crystallises.

The dates in the book's chapter titles are also meant to emphasise the dimension of the here-and-now. Whether you are a player or spectator, football is a sport whose fascination factor has less to do with the pleasure of (involuntarily) re-experiencing the lost moments of the past than with the sporting event's capacity to provoke an experience of being intensely present in the here-and-now. If we were in the world of literature, we would say the sporting experience is more James Joyce than Marcel Proust. The fascination furthermore has something to do with the irreplaceability and fleeting nature of the event. We are witnesses to a number of bodies and a ball that creates patterns, which dissolve in the same second they are complete, never to be seen again. This is football's epiphanic quality, its nature of profane revelation, but also its inherent melancholy.

In more traditional books on Manchester United, the individual events in the club's history are considered as episodes that are illustrative of a larger cohesive (Aristotelian) tale with a natural beginning, a necessary middle and a logical conclusion. The event these tales has chosen to focus on has the aim of emphasising what leads A to B and then C. We are left with the feeling that nothing could be more obvious than Manchester United in 2013 being one of the world's largest and most successful football clubs. *Standing on the Shoulders of Giants* insists that an event might just as well be coincidence; that it can also be a fatal rupture of the otherwise continuous history. However, the fact that Manchester United in its long history has repeatedly balanced on the edge of anonymity and extermination, and that coincidence has also played a leading role in the United drama only adds to people's fascination with the club.

When it comes to coincidences, the St Bernard dog Major, for example, is at least as prominent as Martin Edwards in this book. The former embodies the anecdotal and the random coincidence, while the latter represents the well documented and the purposive. Another example: the purchase of the Dutch attacker Ruud van Nistelrooy can be said to be the result of a purposeful multi-year hunt. But this book also sees a random telephone conversation between Howard Wilkinson and Alex Ferguson as the event catalysing Manchester United's dominance from the beginning of the 1990s right up to the present. Intention and coincidence, rupture and continuity: they all play an equal role in the history of Manchester United.

Yet another final consequence of my insisting that the event does not necessarily need to be seen as a nearly invisible component in a teleological chronology is that it doesn't lose its potential to connect to other events across time. In other words there are sections in this book in which the simultaneous replaces the sequential and in which the cataloguing and paraphrasing will be toned down in favour of the ability of the anecdote and coincidence to either highlight the incoherent or make the unseen coherences visible. Admittedly, on a macro-level the book is built up chronologically, but each chapter is more or less a valid entrance offering many interrelated stories of the club across time and space.

One example: It was hardly 'written on high', as Diderot's fatalist liked to say, that Matt Busby was to be born on 26 May 1909. It is a coincidence that the Champions League final in 1999 was played on 26 May, and thus that Busby would have turned ninety that evening. Through the strange convergence of these two coincidences, a symmetry of almost quasi-religious dimensions occurs, something which Alex Ferguson only contributes to with his eyeing the sky as the final whistle sounds as Manchester United has miraculously turned 0–1 to 2–1 in stoppage time. However, the constellation of 1) Busby would have turned ninety, 2) The Champions League trophy is won and 3) Ferguson's upturned eyes resonates even deeper when you add historical components such as 4) the decimation of The Busby Babes on their quest for European glory and 5) Busby's subsequent ten year hunt for 'the holy grail', culminating at Wembley on a warm evening in May 1968. Such constellations where random events simultaneously come together across time is the metaphysics of the God-forsaken world of football – and Manchester United's history is full of them.

The example shows how memories (Proust) can still play a vital role in our experience of contemporary events (Joyce). Although the fascination about football first and foremost has to do with the intensity that occurs in the experience of a focused here-and-now, memory can definitely play a role (even though secondary), where past and present can resonate in a very enjoyable manner. When we experience a new event, we occasionally hear echoes from the past knocking on memory's doors. As Gumbrecht notes in *In Praise of Athletic Beauty*, memory thereby contributes to make contemporary events more intense, complex, and polyphonic. On the other hand, these contemporary events can help recharge our memory when those same memories had become a little blurred, or even totally erased.

Standing on the Shoulders of Giants has the same dual ambition: to (re)charge the reader's memory in connection with Manchester United's history and, at the same time, to show the richness of contemporary events through the narration of this history.

Newton Heath and the difficult beginning

Births are rarely unproblematic or glorious. All things are difficult before they are easy. This was the case with Manchester United's early history, which in many ways reflects the journey of the ugly duckling, its troubles and travails, before it finally turns into a beautiful swan. This is the story of Newton Heath LYR FC and how, after a bankruptcy in the early 1900s, having been close to becoming Manchester Celtic or Manchester Central, they eventually transformed into Manchester United. It is also the story of a club where the players got changed in the local pubs before they set out to play their home games at lumpy and muddy tracks, greenish in colour not from grass but from the chemicals leaking out from neighbouring factories. Finally, it is the story of how yellow and green colours became the characteristic red and white strip that is so closely associated with the club today.

The year is 1878; the place is Manchester. Thirty-four years earlier, a young Friedrich Engels was coming to the end of his two-year stay in the city. He was in Manchester to investigate the working conditions for what would result in his famous work, *Die Lage der arbeitenden Klasse in England*, published in 1845. As the title suggests, the book deals with the working class's conditions in Victorian England. He chose to analyse Manchester because the city was the cradle of industrialisation. Engels returned to live in Manchester again and if you visit the breath-taking Chetham's Library in the centre of the city's late medieval district near Manchester Cathedral, you can even get to sit at the table (by the window in the Reading Room) where Engels, along with Karl Marx, wrote parts of *The Communist Manifesto*, which appeared in the revolutionary year 1848.

In nineteenth-century Manchester, often given the nickname 'Cottonopolis', textiles were produced and cotton was spun, and in the 1840s Manchester was the heart of the industrial revolution, which started to pick up speed in the second half of the 1800s. The city's landmarks were the smoking chimneys and the soot-black façades, seen in William Wyld's painting *A View of Manchester from Kersal Moor* in 1852 or in L.S. Lowry's *Industrial Scene*, painted a century later. From 'one of the greatest mere villages in *England*', as Daniel Defoe sarcastically wrote in *A tour thro' the Whole Island of Great Britain* (1724–26), Manchester turned into a metropolis of invaluable economic importance to England and its imperialist ambitions. Of particular importance to this book is the fact that the city played a prominent part in the early days of the railway industry from which Manchester United would emerge.

During this time, Manchester was the world's industrial and capitalist centre. The place was an El Dorado, where anything seemed possible. As a 'Mancunian' you were constantly confronted with new industrial processes, new ways of thinking, new religious sects and new ways to organise work. Formidable changes occurred as industrialisation led to Manchester's population growing explosively in the 1840s as a result of massive immigration. Most came 'to serve under the chimney'. Thousands of English peasants and workers walked away from the surrounding Lancashire farms and villages, and made their way to Manchester. Poor people crossed the Irish Sea, and Scots fled from the slums of Glasgow and Edinburgh or from the harsh life in the Highlands and flocked to the city. More settlers arrived from the continent: Jews fleeing from religious persecution; Greeks and Italians escaping from national unrest; and many German businessmen from the Hanseatic towns were attracted by the possibilities of earning good money.

Throughout the remaining years of the nineteenth century the German and Jewish influence was stronger in Manchester than in any other European city: 'Manchester is an immigrant city, and for a hundred and fifty years, leaving aside the poor Irish, the immigrants were chiefly Germans and Jews, manual workers, tradesmen, freelancers, retailers and wholesalers, watchmakers, hatters, cabinet-makers, umbrella makers, tailors, bookbinders, typesetters, silversmiths, photographers, furriers and glovers, scrap merchants, hawkers, pawnbrokers, auctioneers, jewellers, estate agents, stockbrokers, chemists and doctors.' The quote is from the German-Jewish author W. G. Sebald's novel *The Emigrants* (1993) whose fourth part, 'Max Ferber', is about Manchester and the city's German-Jewish connection.

In the 1830s and 1840s the exploitation of the working class was at its highest. The wealthy factory owners sought refuge outside the city, where they built their large houses in idyllic surroundings far away from the appalling conditions that their plants created in the big city. They settled in places such as Alderley Edge and Wilmslow in Cheshire, which even these days attracts the rich and the famous. The workers, however, were tied to the city, where disease and epidemics raged, where extremely long working days affected people's health, and where women and children, as the most natural thing in the world, were also used as labour in the factories. It is a clear evidence of Manchester's magnetism and its status as a pioneering city in the industrial revolution that the city during this period began to appear regularly in English literature. In both Elizabeth Gaskell's *Mary Barton* (1848) and in Charles Dickens' *Hard Times* (1854) we find empathic descriptions of the worker's miserable living conditions in Manchester.

*   *   *

In 1878, the year when Newton Heath LYR FC was formed, working-class conditions had improved in several areas. Ten years earlier the city had hosted the first labour union congress, a huge move forward in industrial relations history in the last decades of the nineteenth century. The last quarter of the nineteenth century marked a golden period in Manchester's history that was defined by large-scale projects like the Manchester ship canal and the development of the railways. This framework contributed to the city maintaining its industrial lead, just as industrialisation brought into being the cosmopolitan atmosphere and vibrant cultural life, which was now very much a part of the city.

Existentially, a very important consequence of industrialisation was the strict organisation and disciplining of people's time. Factories in the early phase of the industrial revolution had required up to eighteen working hours a day, six days a week from their workers. But more efficient machinery and, importantly, the emergence of trade unions resulted in fewer hours per day for the worker. Now workers not only had Sunday, but also Saturday off. Where traditionally Sunday was devoted to religious and domestic duties, Saturday was freely available. One of the most significant cultural-historical consequences was the emergence of the concepts of 'leisure' and 'weekend', and these phenomena, established at the end of the nineteenth century in England, still have an enormous impact on our way of thinking and organising time.

But what has all this to do with Manchester United? This cultural-historical background is significant for two reasons. First, the workers' newly won leisure time led indirectly to the formation of the world's largest and most famous football club and the start of its glorious history. In 1878 a group of workers from a depot owned by Lancashire & Yorkshire Railway (LYR) decided to start a football club. They had to find something with which to fill their time on a Saturday afternoon, so why not football? Second, the new concept of the weekend, an essential prerequisite for the modern entertainment industry, became firmly established in the late 1800s because workers channelled their pay into leisure activities. Besides weekend excursions to the beach, you could also spend Saturdays as a spectator at a football stadium, and Manchester was a football city from day one. In 1851, a survey showed that out of the 400,000 inhabitants of Manchester, 220,000 weren't born in the city. More than half of the city's population came from somewhere else. For the many thousands of descendants of Irish and Scottish immigrants, for those whose families had moved from country to city, for those who were uncertain of who and what they were because they'd cut themselves from their roots in order to survive, for all those people, football, according to Eamon Dunphy, offered a unique opportunity to create a new community and a new shared identity.

The workers' leisure time made both playing football and watching it possible. Those who were not selected for the team were spectators. Newton Heath LYR thus represents a typical example of the way in which accelerating urbanisation and industrialisation processes contributed to the physical, spatial and temporal disciplining of the workers' leisure time at the end of 1800s. There was thus a close connection between Manchester United, industrialisation and the working classes.

The cultural-historical background is also essential on a more general level than the previous one, mainly because this background, with the focus on the working-class, not only relates to Newton Heath's birth as a working-class club with working-class supporters, but also points forward to Manchester United in the twentieth and twenty-first centuries. The club is still largely dominated by its roots in the working class, and this is an example of the continuity and awareness of its traditions, which despite the many turbulent periods and unpredictable events characterise the history of Manchester United.

When Peter Schmeichel in *The Great Peter* (1999) several times emphasised the humility that is generally characteristic of Manchester United's players, we must remember this is not just a random characteristic. Rather, it is a club code, which bears witness to the legacy of an Anglo-Saxon working-class tradition, where concepts such as loyalty, diligence and humility are key. Another example supporting the practice of maintaining the club's roots in the working class is the fact the club has a policy to focus on homegrown players who have been through the club's youth academy. These are often local boys from Manchester and Lancashire's working homes (today, perhaps, rather middle-class homes), where the above virtues also apply. Just think of players like Nicky Butt, Wes Brown and Danny Welbeck in recent times, or Roger Byrne, Eddie Colman and Brian Kidd back in the 1950s and 1960s.

Of course there are counter-examples. Humility is perhaps not exactly the first thing you think about in connection with the aristocratic Frenchman Eric Cantona or Portuguese wonderboy Cristiano Ronaldo. There are two things to say in this context: both are foreigners and therefore didn't embody the code of humility in the same way. But conversely, despite their awareness of their own skills, both acknowledged they were 'only one spoke' – though the most brilliant

– in the big wheel structure. Cantona and Ronaldo represent an equally important tradition in the club: arrogance and individual virtuosity.

*   *   *

After having collected enough money out of their modest wages for a ball and other future small expenses, Newton Heath LYR began their voyage to future greatness by playing against other teams from Manchester. In the beginning they played on a course on North Road in the Monsall neighbourhood a few kilometres north-east of today's Piccadilly Station. United at North Road were almost invincible, but the ground itself was also in a very questionable condition. At one end it was marshy, while the other end was bumpy and rock hard. The change of clothes took place at the local pubs, such as The Three Crown and The Shears Hotel on Oldham Road, more than ten minutes' walk from the course, and the latter hotel also acted as the club headquarters until the early 1900s.

Soon they began to recruit talented football players through the company, which was favoured by the strong economy of the railway industry in those years. The method went under the name 'shamateurism'. Until 1885 it was illegal to remunerate players, but instead you could offer them well-paid jobs in LYR if they agreed to play for Newton Heath, and in this way the club from the beginning managed to dominate the football landscape in Manchester. An early example of this form of recruitment was Jack Powell from Wrexham. He is believed to be the first Welsh footballer who turned professional in England when he arrived at Bolton Wanderers in 1883. Three years later he moved to Manchester, where he received work at LYR. Powell was captain of Newton Heath and was one of the club's first prominent names during its ascent to Football League status.

If you take a look at one of the first team pictures (opposite), you see a bunch of tough men with determined but solemn eyes. From their physical appearance it is quite clear that they are used to hard physical work. Most have the characteristic Victorian moustache. The picture is from the 1890s, and stylistically it can be seen as a form of Darwinian naturalism. It possesses an unmistakable aura that is both fascinating and provides clues about a time before the decolonisation and globalisation in the 1950s and 1960s – a time where England was still 'white'.

On 20 July 1885, after four years of intense debate, the ideologically Corinthian Football Association finally legalised recruitment of professional football players. The legalisation, however, had very restrictive conditions; for example, the player had to be either born or have lived within a radius of ten kilometres from the club's field for at least two years. The introduction of the 'professional' state led, naturally, to an increase in the club's wage bill. Their response to the increase was an attempt to arrange more matches and thus get more spectators through the turnstiles. This led to the formation of the Football League in 1888, at the beginning consisting of twelve clubs from the Midlands and Lancashire. (Accrington, Aston Villa, Blackburn Rovers, Bolton Wanderers, Burnley, Derby County, Everton, Notts County, Preston North End, Stoke, West Bromwich Albion and Wolverhampton Wanderers). The organisation's primary purpose was to replace the existing arbitrary and chaotic match schedule – consisting of the FA Cup, regional and friendship matches – with a developed and thoroughly organised match programme, with fixed home and away games resulting in a stable income for the clubs involved.

Newton Heath's application for inclusion in the Football League in 1889 was rejected in the first round, and instead the club, together with a number of other clubs, created the rival Football Alliance. As the Football Alliance afterwards was absorbed into the Football League, a new structure emerged with multiple divisions. Newton Heath, after their 2nd place in season 1891/92, moved up to the Football League's First Division for the 1892/93 season. On 3 September 1892, fourteen years after the founding of the Football League, Newton Heath played its first match in the top English league. Despite the rain and stormy conditions, eight thousand spectators turned up. Their opponents were Blackburn Rovers, one of the top teams in England at the time. After a disastrous start, Newton Heath went 3–0 down, but the team fought back towards the end and lost 4–3. The Scotsman Bob Donaldson scored the club's first league goal in

Newton Heath: one of the first team photos, 1892.

this match. After a number of further defeats, the club won its first victory in the league on 15 October 1892. The victory is not only historic because it was the first; it's also still the largest to date. Wolverhampton Wanderers were defeated 10-1. Newton Heath ended the season last in the league, but in a play-off game against Small Heath, the club won to remain in the top league.

In their second season in the First Division Newton Heath changed home ground, as several of the visiting teams had complained about the wretched pitch conditions on North Road. The choice fell on nearby Bank Street in Clayton. Bank Street had perhaps better facilities than North Road, but the ground was not in a better condition than its predecessor. It was rough, the surface was slimy brown and there was not much grass to be seen. Right next to the field there were, moreover, some of Manchester's many chemical plants, which sent thick clouds of acrid smoke from their chimneys out on to both players and spectators alike. Behind one goal boilers emitted a lot of steam out on to the pitch. A local poet was so inspired by Bank Street he wrote these immortal lines:

As Satan was flying over Clayton for Hell,
He was chained in the breeze, likewise the smell.
Quoth he: 'I'm not sure in what country I roam,
But I'm sure by the smell, I'm not far from home.'

Newton Heath won a match against Walsall 14-0, but the result has been deleted from the statistics on the grounds of the field's appalling condition. Tradition also says Newton Heath sometimes were saved from imminent defeat by the surrounding plants that were owned by club sympathisers. On certain days with a favourable wind direction they put an extra turbo to work. The chimneys then spat so much smoke out that the referee was forced to stop the match.

After the club was incorporated into the Football League, and with the move to Bank Street, the links to Lancashire & Yorkshire Railway were cut. Now the club was called Newton Heath FC. The second season of First Division football again resulted in the team finishing bottom, but this time they lost the play-off match against Liverpool, and in 1894 the team moved down into the Second Division, where they remained for the next twelve seasons. During the 1890s the club was in financial difficulties, and in January 1902 Newton Heath FC was declared bankrupt.

2 March 1901
Major, Mangnall and the Championship

The club's bankruptcy in January 1902 meant Bank Street was locked up, and Newton Heath didn't have a home. The captain, defender Harry Stafford, refused to accept this state of affairs, however, and he managed to persuade four local business people to each put £500 into the club. The main donor was John Henry Davies, director of Manchester brewery Walker & Homfray, and one of the leaders in the city's business aristocracy. Along with Harry Stafford and his St Bernard dog Major, John Henry Davies symbolises Manchester United's first rebirth. Davies not only put money into Newton Heath, but in spring 1902 he also set about rebuilding the club through his office as club president.

Had it not been for Major, Manchester United would not, in all likelihood, have existed at all today. There are several versions of the story of the St Bernard dog, and a certain mystique surrounds Major's precise role in the club's rescue. The starting point for the various anecdotes about Major is certain, however. In the days between 27 February and 2 March 1901 Newton Heath held a bazaar in St James's Theatre and Exhibition Hall on Oxford Street in Manchester. The bazaar aimed to raise £1,000 to avoid the club going into bankruptcy. Stafford had brought Major, and the dog trudged proudly around with the collection box hanging around his neck.

The version of the story that appeals to me most is both dramatic and endowed with the magic of coincidence. On the last day of the bazaar, the otherwise trusty Major ran off with the collection box hanging around his neck. The dog visited a pub, which happened to be owned by John Davies. Thereby Davies ended up having the dog and the money fall into his hands. The anecdote says Davies gave the dog to his daughter Elsie on her twelfth birthday, but Harry Stafford managed to find Major, and thus he came into contact with John Henry Davies. The director was very impressed with Stafford's enthusiasm to rescue Newton Heath so he offered his services as both economic saviour and future leader.

The story about the bazaar and Major represents not only the club's first of a long series of rebirths, it also is the first important example of the significant role coincidence plays in this tale of Manchester United. However, almost a year passed from Davies's meeting with Major and Stafford before the brewery owner made an appearance as the club's saviour. After the random meeting in March 1901, Newton Heath's bankruptcy in January 1902 was formalised, which allowed Davies to dismantle Newton Heath to make room for Manchester United.

When Davies took over financial management of the club in 1902, he decided that a new beginning would be required. He insisted that name and uniforms be changed, and the club's new headquarters were now the Manchester Imperial Hotel. The board meeting of 26 April 1902 agreed the club's new name and colours. Of the names discussed Manchester Central and Manchester Celtic were possibilities, the latter bearing witness to the Irish–Scottish and Catholic influence in both the city and the club. But, according to lore, it is the nineteen-year-old Italian immigrant Louis Rocca, at this time serving as a kind of errand boy at the club, who deserves to be credited for the name that is so famous today. In the middle of the discussion he supposedly burst out: 'Gentlemen, why don't we call ourselves Manchester United?' On this day the club was resurrected and transformed, no longer as Newton Heath in yellow and green outfits, but as Manchester United in red and white strips. Manchester United FC was registered two days later, on 28 April 1902.

* * *

The first match under the name Manchester United was played away against obscure Gainsborough Trinity on 6 September 1902 and ended with a modest victory of 1-0. As in the previous couple of seasons, the manager was James West, who, however, withdrew from the job on 29 September 1903. West was succeeded by Ernest Mangnall, who was lured to the club from Burnley. Mangnall is the first great manager in the club's history.

Ernest Mangnall belonged to the era in which the football manager was more like a secretary of the club. Mangnall, despite his role as secretary–manager, was in many ways ahead of his time. Behind him he had an active career in football, rugby and athletics. His greatest passion, however, had been cycling. This experience as a sportsman was invaluable in his dealings with the players. First and foremost he knew exactly how to motivate his players, and his other strength lay in his meticulous focus on the physical aspect of the sport. Mangnall belonged to the old-fashioned school of football management, since he denied the players to train with a ball during the week in the belief they would be extra hungry for the ball on Saturday.

In his first season, Mangnall only managed to lead Manchester United to a frustrating third place. But positive things happened in the club this season. In addition to a number of improvements to the facilities at Bank Street, the new campaign also saw a handful of new players brought to the club, players who became the backbone of the team that won the club's first championship in 1908. In addition to the excellent goalkeeper Harry Moger and stalwart John Peddie, it's particularly noteworthy that the legendary half back trio consisting of Dick Duckworth, Charlie Roberts and Alex Bell arrived at Manchester United at this time.

Although too late to play a crucial role in the team's final position during that first season, Mangnall signed twenty-one-year-old Roberts from Grimsby for a record high amount of £600. He then had to listen to some criticism for having paid a high price for such an inexperienced player. But Mangnall made the right decision and Charlie Roberts was to become the first legend in the story of Manchester United. He was captain, and the driving force behind the first championship success; with his huge work rate, he left a herculean imprint from penalty area to penalty area. He was to the club's early years what Duncan Edwards, Bryan Robson or Roy Keane would be in later decades. Because of his speed and pale appearance he went under the nickname 'Ghost in Boots'. He was athletic and aggressive, and his bellicose style endowed him with an aura of the future. Although Roberts was one of England's best players, he achieved only three international caps. The cause of this is to be found in the fact he often expressed himself loudly off the pitch over various topics. He also attracted football's bureaucratic displeasure on the field by not playing in shorts that covered the knees – this was customary at the time.

The Italian coach Vittorio Pozzo, who among other things led Italy to World Cup gold in 1934 and 1938, and for a short time lived in Manchester, described Charlie Roberts as the world's best player. Roberts's dynamic playing style impressed the Italian and was by all accounts one of the direct reasons why Pozzo developed the so-called 'Metodo' formation, where he pulled the two wingers in the 2–3–5 formation back a bit. This led to a modernisation of the game tactically. On one hand, the Metodo formation managed to respond defensively to a greater dynamism and flexibility on the part of the rival team. On the other, the formation also let one's own attacking qualities come to the fore.

In 1906, after twelve years in limbo, the patience with Mangnall paid off as Manchester United finished in second place and moved up into the First Division. Both John Davies and Ernest Mangnall were aware, however, that the club needed to recruit better players to go the distance in the First Division. For this reason the summer of 1906 is one of the most notable in the club's history in terms of recruitment. They didn't even have to look far afield, since Mangnall shamelessly began to prey on their neighbours from Manchester City and hand-picked four of their star players: Billy Meredith, Alexander 'Sandy' Turnbull, Jimmy Bannister and Herbert Burgess.

The coup succeeded because Manchester City had been found guilty in a case of giving the players illegal salaries and bonuses. Five of the club's leaders and eighteen of the players were given lengthy suspensions, and in the wake of this player suspension Mangnall showed ingenuity and drive. The plan was that the City players were to be auctioned to other clubs. The event would take place in the Queen's Hotel in Manchester, but the night before the auction was to take place, Mangnall had made a shady deal to secure his four future heroes. The trio of Duckworth, Roberts and Bell had transformed Manchester United from an average Second Division team into a solid First Division one, but Bannister, Burgess, Meredith and Turnbull were the collective push forming United's first ascent of the Mount Everest of English football.

Despite this, Mangnall wasn't able to use them, because of their suspension, until New Year's Day 1907. On this day, Manchester United played against Aston Villa on Bank Street in Clayton and won 1–0 in front of 40,000 spectators, thanks to a debut goal from Sandy Turnbull and an assist from Billy Meredith. During spring the team clicked into a well-oiled attacking machine and, for the first time in the club's history, Manchester United became a big attraction away from home.

* * *

The year is 1908. The Olympic Games, which for the first time has the participation of female athletes, takes place in London, and in Detroit the first Model T Ford rolls off the assembly line. William Howard Taft wins the presidential election in the United States, and in Bolivia it is believed that Butch Cassidy and the Sundance Kid have been killed by soldiers. An earthquake destroys Messina in Sicily and 75,000 people die. The English writer E.M. Forster publishes *A Room with a View*, and his compatriot H.G. Wells pens *The War in the Air*. 1908 is also the year when Manchester United (with the team shown opposite) wins the English Championship and Charity Shield for the first time.

Manchester United won the league with 52 points, which was a new league record. From his position on the left wing, George Wall chipped in with an impressive twenty-two goals, but Sandy Turnbull exceeded him with twenty-seven goals scored in thirty-four matches. 'He had the habit of asking the goalie for a receipt after scoring!', it was said of Turnbull.

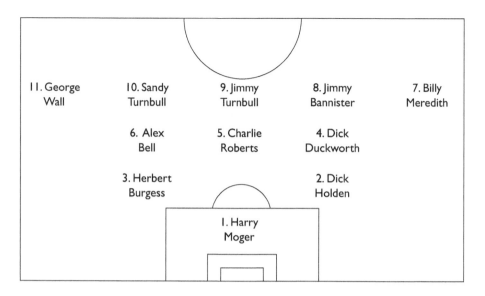

11. George Wall 10. Sandy Turnbull 9. Jimmy Turnbull 8. Jimmy Bannister 7. Billy Meredith

6. Alex Bell 5. Charlie Roberts 4. Dick Duckworth

3. Herbert Burgess 2. Dick Holden

1. Harry Moger

On 27 April 1908 Manchester United met Queens Park Rangers in the first Charity Shield. The match at Stamford Bridge in London ended in a draw at 1–1, and only 6,000 spectators saw Billy Meredith score for United. The re-match was also played at Stamford Bridge and attracted the same low number of spectators, but this time Manchester United won 4–0 without any problems.

Besides the captain Charlie Roberts, the team's other big profile player was Billy Meredith, football's first superstar. In 1926 Meredith also starred in Hugh Croise's feature film *The Ball of Fortune*. At the beginning of the twentieth century, Billy Meredith was an icon almost as well known in Britain as King Edward VII. Their respective backgrounds, however, could not be more different. Meredith came from humble stock in the devout village of Chirk in Wales, and at the age of twelve he began to work in the mines. But, as was the case for so many other talented footballers, football was his way out of the bleak mining shafts.

'The Welsh Wizard of Dribble', as he was called, had a tremendous impact both on and off the pitch. His trademark was a wooden toothpick, which during matches was carelessly left on his lower lip. Meredith claimed the toothpick helped his concentration. Previously, he chewed tobacco, but since the club's washerwomen refused to wash his tobacco spit off his clothes, he replaced his tobacco with a toothpick.

However, it wasn't only because of this media profile and self-confident demeanour that Billy Meredith stood out. On the pitch he demonstrated technical abilities and made dribbling the ball into an art form, and this raised him up into a sphere beyond all others at the time. He was as fast as Theo Walcott, dribbled like George Best and delivered crosses like David Beckham – and moreover he was as bow-legged as Pierre Littbarski! Like his teammate Charlie

The first giant: Billy Meredith (left).

Roberts, Billy Meredith was in possession of an inexorable winning instinct, but where the former's desire for victory was manifested in aggression on the field, Meredith's winning instinct was expressed in a more subtle way. Film clips show Meredith's appearance on the pitch as a mixture of casualness and indifference bordering on outright dullness. But behind this fraudulent outer shell hid an incomparable ability to focus all his energy into cut-throat creative details – for example, his famous and often decisive heel pass. If Roberts's influence was apparent as a continuous presence, then Meredith's felt more like a focused flash of lightning. Meredith's arrogant, casual and anti-authoritarian attitude reminds one of Eric Cantona, while his ability to dribble, on the other hand, can be compared to Ryan Giggs.

Off the pitch, Meredith, Roberts and the reserve goalkeeper Herbert Broomfield helped revive the players' union, which had collapsed ten years earlier. When approximately 500 players were assembled at the Manchester Imperial Hotel on 2 December 1907, it was Meredith who led the meeting. One of the union's most important declarations of intent was to get the maximum wage suspended, or at least raised, which at this time was just £4 a week. This limit came from 1900, that is to say, a time when there were rarely more than 10,000 spectators at the matches in the best English row. But in 1907, spectators started to stream into football, and the players wanted to enjoy part of the escalating gate revenues.

The Edwardian period, which coincided with the European *belle époque*, was in some way more lustrous and liberated than the Victorian, which it replaced in 1901. But the myth of 'the good old days' under King Edward VII is contrasted by the deep poverty, illiteracy, hunger, incest, violence, and slum-like housing conditions experienced by the working class. This is depicted in Robert Roberts's disturbing *The Classic Slum* (1971), a personal report on life in Salford (a city and metropolitan borough of Greater Manchester) in the first quarter of the twentieth century. The period was characterised by unrest and upheaval with strong contrasts between conservatism and radicalism, culture and mercantilism, and liberality and snobbery, all themes that can be found in E.M. Forster's novels. On the one hand, society was permeated with rigidity in the context of class, gender, race and sexuality, primarily a relic from the Victorian era. As Roberts writes about the lower class: 'Whatever new urges might have roved abroad in early Edwardian England, millions among the poor still retained the outlook and thought patterns imposed by their Victorian mentors. For them the twentieth century had not begun.' On the other hand, the period was characterised by a dawning liberalism that was helped by the economic growth that came from industrialisation, technological inventions and radical new ideas, such as socialism and the issue of women's suffrage. The consequence was that it became possible to move upwards socially, despite the inherent conservatism of the time.

In an age when people were encouraged to actively seek their own personal success by offering labour to the highest bidder, it is a paradox that the Football League maintained professional footballers on amateur-like terms and under conditions that were reminiscent of slavery in both a monetary and freedom sense. The Edwardian virtues (every man is the architect of his own fortune) and rules (free-market forces) apparently didn't apply in the world of football, which, in contrast to a traditional and romantic view, mainly worked in accordance with business and economic principles from the very beginning.

The Football League was formed in 1888 with the specific intention of ensuring clubs increased revenues from tickets by organising a developed and scheduled fixture programme. The motive had been the club's profit, not improving the players' condition, and the League's foundation was a direct consequence of players' new 'professional' terms and relatively improved remuneration conditions. The Corinthian amateur principles, which characterised the Football Association in the 1880s, was not necessarily in conflict with the Football League's ideology, as the latter was formed as a response to the implementation of professionalism and not as an initiator of it. In modern days, footballers might be criticised for being greedy and disloyal, but in the beginning of the twentieth century they were deprived of rights. In relation to the revenue they helped generate, they were extremely ill paid, and the free movement of labour in football was a concept that, at best, one could read about in a sci-fi novel by H.G. Wells.

The Football League was an opponent of a lift in maximum wages because they feared the smaller clubs would no longer be able to keep their star players. In his excellent book *The Italian Job* (2006), the former Italian striker and Chelsea manager Gianluca Vialli furthermore points out that in England there exists a historically ingrained view of football as a sport for workers, while rugby and cricket, are considered to be sports for gentlemen. According to Vialli the consequence is a special kind of English morality, which generally frowns upon football players' high salaries.

English football was marked by egalitarian thinking far into the twentieth century, where the best players were spread out over many clubs. Stanley Matthews is the most famous example. He played for Stoke and Blackpool, and in 1956 was the first player to receive the Ballon d'Or prize as Europe's best footballer. In spite of Matthews's undeniable qualities, in the whole of his long career he won only one single FA Cup medal, with Blackpool in 1953. The example of Matthews shows why English clubs and the English national team weren't competitive enough on an international level. Instead of making it possible for the best and richest clubs to gather more of the best players in competitive squads, the union, with its maximum wage, held on to a relatively flat hierarchy among the clubs.

In addition, there is the cultural ideology that dominated the English football world for most of the century. As Vialli notes, the main task of the entire organisational football mechanism in England is to produce 'good people', while other places in Europe, such as in Italy, focus on producing 'good footballers'. In this sense the game's roots in English public schools are apparent. It was at schools like Eton and Winchester in the 1500s that football was taken from the mob and went through a sophistication process, which in the course of the next centuries led to a formalisation of rules and the differentiation of the various forms of football. But it also led to an attention to players' social skills before 'the mob' in England conquered back the sport in the late 1800s. For the English system, football therefore became a medium through which you could impress the right ideals and values on the uneducated working class.

There are many who believe this egalitarian system consisting of maximum wages, morals and sportsmanship was one of the main reasons the English national team and the English clubs in the middle of the twentieth century lagged far behind their continental counterparts. Real Madrid's dominance in the Europe Cup from 1955–59 is one example, Hungary's historic 6–3 demolition of England at Wembley in 1953 a second, and England's humiliating 0–1 defeat to the United States during the 1950 World Cup in Brazil is a third. All three events shook the English's fundamental belief: since England was football's mother country, then the English way was surely the only and most appropriate kind of football.

John Henry Davies and Manchester United, as well as other of the big clubs, looked positively at the players' wishes. A repeal of the maximum wage would mean Manchester United's ability to attract the best players would improve as the club could afford to pay a higher salary than £4 per week. John Davies was persuaded by Meredith and Roberts to be the union president, and together the players and the clubs hoped to pressure the Football League into a change in the rules towards professionalism and freer market conditions. Davies and several other powerful club presidents threatened to form a breakaway league. The Football League, however, met them head on and required the clubs to introduce new contracts not only to maintain the maximum wage of £4, but also to make it more difficult for players to change clubs. In addition, the league demanded that the clubs distance themselves from the trade union. The clubs ended up bending, and not until half a century later, in 1961, did the trade union succeed in lifting the maximum wage.

*   *   *

In addition to John Henry Davies's announcement in March 1909 that he would donate money for the construction of a new stadium at Trafford Park, the season's second positive story was that Manchester United, for the first time in the club's history, took home the FA cup. In the quarter-finals, United met Burnley at Turf Moor. Burnley were a club who fought a brave struggle at the bottom of the Second Division. The favourites did not, however, live up to the high expectations and with twenty minutes left the home team got in front and seemed to have the game completely under control. Once again coincidence played a starring role in this tale of Manchester United. The snowy weather, which had started in the middle of the first half, turned into a genuine blizzard towards the middle of the second. The referee Herbert Bamlett, who in the irony of fate became manager of Manchester United eighteen years later, had to call off the match and thus came to the rescue of the defending league champions. A few days later, on 10 March 1909, United won the re-match 3–2, and in the semi-finals the Red Devils defeated Newcastle 1–0 at Bramall Lane in Sheffield.

In the final on 24 April 1909 Manchester United played against Bristol City. The match was played at Crystal Palace in London and was seen by 71,401 spectators. According to a newspaper headline in the *Daily Mirror* two days later, it was, however, a 'crowd without enthusiasm'. The newspaper's explanation was that Bristol City and Manchester United just weren't able to wake the metropolis's interest. London's cockneys didn't turn up in such a large number as they used to at major sporting events in London, and therefore it lacked atmosphere. The same article also characterises the final as 'a poor game', which may also explain the crowd's lack of enthusiasm.

In the days leading up to the final, Sandy Turnbull had been suffering from a painful knee injury, but on the morning before the match he begged Mangnall to let him play. Team captain Roberts agreed with Turnbull and joined in: 'Let him play. He might get a goal and if he does we can afford to carry him.' Manchester United won the final 1–0, and Roberts's words proved prophetic as the match winner was Sandy Turnbull.

The 1909/10 season is memorable for two reasons. One has to do with the construction of Old Trafford, the other has to do with the dispute between the players' union and the league. This dispute rekindled in the summer of 1909, as the Football League demanded the players distance themselves from the trade union. The consequence of continued membership of the trade union was exclusion from all league football. Shortly before the start of the season it was only Manchester United's cup heroes who stood firm while the other clubs' players had given in to the league's pressure. Aware of the fact that their case would make good press, the players themselves organised their workouts, and called themselves 'The Outcasts FC'.

Manchester was proud of its footballers. Their dual role as spellcasters on the field and rebels off it fitted perfectly into the city's romantic view of itself as a truly unique place. There was actually a real danger that the players, who had won the FA Cup a few months beforehand, would never get to play professional football again. But at the last moment players from Liverpool, Everton, Newcastle, Sunderland and Middlesbrough chose to back up the trade union. This forced the league into a compromise, which not only allowed the players' union to survive, but also Manchester United's players to play for their club again.

In March of 1909 John Davies announced he would donate £60,000 for the construction of a new great stadium at Trafford Park in south-west Manchester. Davies bought the site situated between the Bridgewater Canal, the railway and Warwick Road (today's Sir Matt Busby Way). He hired the young, but already famous Scottish architect Archibald Leitch. Leitch had started his career with both designing and constructing factory buildings in his home town of Glasgow, but in 1899 he received an order from Glasgow Rangers, for whom he was to draw up plans and construct Ibrox Park. Although a grandstand collapsed and twenty-six people lost their lives during the first great battle at Ibrox, Leitch was still a sought-after stadium architect. In the following years, he was involved in more than twenty stadium projects in Great Britain. His style was industrial, more functional than aesthetic, clearly reflecting his first factory projects.

John Henry Davies envisioned a stadium with a capacity of 100,000 spectators, of which 12,000 would be seated. In addition, the stadium would be equipped with luxurious facilities, such as a billiard salon, gymnasium, laundry rooms and a tearoom. Because of budget excess, the capacity was revised to 80,000 spectators. But when the stadium was completed, Manchester United held a modern football arena ready for the challenges of the twentieth century. The name of the new stadium was Old Trafford and the inauguration took place on 19 February 1910. Their opponents were Liverpool, and 45,000 spectators witnessed Sandy Turnbull score the historic first goal at Old Trafford. The party was spoiled, however, as the visitors won 4–3.

* * *

Old Trafford was hailed after the opening as the best football stadium in England, and before long it was also the location of the nation's best team, as Manchester United regained the championship in 1910/11 after a dramatic duel against Aston Villa.

At Old Trafford on 29 April 1911 United played against Sunderland, and the home team did their duty by winning the match 5–1. Charlie Roberts said to the *Manchester Saturday Post*: 'At the end of the game our supporters rushed across the ground in front of the stand to wait for the final news from Liverpool. Suddenly a tremendous cheer rent the air and was renewed again and again and we knew we were the champions once again.' At Anfield, Liverpool triumphed 3–1 over Aston Villa, and with that the Merseyside club had played the championship into the hands of United.

Manchester United's last significant triumph, before a trophyless period of thirty-seven years began, was their victory in the Charity Shield against Swindon Town. At Stamford Bridge on 25 September 1911, Manchester United won 8–4 in the most goal-rich Charity Shield ever. The match is remembered especially for Harold Halse's six goals. 'I'll be back in a minute,' Harold told Swindon's goalkeeper after each of his goals.

Then the journey passed into oblivion. One of the first blows occurred in 1912, when Ernest Mangnall, after nine years and 373 matches as the manager, left the club. What made his resignation even harder to take was that Mangnall was leaving to go to United's arch-rivals, Manchester City. With the departure of Mangnall an era in United's history ended, and his exit also resulted in a gradual dissolution of the team that for almost a decade made Manchester United legendary. Mangnall's era brought stability to the club, leading United back to the First Division, and to their success in winning two championships, the FA Cup and two Charity Shields. In addition, it was an era guaranteeing Charlie Roberts and Billy Meredith status as legends of Manchester United.

T.J. Wallworth and J.J. Bentley succeeded Ernest Mangnall. The construction and operation of Old Trafford, however, meant Manchester United was so

27

financially crippled that Wallworth and Bentley had no real opportunities to maintain a powerful team. In the summer of 1913 Charlie Roberts left Manchester United in favour of Oldham Athletic.

In addition, the First World War's outbreak on 1 August 1914 meant that the 1914/15 season was dramatic in a number of ways for Manchester United. To the club's supporters the season was most of all remembered for the Good Friday scandal, which smeared the club's name and image for many years in the future. But the drama also related to the most nail-biting finale of the season, when United, with difficulty, avoided relegation. The season also offered a manager change, when John Robson joined the club on 28 December 1914 to succeed Bentley.

On 2 April 1915 Manchester United met Liverpool at Old Trafford. It was Good Friday, and a modest 18,000 spectators had turned up to see the battle between the north-west rivals. With two goals by George Anderson, United won 2–0 and secured two vital points in the fight to avoid relegation. Liverpool held an indifferent position in the league and had nothing to play for, so at first there was nothing surprising about the outcome. But a few days after the match, stories began to circulate that the match had been fixed. In the course of play, the referee and several other observers noted a strange apathy from the Liverpool players, and Jackie Sheldon even missed a penalty kick for Liverpool. Rumours were also abounding that bookmakers in Manchester had received many bets on the outcome of 2–0 at odds of 7–1.

Sporting Chronicle followed up on the story and accused a number of players from both teams of manipulating the outcome. The Football League opened an investigation and delivered their verdict in December 1915. Four players from Liverpool, three from Manchester United and one from Chester City were suspended for life. Jackie Sheldon from Liverpool, who for a short time had played for United, was regarded as the ringleader. Of the three United players, the two most prominent names were the long-standing top-scorer Sandy Turnbull and the club's second major goal-thief Enoch 'Knocker' West.

Both Turnbull and Arthur Whalley (the third disgraced United player), and Laurence Cook from Chester, had their suspension lifted after the war as a result of their efforts for King and country. For Sandy Turnbull, though, it was a posthumous pardon, as he died in France on 3 May 1917 during the Battle of Arras. Enoch West, the only one of the three United players who actually took part in the famous battle, never played again. He continued to proclaim his innocence. And in 1945, when he was fifty-nine years old, West was pardoned.

21 December 1931
The long weekend and James W. Gibson's Monday

Shortly before Christmas 1931 on Monday 21 December 1931, Walter Crickmer takes a bus from Manchester centre to the exclusive village of Hale Barns in beautiful Cheshire. Crickmer is Manchester United's secretary and temporary manager, and he is a man on a mission – a rescue mission, to be precise. Seven months previously, at the end of season 1930/31, Manchester United found themselves completely isolated in last place in the league and on the verge of bankruptcy. Old Trafford was moreover a sporting necropolis, where the attendance rarely exceeded 8,000 spectators.

In the history of Manchester United, the period between 1919 (the year when the league was resumed after the war) and 1932 is often referred to as 'the long weekend' or 'the years of depression'. In 1931 it is clear the club needs a miracle along the lines of John Henry Davies's meeting with the St Bernard dog Major thirty years earlier. In fact, a miracle of a kind does occur, although this time the meeting is intentional, rather than coincidental. The new John Henry Davies is the visionary and experienced businessman James W. Gibson, who Crickmer has gone to Hale Barns to visit.

James Gibson tells Crickmer he has a Christmas present for Manchester United. This gift consists of £2,000 and a pot of money to cover the wages, which Crickmer had just visited the bank to withdraw without success. The only condition is that the board is to insert Gibson as chairman and appoint him as the president of the club. Furthermore, Gibson promises that there is more money at the club's disposal when a new board has been elected. On behalf of Manchester United Crickmer gratefully accepts Gibson's helping hand. With Gibson's commitment to the club Manchester United negotiates its way out of oblivion and back to respectability, but within another eight years another world war will bring a temporary halt to the club's ambitions.

* * *

As Justin Blundell notes in his detailed *Back From the Brink* (2006), the years just after the First World War were an era of shoulder tackles, and death on the field as a result of brutality was not a completely unknown phenomenon in the early years of the professional game. Substitutes and Sunday matches were still not allowed, and there were no floodlights, so a midweek kick-off was usually 2.30 p.m. The players didn't have numbers on their sweaters and the goalkeeper didn't use gloves. Both outfield players and the goalkeeper ran around in huge shorts, and the latter wore a thick green polo neck jersey while the field players had thick woollen sweaters on. The ball was still sewn together with thick threads, so there was real danger of getting injured when heading. This happened to Manchester United's twenty-five-year-old Thomas Blackstock in April 1907 when he collapsed after heading the ball during a reserve team match and died soon after in the locker room.

Old Trafford, which at its inauguration in 1910 was, according to *Sporting Chronicle*, 'the most handsomest, the most spacious and the most remarkable arena' in the world, was home in the war years for a Manchester United team participating in the provisional regional leagues. Due to the war and a decreasing number of spectators, the club experienced difficulties in keeping up with the high interest rates and the day-to-day operation. So instead of an enviable income source, John Davies's ambitious project had turned into a financial burden to the club.

After the tiring war years the English people, however, were hungry for entertainment. The Great War had turned football into the British national sport. Both aristocratic officers and working-class privates had played football behind the trenches, on the military bases, and on leave, and the sport had been an invigorating remedy in a sometimes tedious everyday life and a refuge where class differences had been temporarily eliminated. National sport or not, it's still a fact that football in England is being played and watched by working and middle classes today. The class difference is noticeable in English football to a much greater degree than in Italian football, where it isn't unusual for professional footballers to be sons of doctors, engineers or academics. It's possible that the greater degree of academic prowess of footballers in Italy, in relation to England, can be seen in the two countries' styles. The Italian rational cynicism versus the English irrational passion. It's the story of work, brains and skill versus play, heart and values all over again.

One player in particular managed to lighten up Old Trafford on the otherwise dismal match-day afternoons of the 1920s. From Joe Spence's debut on 30 August 1919 to his retirement in 1933 he was one of the club's key players. At thirteen, Spence began to work in the mines, and at the age of seventeen he was drafted into the army, where he served as machine gun rifleman in the First World War. Spence spent 510 matches in the red shirt and scored 168 goals for Manchester United. He was a fast and shoulder-strong winger, who liked to cut inside and score goals. He was often used on the right wing, but his physique and general skills meant he could also be used as an inside forward and centre forward. Spence had a different build than the more typical, scrawny United wingers such as Billy Meredith, David Pegg and Ryan Giggs. Spence was stocky, but because of this he was also physically very tough, and this combined with an opportunistic drive made it difficult for opponents to stop him. He was not the elegant virtuoso, but rather the very strong bomber. In addition, Spence, much like Wayne Rooney, was endowed with the heart of a lion and the aggressive persistence of a terrier, which immediately made him the spectators' favourite.

Joe Spence's arrival at the club was the result of a strategic decision to focus on youth. The decision was, however, less to do with planning than necessity. After the war Manchester United's team was more or less non-existent. Sandy Turnbull was the only casualty, but the rest were five years older. In addition, the war in general had claimed many of the nation's men in their twenties, the age at which one's best football years are enjoyed. When the war was over, Manchester United's manager John Robson launched a policy, called 'players before points'. It was the club's first youth policy, and in the war years Robson went around the region to spot young talent who could step into Manchester United's first team after the war. Joe Spence, Clarence 'Lal' Hilditch, Fred Hopkin, John 'Jack' Silcock and Charlie Moore were some of 'Robson's Rookies'. They had debuts at a young age for the club in their first league match after the war. The four of them were still playing for Manchester United in the early 1930s.

* * *

The years after the war were marked by massive unemployment, and those who had work often went on strikes. There was also a shortage of food and money. The world of football continued, however, to rotate about its own axis, and was not only a reflection of society, but also a counter-image of it: Manchester United in 1920/21 was, according to Blundell, a financial goldmine, because the crowd flocked to Old Trafford. It was the first time since the opening of the stadium in 1910 that John Davies's megalomania vision seemed to be justified.

John Robson's team, however, were no more than average at the beginning of the season. The board had not been willing to invest the profit in star players capable of lifting Manchester United up with the best. But when 50,000 spectators turned up to the season's first match at Old Trafford, John Henry Davies decided it was time to invest in the team. He said: 'The club is still handicapped financially for reasons pretty well known, but the great following the team has makes it clear that there ought to be a wonderful period of prosperity before Old Trafford. We hope that Leonard and Miller will make our forward line one of the best in the country. Indeed, we owe it to that splendid young defence of ours to see that other departments are all right.' Davies was alluding to Harry Leonard, a centre forward from Derby, and Tommy Miller, an inside forward from Liverpool. However, both Miller and Leonard only lasted one season in Manchester.

In 1920/21 the relationship between Manchester United and Manchester City suffered great damage. City's stadium on Hyde Road was in a deplorable state and, at one point, one of the grandstands caught fire. Earlier in the season, John Davies had already offered Old Trafford to City for free, but had been rejected. When the fire led them to change their minds, Davies demanded either City paid United the excess revenue in relation to the revenues from the previous season or the normal 10 per cent of the entrance earnings. City indignantly refused to accept Davies's otherwise reasonable conditions and decided to stay on in Hyde Road. The local media sympathised with City and were offended by what they saw as United's greed and lack of responsiveness to their neighbours. When Mangnall's Manchester City on 27 November 1920 defeated United 3–0 on Hyde Road, among City fans and the local media there was a feeling that justice had been done.

The year of 1921 marked another end of an era. The legend Billy Meredith finally obtained the free transfer he had asked for the year before. With Meredith out of the picture the last connection to the Mangnall era had been cut. Back then Manchester United symbolised style, stardust and silver. All that was left now was a giant stadium, a large and loyal fan base, and a team unable to match either its venue or its crowd's expectations.

* * *

In 1921, John Robson was, in spite of modest rankings both before and after the war, considered a miracle worker among Manchester United's fans. It was with him in charge the club got out of its financial crisis; he built a new team and created a talented reserve team for no money. He managed to keep the club in the First Division, and he attracted lots of spectators. Robson's strength was to act relatively invisible in chaotic or, at the very least, difficult conditions. However, the board questioned whether Robson was the correct type to lead the club to the next level. He lacked media appeal, and he didn't manage to bring in big stars to the club. Manchester United was looking for a new Ernest Mangnall. A manager who through his ability to attract stars and create publicity could legitimise the media's depiction of Manchester United as a flamboyant club that played entertaining football. On 16 September 1921 John Robson resigned his post as manager because of failing health, but continued in the newly created role as assistant manager. For Manchester United this was an ideal solution, because the club was able to retrieve its showman without losing Robson's 'know-how', administrative skills and excellent ability to spot talent.

On 31 October, Manchester United presented John Chapman as their new manager, the club's first Scot in charge. Unfortunately, the new coaching partnership did not bear fruit, since Robson died of pneumonia on 11 January 1922. Furthermore, John Chapman turned out not to be the showman Manchester United had in mind. He came from Airdrie, where in fifteen years he'd not only been manager, but also 'a guide, philosopher and friend', as the *Athletic News* wrote upon his arrival at Old Trafford. He also brought a reputation as a sly and experienced manager with an ability to spot new talent and bring them up through the ranks. Instead of a new Mangnall, Manchester United had got its hands on a younger version of Robson. Chapman got off to a disastrous start at Old Trafford and in his first fifteen matches he only won a single game, and the season ended with the team at the bottom of the First Division.

*   *   *

Manchester United were relegated to the Second Division, which they had not been in since 1906, and the hopes of a rapid return to the top league soon turned out to be unrealistic. At Old Trafford United had it hard, since one away team after another seemed inspired by the imposing surroundings and delivered their best performances. Joe Spence even suggested the field should be dug up to see if one could find 'the remains of a policeman or a Jew or something casting an evil spell over the club's doings.' A second (and perhaps more plausible) explanation is that players like Ed McBain, William Henderson, Hilditch and Teddy Partridge suffered under the harder and more physical game played in the Second Division.

In the summer of 1922, when the club had been relegated, Manchester United managed to buy the former blacksmith Frank Barson from Aston Villa for a record fee of £5,000. Barson was the sheriff the team had lacked since Charlie Roberts was sold in 1913. Barson was a centre half like Roberts, and he filled his position as the team's centre of gravity like a colossus cast in granite. Quite simply, Frank Barson looked scary! He was tall and wide, and his crooked nose was a result of the close combats he had thrown himself into. At a time when sendings off were considered to be shameful for both the player and the club, Barson had already been sent off twelve times before his arrival at Old Trafford. His disciplinary list of transgressions, however, was partially the result of his remarkable honesty. If an opponent committed fouls, Barson immediately vowed to retaliate, but he also told the referee exactly what he intended to do so his intentions couldn't be misunderstood.

Frank Barson was what most football experts considered to be England's best centre half: play-maker, strong as an ox, the team's motivator and a fantastic heading ability. Hence, it may seem puzzling that Manchester United succeeded in getting Barson to Old Trafford, a Second Division club. But perhaps Barson was persuaded by the bizarre package United offered him. Barson would be rewarded with a pub if he led the club back to First Division within three years – and he succeeded!

* * *

Manchester United's return to the First Division in 1925/26 saw them to a respectable ninth place; the Devils had even been fighting for the title until March. It happened in a season where changes to the offside rule made the campaign perhaps the most unpredictable ever. Previously, an attacking player would be offside if there were no more than three opponents, including the goalie, between himself and his opponents' half at the moment of passing. Now there only had to be two opponents, including the keeper. Earlier, in theory one of the defenders could stay together with his goalkeeper down by the goal line and still play the opponent's attacking player offside, but if a defender now withdrew deep in his own half the attacking player could follow him without making it a punishable offside.

The rule freed the attackers and resulted in more goals, but gave the defenders more headaches. In addition, it increased the workload for the three backs, particularly for the centre half. Previously, the centre half had to act both as defender and attacker, but now he was forced to act more as a third defender. It also meant the half backs were pulled in more centrally, and the two inside forwards were pulled further behind. The traditional 'pyramid' formation (2–3–5), where the centre half appeared in the midfield, and where the forward line was just a straight line, now was replaced by the so-called 'WM' formation (3–2–2–3), credited to Herbert Chapman. This represented a more flexible structure than in the past. Compare, for example, the two line-ups shown opposite, from 1908 (top) and 1926 (bottom).

In 1926, Manchester United once again got involved in a scandal, smaller than the Good Friday scandal of 1915 but significant nonetheless. On 8 October, John Chapman was suspended by the Football League on the grounds of non-defined criminal offences. The official and vague wording said 'improper conduct'. The secrecy from the FA's side only reinforced the sceptics' view that Chapman was innocent, and that the judgement was delayed revenge on the affair with 'The Outcasts' in 1909. The Chapman case remained obscure and mysterious, and only the journalist Alf Clarke, who was a trusted friend of Chapman and later one of the victims in the Munich air disaster, was able to

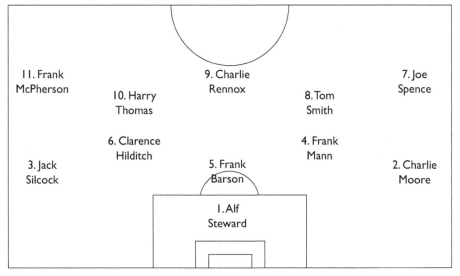

throw a little light on the matter in the club's history from 1948. He said: 'I know full well all the circumstances, and I know that had John come out into the open he would have cleared himself very easily. But a player was involved and John Chapman preferred the matter to rest at that.'

Chapman's suspension was a hard blow to Manchester United, as it came at a time when he had led the club to promotion, an impressive ninth place in the top league and a semi-final place in the cup. In addition, Chapman could boast generating a surplus of £21,000, and he also enjoyed a great reputation among the players. The suspension led to Clarence Hilditch succeeding him as manager, the first player–manager in the club's history, and Walter Crickmer was hired as club secretary. Hilditch, however, was a temporary solution and only stayed until April 1927 when the club engaged Herbert Bamlett as the new manager.

There were high expectations of the new manager, because at Middlesbrough Bamlett had set the highest goal-scoring record in the Second Division with an offensive-minded team. At Manchester United he attempted to continue with this philosophy.

* * *

The 1926/27 season ended in a sloppy fifteenth position, which triggered an increase in the number of critical voices in local newspapers, primarily from fans, who were dissatisfied with the board's inaction on the transfer market. However, John Chapman's profit was earmarked for buying up Old Trafford from John Davies's Manchester Brewery Company and in June 1927 the trade went through. Manchester United now owned Old Trafford, but the profits from Chapman's era were gone.

In October 1927 John Henry Davies died, aged just sixty-three. In 1902, he had headed the club's revival, saving the club from economic ruin, but also changing its name to Manchester United. He furthermore secured the services of Ernest Mangnall to the club and together with Mangnall he stood behind the club's first championship and cup success. Last, but not least, John Henry Davies built Old Trafford and moved the club's base from the north-east to the south-west of Manchester. Just before his death he fulfilled the club's wish to own Old Trafford, when his brewery sold the ground including the stadium to Manchester United.

But why didn't the successful businessman John Davies manage to keep the club at the top of English football? Without doubt, one of the reasons was that since 1910 Davies had not held an autocratic position, a position he had previously held with success. His withdrawal to a more anonymous role was the result of the Football League's witch-hunt against Manchester United in 1910, a hunt most considered to be a revenge for 'the Outcasts' affair. The pursuit resulted in the league publishing the club's illegal salary and bonus payments in the period 1903–1909. In the light of these revelations the FA demanded the club make organisational changes. This reduced Davies's absolute control and made it possible for the public to gain insight in the club's accounts and influence on the club operation. It was an unprecedented use of force, since the Football League in this way meddled with the club's internal organisation.

Davies's voice was thus no longer the only one heard after 1910, but the club had, however, been dependent on the Davies family's financial donations on several occasions. When Davies died in 1927, the board was of the belief they could get by without a saviour, but they were mistaken. In the following four years the gap between the supporters and the club increased, mainly as a consequence of the board's inaction on the transfer market and the arrogance they showed towards the supporters by refusing to engage in dialogue with them. It was as if in these years they built a growing barrier between the club and the fans, and it was only with James W. Gibson's commitment to the club at the end of 1931 that the barrier fell and the wounds began to heal. The fans' frustration and invitation to take action were in the first instance due to the results and the game played on the field. Herbert Bamlett attempted to transfer his attacking philosophy to Manchester United, but he didn't have the right players to do so.

In Bamlett's first full season at the club they returned to their original red shirts, having played in white shirts with a red V on the front since 1922. Not that it helped. In 1927/28 the club lay in the bottom half of the table for most of the season, and it was only a strong finish that saved them from relegation. Bamlett's biggest test in 1928/29 was to replace Frank Barson, and his choice fell on Billy Spencer, who was bought from Newcastle for £3,250, but immediately after his arrival at Old Trafford Spencer was diagnosed with malaria. Bamlett's battle with the previous year's defensive pragmatism in favour of a kind of utopianism, accentuating offence over defence, exhibited a laudable ambition. All very well, but with the available players this style only threatened to send the club back to the Second Division.

When Manchester United managed a record showing of sixteen league matches without victory, a possible place in the top six was replaced with a view from the bottom. With the purchase in February of Tom Reid from Liverpool the club's fortunes turned, ironically enough, against Liverpool. Tom Reid scored fourteen goals in seventeen matches in his first season, and in his one hundred and one matches for the club he scored an impressive sixty-seven goals. Reid was a physically strong and unflinching attacker. He was also a born leader, and leadership was in short supply at this time.

Manchester United ended the season in a respectable twelfth place after the season's last six matches achieved five victories and a tie. The formidable finish even made the optimists talk about Manchester United as the upcoming season's 'dark horse', but the reality, quickly proved to be completely different. In the season when the stock market collapsed on Wall Street in October 1929, Manchester United acted, according to Blundell, in the same way as the British government. They cut down on expenses, battened down the hatches and waited for the storm to subside.

* * *

In his first three seasons as manager of Manchester United, Herbert Bamlett had narrowly escaped relegation each time, as well as managing a record-breaking series of matches without victory. Bamlett in the summer of 1930 was a candidate to the title as the club's worst-ever manager. But in fairness to Bamlett he had also worked under the toughest conditions. Examples included a board-led ostrich policy and fear of contact with the transfer market, a global economic depression, an endless series of player sales and also a few career-damaging injuries to promising talents, such as Chris Taylor and Jimmy Hanson. But the fact is that the 1930/31 season didn't change Bamlett's reputation as the most unsuccessful Manchester United manager, it cemented it.

The season ended with a clear relegation. It was, in terms of the results, their worst season ever. The team started by losing the first twelve matches, and when they finally won, 197 days had passed since their last league victory. After the season's forty-two matches Manchester United were left with seven wins, eight draws and twenty-seven defeats. They were completely isolated at the bottom, nine points off Leeds. By the end of the season the club had already disposed of Bamlett.

Just a month into the fatal season the legend Charlie Roberts criticised the board for their lack of drive and warned them that the club was doomed to relegation if they didn't acquire nine new players. Admittedly, they didn't have luck on their side. According to the *Football Chronicle*, 'Manchester United are the unluckiest team in the country as regards injuries to players and they are, perhaps, the worst team in senior football.' United's scouts (with Louis Rocca in the lead) were at this time so desperate they reportedly retrieved Tommy Parker to Old Trafford directly from a construction site on Oxford Street where he was working as a plumber. Parker was the latest man to fill the vital space at centre half and was immediately proclaimed the club's new shooting star. He delivered a decent piece of work, but to wrestle the club free from the bottom, let alone eliminate the team's inferiority complex, was just too much to ask of one person.

The 1930/31 season also stands out because of one of the most remarkable incidents in Manchester United's history. At one point during the season the miserable results didn't seem to be the most urgent problem for many United fans, which, rather than focusing on the battles on the field, increasingly began to focus on the fight for the club's soul. According to the more political fans, the club's soul was in the process of being eaten up from the inside by a bunch of inept board members. With George Greenhough in charge, a series of meetings was arranged around Manchester in September 1930, where the club's management and future were discussed. The meetings were well attended, and they all ended up with a vote of censure to the board. Since the board still refused any form of communication with the dissatisfied fans, the latter resorted to an unconventional plan that was to boycott a match with the aim of demonstrating their strength. The choice fell on a home game against glamorous Arsenal on 18 October 1930.

The boycott had, given the standards back then, huge media attention. Most of the local media were sympathetic to the fans' concerns about the club's future and the team's ambition, and they were critical of the board's silence. However, they strongly disapproved of the idea of a boycott. The Arsenal match was watched by 23,406 spectators, which indicates the boycott didn't succeed. For a short time, Manchester United and the club's management were the country's sweethearts, since the intended boycott and the last few weeks of media stunts hadn't strengthened the fans' reputation around the country. Time justified the fans' actions as in the subsequent months every football fan with the slightest insight into the game had to admit things were not as they should be at Old Trafford. The original demands regarding a better scouting system, new players and an issue of shares for the purpose of obtaining transfer funds began to seem more and more equitable as the weeks passed and the defeats accumulated.

In May 1931 Manchester United was in a deplorable state, even worse than the situation of 1922, when the club was relegated to the Second Division. At that time, the club had money, first and foremost secured via John Davies's safe deposit box. Crowds flocked to Old Trafford, and the team consisted of a number of players on an international level. The reserve team consisted of a bead of talented young people, the defence was a class act, and it seemed inevitable that United would return to the First Division quickly. In 1931, however, it seemed that the club might move all the way down to the Third Division, as the board led an idle head-in-sand policy. The support from the crowd had fallen dramatically, both in relation to the number of attendees in the stadium, but also among the fan club's inner core. The debt grew and grew, the team was decimated, new talents suffered from their all-too-quick introduction into the first team, while the experienced players now had exceeded their sell-by date.

* * *

It's possible the 1930/31 season was the most disastrous in the club's history, but actually the 1931/32 season started almost as badly. On 3 October 1931 United lost 0–2 to Burnley and was third to last in the Second Division, the lowest place ever in the club's history. In addition, no one who knew anything about running a club wanted the job as manager at Manchester United. When the club during the summer of 1931 announced the manager post was free, they reportedly received applications from textile workers, removers, bricklayers and grocers – in fact, from everybody except real football managers.

The chronic absence of spectators finally got the board to act. Billy Meredith was hired as coach for the reserve team, ticket prices were lowered, the main grandstand was covered, and a special unemployment rate was imposed. But at the same time, both deficits and debt increased, and the club was forced to borrow £5,000 from John Davies's widow for salaries.

During the annual shareholder meeting in November 1931 G.H. Lawton, the chairman of the board, informed the shareholders the club lacked money and was no longer in a position to buy new players. He appealed to influential gentlemen to come to the club's rescue. No one came forward immediately, and when Walter Crickmer on Friday 18 December 1931 was told by the bank they had no more credit, he had neither the money to pay the players' salaries nor to purchase the employees' Christmas turkeys. If a Santa Claus had not come during the course of this weekend, the club would in all probability have collapsed and been forgotten.

And now we return to the beginning of this chapter. 'The long weekend' is over, it is Monday 21 December 1931 – James W. Gibson's Monday – and Manchester United is on the threshold of one of the club's many rebirths. Fifty-four-year-old James Gibson isn't the most obvious saviour of a football club. He is wealthy, but he has not previously taken an interest in football. What Gibson has, however, is a weakness to take over ailing companies and make them profitable. He is also in possession of a considerable portion of bourgeois pride and local patriotism – and he knows that Manchester United is absolutely one of Lancashire's most prestigious enterprises. He says: 'I do not think it would help Manchester business and Lancashire trade in general if such a famous club as United was allowed to drop out without some definite stand being made to resurrect it.'

In December 1931 Gibson promises to take care of the club from 16 December to 9 January. He makes it clear his commitment to the club stops in January unless he is given a clear statement from the club supporters showing that they are behind him. With the successful businessman's typical self-confidence Gibson says to the local newspapers: 'My only concern is that the public will respond to my appeal. . . . For a month I am at the disposal of Manchester United and during that time I want to see if the public of Manchester desire football at Old Trafford. If in the course of that month I find them coming down to the ground I will redouble my efforts. Although I have undertaken to see United through the coming month, I am not going to be a milch cow.' If Gibson gets the desired response from the public, he would, as he said, 'place Manchester United, if possible, on a level with the great teams in the country, such as Arsenal.' He goes on: 'And I also want to see the Pop Side people at Old Trafford afforded some protection from the bad weather . . . and I will also see that United have a manager who will be one of the best in the country and will be paid accordingly. . . . I shall then look at the first team. United want a good centre-half, a centre forward and two wingers. Money ranging anywhere from £12,000 to £20,000 must be expected to be spent in securing players.' Clear speech and clear priorities. Gibson knows precisely where it hurts, what it takes and how much it will cost, and he is also aware of why it has come to this. The board has been unforgivably sluggish, just as they have wrongly refused to communicate with the supporters.

On 21 December the board announces they are willing to step down after 9 January, if Gibson wants to continue his commitment to the club. In the following days the FA give their blessing to the takeover. What perhaps is more worrying is that Gibson is also given the green light to select the team. But Gibson is sly, both in PR and in football terms. In a conciliatory gesture he teams up with the rebel George Greenhough, who proposes to Gibson the responsibility of the team line-up should be shared between Walter Crickmer, Jack Pullar and Navigator, the secretary of the club, the coach and a football writer from one of the local newspapers. From today's perspective this approach seems a bit amateurish, to put it mildly, but we must also remember the club is a sinking ship. For a start, the fact the selection of the team is now carried out by three football-competent gentlemen is more than can be said about many of the clubs in the First Division at this time.

With regard to the choice of the manager, James Gibson reveals to Greenhough he is looking for someone who is ready to assume full control of all aspects of the playing side, while he himself will oversee the business aspect. For the manager's position, Gibson is thinking of ex-players who through their own experience can take hold of the ball and demonstrate to the players, what they may be doing wrong. The idea of dividing the club into football and business sections, plus the idea of a manager in a tracksuit, is still a little way off. This would be first realised with the recruitment of Matt Busby in 1945.

Gibson's plea to the public is put to the test on 25 December 1931, when Manchester United play at home against Wolverhampton Wanderers. Six days earlier only 4,697 spectators had turned up, when United lost 0–1 to the absolute bottom club Bristol City. Wolves are the division's top team, later to be crowned champions, and in a match that United surprisingly win 3–2, over 33,123 fans have turned up. The test has been passed and Gibson given a clear indication of the public's support. On 5 January 1932 Gibson accepts the debt of more than £40,000, and on 20 January the new board with James Gibson as chairman is inaugurated. A week later he is appointed president.

The results continued to be poor during the spring, but Gibson kept his word and invested £13,000 in nine new players during the course of the season's last three months. The purchases sent a clear signal of grit and determination, but most of the players did not have the ability to succeed at Old Trafford. Off the pitch the club seemed to be on the road to becoming 'United' again. The peace process had begun when Gibson had invited Greenhough on-board, just as he had also recognised the fans should not be penalised for anything regarding the boycott. The Supporters' Club now announced plans to organise trips to Manchester United's away games, just as they would help to improve the facilities of the stadium. As a gesture of thanks, the Supporters' Club was made an official fan club, and an office and meeting place was built on Old Trafford's grounds.

* * *

Scott Duncan had been a star player at Newcastle and Glasgow Rangers, and had managerial credentials from the Scottish club Cowdenbeath when he arrived at Old Trafford in the summer of 1932 as Manchester United's new manager. In addition to Duncan's arrival, Gibson's desire to spend big and the general reconciliation between club and fans there was one more element giving great promise for the future. Manchester United joined a junior team coached by Clarence Hilditch to the Manchester League, and thereby started what in 1938 became Manchester United Junior Athletic Club, the foundation on which Matt Busby and Jimmy Murphy later built the famous Busby Babes.

But all the talk about a speedy return to the First Division proved to be too optimistic. In his first season at the club Scott Duncan led Manchester United to sixth place in the Second Division. In a disastrous second season he was only ninety minutes from leading the club into the Third Division. Only a 2–0 victory at Millwall in the last game of the season saved Manchester United from total humiliation. In his fourth season the Scot finally succeeded in winning the Second Division and thus secured the longed-for return to the big table.

In addition to investing £35,000 in the modernisation of Old Trafford, James Gibson also succeeded in 1936 in persuading the local authorities to place a train station right next to the main entrance of the stadium. The club's first season in the First Division after five years away ended with another painful relegation and the club had to visit the Second Division again. In September 1937 Scott Duncan stood down as manager, and Walter Crickmer once more demonstrated his loyalty to the club when he temporarily took over the manager's post again. Crickmer managed to lead the club straight back up to the First Division.

In 1937/38 the club had secured the players that were to play a leading role in climbing football's peaks after the war. Louis Rocca had been on a spying raid in Dublin where the club's Irish scout Billy Behan had spotted the young inside forward Johnny Carey, and Rocca bought him for £250. Then, during a holiday on the south coast, James Gibson attended a match where a talented attacker by the name of Jack Rowley stood out for Bournemouth and Gibson tempted him immediately to Old Trafford. A pre-war ascent didn't lie in the cards as in 1939 United finished in fourteenth place in the First Division. But the purchases of Carey and Rowley showed the club's scouting system had been improved, and in 1938 Gibson, Crickmer and Rocca created the famous

Manchester United Junior Athletic Club (MUJAC). It was the most ambitious formalisation of youth players in the entire country and an essential element in the club's hierarchy.

Three matches into 1939/40 Adolf Hitler put a stop to league football in England, and the league wasn't resumed until six years later. With its location close to the industrial estate of Trafford Park, Manchester Ship Canal and the railway, Old Trafford was exposed when the German Luftwaffe bombed Manchester. During the blitz in March 1941, Old Trafford was bombed twice, and the entire main stand was destroyed, just as part of the pitch and other stands were hit.

15 February 1945
Matt Busby's arrival at Old Trafford

'Bryn boru' was, according to Rick Glanvill, the prophetic words by which Sir Matt Busby's grandfather used to call his grandson, when he was playing with the street's other children. This was in the small coal-mining town of Orbiston in North Lanarkshire in western Scotland. The words mean 'a leader of men', and this was the distinction that characterised Matt Busby throughout his life: as a child, as a footballer at Liverpool and Manchester City, as a soldier during the Second World War, but, first and foremost, as Manchester United's legendary manager for twenty-five years. From the day Matt Busby walked into Manchester United to his death in 1994, he was revered by the people of Manchester in a degree only granted to respected priests in Catholic communities, as Eamon Dunphy remarks in his excellent biography on Busby, *A Strange Kind of Glory* (1991).

On 15 December 1944 the Italian Catholic immigrant Louis Rocca sent a letter to his friend the Scottish Catholic immigrant Matt Busby. At this time Busby was Company Sergeant Major Instructor and still on contract in Liverpool as playing coach:

Dear Matt,
No doubt you will be surprised to get this letter from your old pal Louis. Well Matt I have been trying for the past month to find you and not having your Reg. address I could not trust a letter going to Liverpool, as what I have to say is so important. I don't know if you have considered about what you are going to do when war is over, but I have a great job for you if you are willing to take it on. Will you get into touch with me at the above address and when you do I can explain things to you better, when I know there will be no danger of interception. Now Matt I hope this is plain to you. You see I have not forgotten my old friend either in my prayers or in your future welfare. I hope your good wife and family are all well and please God you will soon be home to join their happy circle.

Wishing you a very Happy Xmas and a lucky New Year.
With all God's Blessings in you and yours

Your Old Pal,
Louis Rocca

The letter is unceremonial, but with an unmistakable religious touch and a characteristic Italian Catholic care in relation to the family. Matt Busby's contractual relationship with Liverpool led to Rocca informing Busby of the vacant manager's seat at Manchester United without elaborating upon it. It appeared Busby was very much interested in returning to Manchester with its cosmopolitan atmosphere and its huge share of Catholic immigrants from Ireland and Scotland. Manchester United also appealed to him as a club. It had it all – except sporting success.

The war was not yet over when on 15 February 1945 Busby turned up to an interview with James W. Gibson. It would prove to be one of the most important meetings in the club's history. It was not as random as the meeting between the dog Major and John Davies forty-four years earlier, but just as important. During the conversation thirty-five-year-old Busby insisted he himself would be in charge of the recruitment of his closest employees, and he demanded full control over all aspects regarding football. Gibson was impressed by the sincerity and uncompromising approach in Busby's vision of the new manager role. On 19 February 1945 Manchester United recruited Matt Busby as manager. However, Busby didn't start as manager until October that year, as he wasn't demobilised from the army until mid-autumn.

The recruitment of Matt Busby was, as Stephen Wagg (a professor of sport at Leeds University) points out, the club's entrance into modernity. It was under Busby the uniqueness and the legend of Manchester United was born and consolidated. It was in this period the values we associate with the club (entertainment, youth, glamour, Europe and the English–Celtic) began to settle in people's collective consciousness. Since its founding in 1878, Manchester United had been just another provincial club with a limited national fan base. Manchester City had been more successful, if you take out United's short reign 1908–11 when Mangnall led the club to two championships and one FA Cup triumph. During the Matt Busby reign the club transformed not just from being little brother to big brother in Manchester but also from mediocre to mammoth in England. And from being permanent front-page news in the *Manchester Evening News*, the club's name was now often mentioned on the sport pages in Madrid, Montevideo and Moscow.

Matt Busby incarnated a new kind of egalitarian modernity, which was half-revolutionary, half-zeitgeist, but at the same time his paternal style endowed him with a certain traditionalism. The prototypical image of Busby pictures him with pipe in hand, wearing a Crombie and Trilby. He was stylised as the authoritative patriarch: 'Matt the player was dignified and charismatic; Matt the manager was powerful, a paternalist in an age of authoritarianism. A man of action and a visionary, a football man to the core, with the bearing and political instinct of a cardinal,' says Dunphy.

During the 1940s and 1950s the football manager increasingly became synonymous with the team and its performances. With Herbert Chapman (Huddersfield 1921–25, Arsenal 1925–34) and Frank Buckley (Wolverhampton 1927–44) the prototype of a new type of manager had appeared before the war. The old generation of desk managers who worked from eight in the morning until four in the afternoon and carried a pocket watch in their suit gave way to the strategist who prepared the players' performance and operated rigid tactical systems. Busby was a new kind of 'boss' in tracksuit and muddy boots who even participated in the training. By replacing the office with the training grounds, and through his past as a professional footballer, Busby reduced the distance between himself and the players, creating a more egalitarian culture. On the training pitch the new manager type and his coaches worked seriously with the players' technique and tactical understanding in order to 'organise victory', as Herbert Chapman described the new practice. Before the new regime, it was a widespread attitude that players should not train with the ball during the course of the week because they would be tired of it before Saturday's match. Busby revolutionised this side of the workout and included the ball in most exercises. One of his mantras was: 'The ball is round to go around.'

Previously the manager had been the board's extended arm, a kind of secretary, who just completed orders from above. Matt Busby's redefinition of the manager transformed this from henchmen to autocrat in the matter of tactics, transfers and coaching. The manager's position was thus moved slightly away from the board and closer toward the players. An incident in connection with one of Busby's first matches as manager of Manchester United, illustrates very well this new type of manager, as well as reflecting Busby's tactful but uncompromising attitude. During one match Busby overheard Harold Hardman, a prominent member of the board, loudly criticising his stubborn faith in an out of form Johnny Carey. Busby decided to confront Hardman, but rather than do it right away, he waited until half time. In the men's room he told Hardman in no uncertain terms that he did not tolerate interference in his business, that is, in all matters regarding the football side of the club. And he did not want to find that his decisions were questioned in the presence of outsiders. The story, which Busby himself has told, is an important component in the myth of Matt Busby as 'the first great football manager', the sovereign leader and the brains behind his team.

Busby's reaction would have been impossible ten years earlier, but the football community was changing in the years after the war. Busby had an ally in the board in James Gibson. The two were mutually dependent. Gibson needed a type like Busby, a professional that could realise his dream of Manchester United as a new football superpower that developed its own players. Busby needed Gibson, a guardian angel, who was able to secure him the optimal working conditions that he needed.

* * *

There were more minorities in Manchester than in most other cities of the United Kingdom, and the town's heterogeneous population resulted in a relatively tolerant, open-minded and cosmopolitan atmosphere. In Orbiston, before Busby moved to Manchester to play for City in the 1920s, as a descendant of Irish Catholics among Scottish protestants he had experienced first-hand the sectarian and ugly face of bigotry. From his earliest days, Busby felt like an outsider, but in Manchester he was at home among other outsiders; the city's Jews and Catholics (Italian, Scottish and Irish) all shared this feeling.

Manchester was not like a forest, where the trees' roots grew deep into the ground and where the hierarchy between large and small trees was predetermined. Rather, the town was defined by its channels, where the constant flow of water ensured things didn't stand still. In such an environment, the human identity was determined more by what you did, rather than which tribe you belonged to. For both Jews and Catholics, Manchester was a good place to plant new roots.

As Dunphy notes, it seemed as if the Italian charm and the Irish laughter had softened the potentially rigid mass of English protestants, so that Manchester's blood was a well-proportioned hodgepodge of different nationalities, religions and cultures. The world of arts, the entertainment industry and sports were contact zones in a city characterised by its *joie de vivre* and unrestraint. At Old Trafford on a Saturday you could find painters, clerical officers and factory workers, just as it wasn't unusual for the self-created businessman to witness the première of Samuel Beckett's new stage play.

Football played an important role in the creation of the city's self-awareness. Billy Meredith's flamboyant style and his romantic rebellion against football's conservatism and its 'little shopkeepers' at the beginning of the century had, as Dunphy also notes, clearly found an echo in Manchester's soul. The triumphant outsider simply appealed to this city, which to a greater extent than most other cities consisted (and consists) of hikers and the maladjusted. A modern example is of course Eric Cantona, a Frenchman by birth, but spiritually a Mancunian: 'I feel close to the rebelliousness and vigour of the youth here. Perhaps time will separate us, but nobody can deny that here, behind the windows of Manchester, there is an insane love of football, of celebration and of music.'

*   *   *

Billy Meredith had in the beginning of the twentieth century redefined the professional footballer's identity, and Herbert Chapman had before the war been tactically innovative. Matt Busby set about an even more radical approach. His analysis of football's problems didn't stop at the individual player, at the team, or even at the manager: it went all the way to the trunk from which the player, the team and the manager grows. Busby said: 'I did not set out to build a team. The task ahead was much bigger than that. What I really embarked upon was the building of a system, which would produce not one team, but four or five, each occupying a rung of the ladder the summit of which was the first XI.' Busby radically redefined the manager role, but the redefining was inextricably connected to and was a by-product of his vision of the modern football club as a living organism, where all parts were dependent on all the others.

Busby's paternal physical appearance, the pipe, hat and coat, is closely linked to the manager culture and the club ethos, which he introduced at his arrival at Old Trafford. He succeeded in creating a true family atmosphere and an egalitarian, 'one-for-all and all-for-one' culture at Manchester United, where no one was bigger than the club, and where the players were regarded as human beings. According to Dunphy, Busby had brought this strong belief in community and solidarity with him from Orbiston. The sectarianism that Busby had seen overground in Orbiston was incompatible with the mining work underground, where everyone was equal and dependent on each other. The autonomy and individualism in the mine were downplayed to the benefit of a necessary collectivism, and this life had given Matt Busby a dose of socialism. In addition, Busby lost his father during the First World War, and family was almost a phobia to him. The Old Trafford family was the replacement for the family he experienced only briefly as a child before it fell into pieces with his father's death and the entry of the stepfather in the family.

Matt Busby revolutionised Manchester United and football in several ways. On the pitch he guided the workout, which through exercises with a ball focused on tactics and in particular technique, and off the pitch he transformed the club into one large family with himself as head. Busby's intention was to humanise football and clean it of some of its evils. It meant making football professional on an intrinsic level. Busby was seeking players and staff who possessed character. To Busby a player showed character if he fought to the last whistle, but character also had something to do with how the player trained. How he behaved in the locker room towards young players, how he lived his life outside of the pitch, and whether he was still excited of the game's inherent beauty and uncontaminated by cynicism.

* * *

In October 1945 thirty-six-year-old Matt Busby arrived at a club whose basic construction and external frame showed clear signs of metal fatigue and even damages. That not all the players had yet returned from the war was also the case with all the other clubs in the league, not just Manchester United. The other clubs likewise shared the general uncertainty about the constitution in which the players would return. But with a bombed Old Trafford, where trees and weeds grew up through the concrete and where the field consisted of several bomb craters, Manchester United was undoubtedly hard hit. In addition, Busby took over a club that had a debt of £15,000.

The critical state of the stadium was not only an inconvenience but it also helped Busby create a shared atmosphere of a new beginning. Because the club was on its knees it was easier for Busby to leave his mark on it. It's also important to note that Busby – in spite of some cracks in the concrete – took over a good foundation that James Gibson, Louis Rocca and Walter Crickmer in the last decade before the war had worked hard to build. The formalisation of the youth work was one element, the slow creation of a team a second. The right ingredients were already there, so to speak, but the recipe was missing.

Busby's first manoeuvre as manager is considered by many to also be the most important: the recruitment of Jimmy Murphy as an assistant. In Italy during the war Busby had overheard Murphy's electrifying team talk to a squad of soldiers, and he had become convinced the Welshman's enthusiasm and raw energy would be a good addition to his own more calm and diplomatic style. In the following twenty-five years Busby and Murphy formed an unbreakable unit on the basis of a random meeting somewhere in the south of Italy.

To the players, who one by one returned to Manchester United after the war, the idea of a manager in a tracksuit was almost impossible to grasp. In addition, the players were told that Busby's door was always open, even for problems of a personal nature. This 'open door' policy supported the community ideology Busby launched upon his arrival at the club. The hierarchy wasn't dissolved but, in contrast to the past, it was emphasised that all played an important role and all were treated as human beings.

In the summer of 1946 Manchester United got ready for their first season after the Second World War. In England, Clement Attlee of the Labour Party had just won a landslide victory over Winston Churchill. It seemed that the English people had rejected the victorious warlord Churchill and the old Conservative values. Attlee's intention was to create a new and more just society based on equality. Although austerity was a large factor in the English society of the post-war years, the British felt new times were on their way, and this sense of a whole new social order was, according to Dunphy, reflected on Manchester United's training fields. Clement Attlee, one of the most popular prime ministers in England's history, was head of a popular and socialist government, and Attlee embodied a democratic leadership style. Busby's project to reconstruct Manchester United as a big club on both a mental and structural level mirrored Attlee's national reconstruction's project.

One of the reasons for the fascination in the Busby myth is undoubtedly its flexibility. If Busby's merits cannot be doubted, and if his revolutionary vision of the manager's role and the club as a family can't be debated, then his tactical intelligence is still a disputed question. In the early 1960s, shortly before a match, Noel Cantwell asked Busby 'How do we play?' and Busby supposedly answered: 'We play football.' The exchange of words between the captain and the manager symbolises the semantic diversity, or perhaps ambivalence, that is deeply rooted in the myth of Matt Busby.

Busby's critics interpret the answer as a testament to his tactical shortcomings and sloppiness. But to Busby's proponents the answer is a testament to his exceptional charisma and several players have stated that Busby always had a strong awareness of how the team should play. The real truth of Busby probably lies somewhere in between. It would be wrong to call him sloppy, but with today's eyes there is no doubt Busby didn't go into detail with tactics. He was operating with a general purpose (to win in style), he had a method (to indoctrinate a series of simple, but fundamental 'truths' in his team, such as 'the ball is round to go around' and 'make it simple, give it to a red shirt') and he implemented a structure (in the beginning the traditional 2–3–5 / 3–2–2–3, later the new 4–2–4), but he rarely focused on the opposing team's strengths and weaknesses. Behind Busby's laconic reply to Cantwell hides the fact that he and Jimmy Murphy in the course of the week again and again had implanted the players with their football philosophy. As Busby has said himself: 'When I came here, I set out to have a team play methodical and progressive football. . . . This will always be my policy, so I leave it to the players to supply the answer.'

On one hand, this seems to point to Busby's implementation of a methodical master plan. On the other hand, Busby suggests his players were not mechanical robots. They were expected, via their instinct, intelligence, and intuition, to come up with creative and individual solutions to the ad hoc 'questions' that occurred in the course of the match. Thus, it was a characteristic of Busby that he gave his creative players both a long and loose leash on the field. Expressed in a more philosophical way, it was not so much the geometric fascination as the existentialistic gesture that had weight in Busby's football philosophy. Rather than being programmatical and strategical as a chess player he accepted that *football is intentions dancing with contingency*, and that the beauty of football, therefore, is inextricably linked to elements of randomness, chaos and unpredictability.

We can therefore argue that Busby – if you disregard the elementary, constitutive principles – barely interfered, as his aim was to let the players focus on what they did best. From this perspective he represents the great reconciler and is also a transition figure who, through his charisma and prudent perceptiveness, according to Wagg, managed to combine science and art, coaching and nature, organisation and spontaneity, tradition and modernity. On one hand, Busby is the very image of a world where the word 'gay' was still used in its original sense of being bright or lively, but on the other side he was also fond of saying 'express yourself' to his players, forty years before Madonna made it her post-modern mantra.

It is therefore possible that Matt Busby's tactical profile didn't correspond to the strategist who 'organises victory.' Busby was not a Herbert Chapman, an Alf Ramsey nor a José Mourinho. He was no cynical optimising calculator and risk minimiser. But he had a main football philosophy, which was to allow the players to express themselves creatively. This philosophy also meant that Busby's Manchester United was the first British team who consistently tried to play football 'from the back'. When he arrived at Old Trafford, one of Busby's most inspiring tactical manoeuvres was to transform offensive-minded players into defenders. Busby's retraining of both Johnny Carey and John Aston Snr from inner wing to back triggered not only a tremendous blossoming of these players but also resulted in a new form of football that people flocked to the stadium to watch.

Therefore it's possible to say that in tactical terms Busby didn't focus on the details, and he couldn't (or wasn't prepared to) adjust to the opponent. But the shifting positions he implemented in Manchester United's post-war squad, bears witness of his overall philosophical aim in football – to play entertaining football with emphasis on passing and technique – but also of his tactical intelligence as he shifted through the positional that created a better and more powerful team. He also provoked the emergence of previously hidden potentials in the involved players, who for their part, thrived in their new positions. If the ingredients were already present in the team, then the answer to the missing recipe was the positional shifts and the methodological indoctrination.

* * *

In Matt Busby's first five seasons as manager of Manchester United they achieved four second places and one fourth. The media, Busby himself and many within the club began to wonder if Manchester United would ever succeed in winning the championship, but in spite of the lack of gold medals it was Busby's United people were talking about and wanted to see. In the seasons after the war spectators flocked to Maine Road and Old Trafford to watch Manchester United's attractive football. On 17 January 1948 the team played out a 1–1 draw against Arsenal in front of 81,962 spectators at Maine Road, which is still a record for a league match in England.

The 1947/48 season also brought the coveted FA Cup back to the club after almost thirty-nine years. On 24 April 1948 Manchester United wins 4–2 against Blackpool in the FA Cup final at Wembley. Around 99,000 spectators are witnesses to perhaps the best final ever. Outside Wembley before the match, a tout attempts to sell three-shilling tickets for £6 but, as a newspaper reports, the crowd is appalled at his shameless greed. Amid the commotion the poor thing ends up losing all of his tickets. Inside the footballing cathedral Matt Busby lines up the following team:

In addition Manchester United, surprisingly, are playing in royal blue shirts. The match is remembered especially for being extremely well played. The day after, the *News of the World* acclaim the contest as 'Wembley's finest final'. In addition, the final goes down in the history books because Manchester United dramatically turn a 1–2 into a 4–2. The metamorphosis from a threatening trauma to a defiant triumph in the last twenty minutes of the match is referred to in the history of football as 'the Manchester miracle'. The team's impressive comeback invariably brings one's mind to another Manchester miracle, namely at the Camp Nou in 1999 against Bayern Munich.

At Wembley, Blackpool have been dominating the match for seventy minutes, but as Jack Rowley with his second goal equalises Blackpool's 2–1 lead with twenty minutes left of the match it is as if only one team can win. Rowley's performance is an epic allegory, with 'Opportunism' in the lead role. Rowley's first goal is the result of a seemingly hopeless chase after the ball, but since Hayward and Robinson, Blackpool's goalkeeper, misunderstand each other, Rowley ruthlessly cuts through in between them and intercepts the ball, after which he elegantly slides past Robinson and equalises. Rowley's second goal is a spectacular header: with a predator's one-dimensional determination he throws himself towards Charlie Mitten's free kick and heads the ball unstoppably into the goal.

The germ of Manchester United's remarkable resurrection has already been planned shortly after the beginning of the second half, when with subdued voices the captain Johnny Carey and centre-half Allenby Chilton hold a tactical meeting in the middle of the field. As a general and his lieutenant on the battlefield consulting on the strategy, Johnny Carey was Matt Busby's alter ego: the calm, pipe-smoking 'Gentleman Johnny' off the pitch, the indestructible and stoic leader in the field. Carey wasn't the aggressive motivator as, for example, Roy Keane was later on. That role belonged to the former coalmine worker Allenby Chilton. Chilton was the verbal stalwart in the locker room and on the field, a physical giant of an unostentatious midfield stopper in the style of Mark Jones and Jaap Stam. Along with Carey he formed a leadership of two, with equal shares of physical aggression and mental nerve.

Carey's intelligent message slowly spread to the rest of the team this afternoon at Wembley: 'Keep on playing football. Fight, but *play* football. The goals will come.' And they did. First with Rowley's equaliser, and then a few minutes later with Stan Pearson who puts United in front 3–2. The goal is merciless, as it falls just a few seconds after Stan Mortensen has spurned a chance at the other end of the field. John Anderson is United's last goal-scorer of the game.

The match shows Matt Busby's mark on the team, which in adversity reacts as a strong collective. Johnny Carey displays an Olympic calmness throughout the match and his confidence has an impact on the rest of the team. Johnny Morris is tireless in his attempts to penetrate Blackpool's defence; Stan Pearson, a local boy from Salford who came to the club in 1936 and made his début as a seventeen-year-old, was usually the team's brain. On this day he is full of creative ideas. John Aston, who plays directly opposite Stanley Matthews, looks like he has played left back all his life. But most importantly of all, the team believes Busby's proverb 'the ball is round to go around' in time will lead to goals.

On 24 August 1949, after three years in exile at Maine Road, Manchester United return to Old Trafford. They celebrate by winning 3–0 against local rivals Bolton Wanderers. The day marks yet another of those moments where the club, or in this case their famous arena, rises from the ruins.

* * *

After their FA Cup triumph in 1948 the question of wages surfaces again, just as it had done four decades earlier during Meredith's and Roberts's agitations. In 1948 the maximum wage was only £14, and the maximum bonus for a victory was £2, an amount that had been set during the 1920s. Many clubs were circumventing the restrictions by paying illegal bonuses, but Busby was not prepared for such steps. Instead he tried to get perks for the players, for example free cinema tickets and access to Manchester's clubs, as well as organising an annual outing for all employees of the club. In addition to the turbulence with the players' wages, there was in these years also a growing feeling that the team was in need of new blood.

It created headlines in the summer of 1950 when Charlie Mitten was the key figure in one of the most bizarre transfer sagas in football history. Mitten was without doubt one of English football's most talented wingers. He was rough and extremely obstinate, two character traits that may have made his play unpredictable, but did not always helped his game. Mitten was, however, a favourite of the spectators. When he took penalties, for example, he asked the goalkeeper to tell him where he had to kick. Mitten always went by the goalie's directions, but this didn't stop him from scoring.

Disillusioned with the poor wages in English football, Mitten broke his contract with Manchester United. The FIFA rules of the time banned Mitten from playing for other clubs, but since Colombia was not yet a member of FIFA, Mitten could freely travel to Bogotá and play for Santa Fe. Mitten said that just by signing the contract with Santa Fe he had already earned as much as he had done during the last fourteen years at home in England. As Colombia a year later became a member of FIFA, Mitten and the other European players were forced to return to their clubs again. Busby gave Mitten a fine of £250 and a suspension of six months, after which he sold him to Fulham for £25,000.

In spite of the general feeling of break-up Busby maintained his belief that many of his players still had what it took to win the championship, and in the season 1951/52 they finally succeeded. The championship was the old guard's swan song. One new face from MUJAC established himself in the team this season: Roger Byrne, the first 'Babe'. In the second last match against Chelsea the Red Devils retained their nerve and won 3–0 at Old Trafford. The result meant only Arsenal were able to catch them, but they needed a victory of seven goals in their mutual showdown in Manchester on the season's last match day. Amazingly Manchester United won 6–1, and 53,651 overexcited fans could thus celebrate the club's first championship win since 1911. Apart from Rowley, Pearson, Johnny Berry and Byrne, the driving force of the team was the reliable and rock-solid Chilton, the captain Carey, the agile Henry Cockburn, goalkeeper Reg Allen and inside forward John Downie.

James W. Gibson didn't see Manchester United win the championship as he died in September 1951 from a stroke. Over a period of twenty years Gibson had been the architect behind Manchester United's recovery, and he had also been Busby's ally on the board. With Gibson away and Harold Hardman in the role as the new chairman Busby feared a more sluggish and conservative board of directors, which in the worst case scenario would be able to block his vision of Manchester United as one of Europe's leading football teams. Busby's counter move was to recruit Louis Edwards, a local businessman, who Busby believed could serve as his new ally in the corridors of power, and whom he hoped one day to see in the head chair. It was not until 1958 Busby's man managed to be elected to the board; it happened in the days after Munich.

9 June 1952
Duncan from Dudley
and Busby's Babes

It is Monday afternoon. We are in Manchester in the early summer. The date on the calendar is 9 June 1952. For many fifteen-year-old boys school is now a closed chapter, but for a few the end of the school year also means the beginning of a new adventure, where pencil, desk and school uniform are replaced by ball, training ground and the red and white of the club uniform. In these weeks Manchester United is like a powerful magnet that pulls the best young football players across the UK towards it. This attraction applies to Gordon Clayton and his young friend this Monday afternoon in June. Together they have taken the trip to Manchester from Dudley, a city located between Birmingham and Wolverhampton some 100 kilometres away. Manchester United's youth coach Bert Whalley meets them at London Road Station, today's Piccadilly Station, in the heart of Manchester. He is full of expectations, as he, like all the others in the club, has great hopes for the two lads, especially for Clayton's companion.

His name is Duncan Edwards, and in football circles he is already well known. Edwards certainly seems to be predetermined to have his name engraved on football's starry sky. All the big clubs have tried to entice him with a contract, but for Duncan Edwards there is only one club: Matt Busby's Manchester United. Many today believe Duncan Edwards to be the best footballer England has ever produced. But 'Munich' took his life when he was only twenty-one years old. In the summer of 1952, this tragic event, however, is still six years away; Duncan Edwards has not yet turned sixteen.

* * *

In 1931, when James Gibson came to the club's rescue, one of his clear objectives was to create a Manchester United with players from Manchester. In a board meeting that year Gibson spoke on 'the advisability of running a colts or nursery team from next season'. The work to create young players, said Gibson some years later, 'must be thoroughly done to be effective. This is so that a common idea and technique shall unite the junior with the senior members of the playing staff. . . . It is from these unusually comprehensive nurseries that the club hopes an all-Manchester team to some distant period might be produced.'

After the war, Busby and Murphy advocated the same philosophy using the same vocabulary. The horizon was no longer so strictly local, though, and where Gibson's vision was endowed with a glow of local patriotic ideology, Busby knew that it was also important to make a virtue of necessity. The club was struggling with growing debt, and from a financial point of view it was advisable, even imperative, to invest in their own players. Busby was not free of ideology, and he attributed to the youth academy an important ideological double function: to imbue young talents with Manchester United's flamboyant football style and to plant a strong club loyalty within them.

The history of Manchester United can be said to be a long red thread, but there are incidents and events in the club's history that threaten to break it. It is this continuity combined with these ruptures that make Manchester United a very special football club. The academy and youth work is one of the main elements of the continuity. An example that can support this claim is the fact that Manchester United in 1968, three decades after James Gibson's declarations of intent and the creation of MUJAC, won the European Cup with a team that included eight players who were a product of the club's academy. The example becomes even more striking when you consider that just ten years before the triumph at Wembley in 1968 the club experienced the tragedy of losing a whole team in the disaster at Munich. A more fatal breach than the Munich disaster is unthinkable, but for that very reason, one cannot imagine a more striking example of the red thread's strength, that is, the survival instinct of continuity, than the victory over Benfica in 1968.

In 1945 Busby took over as manager in a club that had already been at the forefront of youth work, but where the war had ended the development. If MUJAC had not yet produced a clutch of young players with championship team potential, and perhaps didn't seem to do so in the near future, then it is important to point out that Busby arrived at a club that already had the intention of working seriously with its youth. The club's fundamental values were thus consistent with Matt Busby's ideas. Busby was not the inventor of modern football's youth policy, but, as Arthur Hopcraft, author of *The Football Man*, rightly states, more than any other he invested his conviction and his reputation in the youth work.

It took seven years before this work began to bear fruit. In the championship season of 1951/52 Matt Busby introduced two players from MUJAC into the first team: twenty-one-year-old Roger Byrne and eighteen-year-old Jackie

Blanchflower. The year before, during the 1949/50 season, the seventeen-year-old Mark Jones had already played four matches. Busby had even given sixteen-year-old Jeff Whitefoot his first team debut, which was completely unheard of at the time.

If you look at it from the perspective of 1952, there is no doubt the first Championship in forty-one years was a huge redemption for Manchester United, whose name in the post-war years was almost synonymous with silver medals. But if you look at it from the perspective of today, the 1951/52 season is remembered primarily because the English population for the first time was introduced to the concept of 'Babes'. On 24 November 1951 Manchester United met Liverpool at Anfield. The result was not particularly spectacular (0–0), but the introduction of Jackie Blanchflower and Roger Byrne in the away team's defence line was. Their performance made Tom Jackson from the *Manchester Evening News* write the following statement, which has gone down in the history of football journalism as a classic: 'United's "babes" were cool and confident' (some attribute, however, the invention of the term 'the Busby Babes' to Jackson's colleague Frank Nicklin).

Jackson (or Nicklin) was thus the first who captured a phenomenon that in the following years set the agenda in the English and international football world. On a cultural-historical level the Busby Babes reflected the emerging youth culture of the 1950s and, with their youth and energy, optimism and faith in the future emanated from them in the austerity-ridden post-war England. According to the English playwright John Osborne, one of England's 'angry young men' and the author of *Look Back in Anger* (1956/1958), the English society in the 1950s was unimaginative, colourless and petrified. Busby's Babes were the antithesis of this characteristic.

The 1952/53 season represented in many ways an anti-climax after the championship of the year before, when Manchester United finished in a disappointing eighth place. Matt Busby realised the old guard had peaked, and during the season the 'Busby Babes' rooted themselves in people's collective consciousness. It happened as Busby extended the previous season's Babe-list with seventeen-year-old David Pegg, twenty-one-year-old Tommy Taylor, nineteen-year-old Denis Viollet, twenty-year-old Bill Foulkes and sixteen-year-old Duncan Edwards.

Tommy Taylor stood out from the other players on the list, by not being from the club's own academy. As a result of the extensive investment in youth work he was the only player Busby purchased between 1953 and 1957. The purchase of Tommy Taylor was 'breaking news', and a TV station even produced a small film about Taylor. Taylor was bought from Barnsley for the record-breaking amount of £29,999. It was Busby who persuaded Barnsley's manager to take one pound off the price, so Taylor would not feel weighed down by being the first player who passed the £30,000 limit. This manoeuvre had the intended effect. The fans were excited about their new attacking comet and named him immediately 'The Smiling Executioner' because of his contradictory attributes of being a constantly happy boy and merciless goal-scoring executioner. Taylor, who was a classical strong-in-the-air number 9, proved to be the ideal replacement for the predator Rowley, and in 191 games for Manchester United he scored 131 goals.

Although Chilton, Rowley, Cockburn and Pearson still played a role in the season 1953/54, statistics clearly show it was players like Byrne, Whitefoot, Taylor, Foulkes, Viollet, Blanchflower, Edwards and Pegg who increasingly represented the team's backbone. In a 0–0 away match against Huddersfield on 31 October 1953, Manchester United's team included seven players in their teens. In the next season only Chilton and Rowley of the old guard made the cut. On the other hand, both Albert Scanlon and Liam Whelan announced their arrival. When Eddie Colman joined the team during the 1955/56 season the transformation was complete. The Babes were now ready to conquer England and Europe.

*   *   *

But what was it that got Duncan Edwards to choose Manchester United? One of the main reasons for the club's magnetism was Busby's charisma and the aura that surrounded the club. It was an aura with roots all the way back to the beginning of the century, when Meredith, Roberts and Mangnall represented the club's profile. But the aura in the early and mid-1950s primarily originated from the team that with a fluid attacking style won the FA Cup final of 1948 and the Championship of 1952.

In addition there were, according to Tony Whelan, at least four other factors in these years that motivated young players to play for Manchester United. (1) The club simply were 'a big club'; (2) the club's academy had a reputation of making the boys better footballers; (3) the road from youth team to first team was shorter than at other clubs; (4) the club had a reputation of being a family club. We have already touched on the family club in the previous chapter, but let us look at what Manchester and Manchester United was like for the talented footballers who arrived in the city, and how their arrival came about.

Matt Busby's project to build the club's youth department was dependent on his network of scouts. It was scouts, who found talents, often before they were discovered by the scouts of other clubs, and it was also them, who took the first and crucial contract to the boy's parents. Manchester United's chief scout in these years was called Joe Armstrong, an unsung hero in the traditional tales of Manchester United. Through his job at the General Post Office Armstrong can be compared to a hyper-sensitive spider in the centre of a far-reaching and close-spun web. This communication and information network stretched out across the United Kingdom and Ireland. Out in the web's peripheral regions scouts and schoolteachers sat and fed Armstrong with information, which he immediately sorted and responded to. Of these other scouts Billy Behan operated in Dublin, where he found Johnny Carey, and Bob Harper and Bob Bishop covered Northern Ireland. The latter can be credited for having spotted George Best, Sammy McIlroy and Norman Whiteside. The qualities that the scouts first and foremost were looking for were, according to Whelan, fundamental technical skills, discipline and an innate instinct for football. Also important was an obvious enjoyment of the game, a real desire and willingness to play for Manchester United and an impeccable lifestyle away from the pitch.

In England during this time football for school-age children was organised through their schools. Young boys were allowed to be recruited by clubs when they had finished school as fifteen- or sixteen-year-olds. The club's recruitment basis was therefore school football, which was played on a local level. The schools then acted as a food chain for the local team, and the next level was the England Schoolboys team. Often, the players reaching regional teams, and in particular the national squad, had already been spotted by several scouts. Joe Armstrong and the other United scouts therefore mostly focused on the local level, where players had not yet been discovered. In this context, Joe Armstrong's job at the GPO played an important part, as he had the opportunity to gain access to the addresses of many of the sites where the most obscure youth matches were played, as well as access to the phone numbers of various informers, who were often schoolteachers.

A substantial part of Joe Armstrong's success was due to his endearing personality. In an interesting cultural shift, scouts today most often need to persuade the father to secure a young talent, but in Armstrong's time it was the mother. In his charming way the postal official made the persuasion of mothers into an art form. It is said that each time a talent scout from a competing club came knocking on a football talent's door, Joe Armstrong was already sat in the kitchen and drinking a cup of coffee.

Bobby Charlton doesn't hesitate to ascribe Armstrong a large part of the credit for the fact he ended up at Manchester United. 'I signed for Manchester United . . . mainly because of that wonderful little man Joe Armstrong, their chief scout. He had watched me long before I was in any schoolboy internationals, and he always said he wanted me to come and play for United, not to come for trials. Besides, United were just starting to put youngsters into the first team, which was unheard of, and the idea of going to Old Trafford was exciting. The first thing you realised was that it was a family club', Charlton said in an interview given to the *Sunday Telegraph*.

Another essential component in the entire family club concept was the fact the young players who arrived in Manchester from Lancashire, northern England, Scotland, Ireland or Northern Ireland were boarded in groups at a number of houses run by trusted hostesses. They acted as a sort of surrogate mother, ensuring the boys were given protection, care and the right diet, that they kept to their bedtime. These boarding houses formed the framework of a number of friendships between the players, and resulted in linking the great team collective together in an often unbreakable unit. In their leisure time the players enjoyed some of the privileges Busby had secured them to compensate for the wage limit, which meant some of the best footballers in the world didn't earn more than a skilled worker.

Several times a week the club's players visited Manchester theatres, where United players got a discount or even went for free. Here they could see Alfred Hitchcock's *Rear Window* with James Stewart and Grace Kelly, Billy Wilder's *The Seven Year Itch* with Marilyn Monroe and Nicholas Ray's *Rebel Without a Cause* with James Dean. At the weekend, many of them were seen with wax in the hair at some of the city's many dance and music establishments where bebop jazz, rock 'n' roll and jive were played. Among the songs that were a hit in those years were 'Shake, Rattle and Roll' by Bill Haley and the Comets, 'The Great Pretender' by the Platters and Elvis Presley's 'Hound Dog'.

The example of Tommy Taylor's transfer was evidence of an accelerating media exposure of Manchester United's shooting stars. As a foretaste of David Beckham's trendsetting styles at the turn of the millennium, you could get 'a David Pegg cut' in the mid-1950s in any hair salon in Manchester. With his light wavy hair in its distinctive backswept style, Pegg looked like a movie star, but when it came to clothes, Eddie Colman was the trendsetter. Colman was the first of the Babes with pointy shoes and tight-fitting trousers, the so-called 'drainpipes', made famous and infamous by Elvis as he performed his trademark and daring hip movements. The Babes also began to appear in advertisements and thus contributed to the blurring between the cultural and commercial worlds, which is characteristic of post-modern society. The teenagers of the time could identify themselves with the Busby Babes, who after all symbolised youth and the divide between generations, but the Babes were also made of a particularly heroic substance, which gave them the necessary distance to be idolised by the youth. In that sense, the Busby Babes were the first non-musical megastars.

The young talents and the youth team hadn't only the attention of the media, but also had attention within the club. Bobby Charlton tells how Jimmy Murphy always used to say the youth team was the icing on the cake of Manchester United. 'Forget about the first team, the FA Cups and all that. *This* is the most important thing. And I can remember that I would never go to bed the night before a youth match, because I had been brainwashed and indoctrinated into believing that this was the most important match that you would ever play in your whole life.' It is possible Real Madrid won the Champions' European Cup the first five years of the tournament's existence (1955–59), but Manchester United on the other hand won the English Youth Cup during its first five years (1953–57). And in many ways it was an achievement that the club was just as proud of, as if it was them who had won the Champions' European Cup five times in a row. Of course, this is a slight exaggeration, but to understand the ethos that characterised Manchester United in these years, it is essential to recognise the enormous attention given to the youth teams. It was not unusual for 25,000 spectators to see Manchester United's youth team play, and the final was seen by many more.

*　　*　　*

When Duncan Edwards arrived at Old Trafford in the summer of 1952, he had already played for England Schoolboys three years in a row. No one had done this before him. Edwards was not one of the many talents that Armstrong and the other United scouts had discovered on a local level. Edwards was high on the wish list of most English top clubs already in 1950, when as a thirteen-year-old he played for England Schoolboys for the first time. Busby was made aware of Edwards in 1950 by the then captain of Arsenal, Joe Mercer, who had been in charge of the training of the England Schoolboys for a week during the summer.

As already mentioned, Edwards had a burning desire to play for Busby and Manchester United. At first, Edwards joined on amateur terms in the summer of 1952, but on his seventeenth birthday on 1 October 1953 he signed his first professional contract. On 4 April the same year, at the age of just sixteen years and 185 days, Duncan Edwards made his debut for Manchester United when the team met Cardiff at Old Trafford and lost 1–4.

The best way to understand what kind of footballer Duncan Edwards was is to imagine Jaap Stam, Bryan Robson, Roy Keane, Mark Hughes and Eric Cantona in one and the same person. 'Duncan Edwards was the only player that ever made me feel inferior. . . . If I had to play for my life and could take one man with me, it would be Duncan Edwards', Bobby Charlton once said. Duncan Edwards was simply a colossus, unconquerable in the defence and unstoppable in the attack, the greatest of the greatest. He was a nuclear power plant built in the middle of a football field. According to Busby, Edwards was the world's best player. He had no weaknesses and was blessed with an almost inhuman stamina. He was furthermore naturally athletic and therefore also flexible. His technique was good, he possessed a fine balance, and he shot good and hard with both feet. When Edwards was tackling, it sounded like thunder. In the air he was Manchester United's version of Manfred von Richthofen, 'The Red Baron', Germany's legendary fighter pilot during the First World War. In addition,

Edwards, just like Roy Keane and Eric Cantona, possessed an exceptional winning mentality, but in contrast to the Irishman and the Frenchman he had a calm temperament. His presence on the field was felt by players, opponents, coaches and spectators alike. It was as if he himself incarnated gravity on the field, given the ball relentlessly seemed to be drawn to his feet. Duncan Edwards's light simply burned brighter than all the others.

As Arthur Hopcraft notes in *The Football Man* (1968), Duncan Edwards's performance on the field was often accompanied by the quiet admiration you can observe from fathers when they talk about their sons to their neighbours. In this context one could even trace a distressing sympathy with the opponents, who were outplayed by Edwards. Hopcraft remembers very well an incident from a match at Old Trafford: 'beside me was a supporter in his fifties, who shouted little, but nodded his head nearly all the time in deep satisfaction, letting out occasionally an equally deep sigh that was eloquent in its pleasure. By the middle of the first half one of the opposition's inside forwards . . . was reacting furiously to the frustration of being treated like a small child by Edwards, firmly but without viciousness or even very much concern. The player threw himself several times at Edwards, either missing the moving body entirely or bouncing off it, and on each occasion the man beside me sucked in his breath, shook his head and said softly: "Nay, lad, not with 'im, not with 'im."' It was the decent, absorbed football fan like this one for whom Winterbottom was speaking when he called Edwards the spirit of British football.

On 2 April 1955 Duncan Edwards made his debut at a record low age in the abovementioned Walter Winterbottom's team in a match against Scotland. He was eighteen years old and 183 days. Edwards played eighteen international matches and score five goals before the Munich accident. One of the goals is remembered in the history of the national team as one of the best goals ever. The goal was scored on the Olympic Stadium in Berlin on 26 May 1956 in a match against the reigning world champions from West Germany, where nineteen-year-old Duncan Edwards, an unstoppable juggernaut, ploughed his way from the centre line to the German penalty area. On the way he flicked off three German players as if they were flies before he fired the ball down in one corner of the goal. The action was emblematic of the brute strength, technique and opportunistic mentality Duncan Edwards possessed.

* * *

In the 1955/56 season the Busby Babes won their first championship. The average age of the team was just twenty-two years. Roger Byrne and Johnny Berry, an excellent right wing, who Busby bought in 1951 to lubricate the rusty 1948 team, were the only two remaining from the 1952 championship team. Berry, Tommy

Taylor and the goalkeeper Ray Wood were the only players who were not from the academy. The team this season usually looked like this:

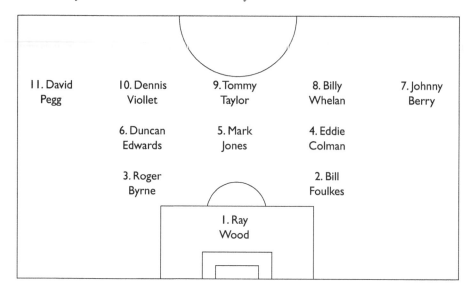

11. David Pegg — 10. Dennis Viollet — 9. Tommy Taylor — 8. Billy Whelan — 7. Johnny Berry

6. Duncan Edwards — 5. Mark Jones — 4. Eddie Colman

3. Roger Byrne — 2. Bill Foulkes

1. Ray Wood

The painter Harold Reilly says in the documentary *The Busby Babes: End of a Dream* (1998) about Busby's young team: 'It's like, you know, when a great painter flicks up some colour from his pallet, the amalgam of some two or three colours sometimes . . . there's some accident, some magic in it that happens. There was with that group, because you had a terrific balance of Colman and Edwards, you've got Byrne and you've got Bill Foulkes in the back, and right in the middle you've got that rock of Mark Jones.'

Manchester United won the league by a record lead of 11 points over Blackpool. The championship was secured in their third last league game on 7 April 1956 against Blackpool at Old Trafford. Film clips from the match show a slightly muddy and uneven field, and all the way around the track it seems almost as if the massive wall consisting of 62,277 spectators could flood the pitch as a tidal wave at any time – not least at the moment when Blackpool's goalkeeper drops a cross from Johnny Berry at the feet of Tommy Taylor, who lives up to his nickname as the Smiling Executioner and ensures United the victory of 2–1, and thus the Championship.

In the 1956/57 season Manchester United regained the Championship. If the football the previous season at times had been spectacular and dynamic, then this season the young team seemed to lift it to new heights. The season also welcomed a new face, someone who came to play a great role for the club the next seventeen years. On 6 October 1956 the eighteen-year-old Bobby Charlton made his debut in a home match against Charlton Athletic. He replaced an injured Tommy Taylor and contributed two goals to United's 4–2 victory.

Today England, tomorrow Europe

It is considered to be 'the night of nights' for the Busby Babes. It is Wednesday 6 February 1957, exactly one year before the Munich air disaster. It is a cold and foggy evening, and the breath of the spectators mixes with the fog of a grey Manchester evening. 70,000 have turned up at a floodlit Maine Road to see Manchester United play against Athletic Bilbao. In spite of the moist cold, the atmosphere in the city is electric. Manchester United is the first English team to participate in the European Cup, and the inhabitants of Manchester have welcomed this exotic adventure with a mixture of northern English pride and much excitement.

Three weeks before the showdown against Athletic Bilbao at Maine Road the Basque team had beaten Manchester United 5–3 in Spain. But, carried forward by an enthusiastic home audience, a lively Manchester United puts Athletic under extreme pressure right from the beginning of the match. Four minutes from the break Dennis Viollet picks up a return ball just outside Athletic's penalty area. He drifts inside the box and with his right foot hammers the ball into the top of the net, giving the 70,000 freezing fans a much-needed hot toddy. In the second half a constantly dangerous Tommy Taylor scores a second from a free kick. The match is Taylor's greatest achievement in his career. In the remaining part of the game Manchester United press for the crucial third goal. With the clock ticking down, Johnny Berry scores at the very end to make it 3–0. Maine Road explodes into euphoric and deafening cheers. The crowd of 70,000 has been witness to one of the most dramatic last-minute comebacks in Manchester United's history. Brian Hughes, a lifelong fan of United, says in *The Busby Babes: End of a Dream*, that the game's intensity was similar to what he experienced at the births of his four children. He said: 'I was at Maine Road that night. And I remember it. It was the most pulsating, tense occasion that I have ever been in. And you lived on that for months. It kept you buzzing.'

Manchester United in Europe was the result of a visionary and steely Matt Busby. In 1955 Chelsea won the English Championship, but the Football League had advised the London club against taking part in the first European Cup, and Chelsea obediently gave in. The Football League feared Chelsea's continental business would disrupt the club's commitments in the domestic league. The general attitude among English football's bureaucrats was that the continent couldn't teach the English anything. England and the other British countries opted out of FIFA in 1920 because, among other reasons, it was considered to be an unwelcome foreign influence on the game from both the southern European and South American leagues. But twenty-six years later the British teams accepted FIFA's invitation to resume their membership. In 1950 England took part in the FIFA World Cup for the first time, where the shocking 1–0 defeat to the United States shattered the illusion of England being the world's leading football nation.

Up north in Manchester the Football League's ban on participation in the European Cup was regarded as a reactionary and narrow-minded islander mentality. Busby felt Europe was the necessary next step in the development of his team and his club. 'Prestige alone demanded that the continental challenge should be met, not avoided,' said Busby. Manchester United's entry into Europe as the first English team is one of the factors that contribute to the club's aura and international magnetism. Busby's battle against the football authorities also enhanced the image of him as a tenacious Celtic outsider. Finally, the fans also saw United's European ambitions as a tribute to a more humble and cosmopolitan Britishness, rather than the insular and haughty Englishness represented by the Football League. For the fans, Manchester United simply represented a more positive 'Englishness': the horizon was global, but at the same time they proudly upheld their local northern English roots.

Three years earlier, English pride came before a fall when England were outplayed by Gusztáv Szebes's Hungary. England had never lost at Wembley against teams outside the British Isles, but Hungary were the defending Olympic champions and had been undefeated for three years. At Wembley the Hungarian upstarts beat the English progenitors 6–3, and six months later they sent football's inventors home from Budapest with a painful loss of 7–1. It wasn't just the results that were an eye-opener for several British managers and players, it was also the way in which victory was won. It was clear that on the continent, football had reached a technical and tactical level that the British were unable to match. The Hungarians' flexible style meant the English were chasing shadows for most of the time. The Hungarians played with two central attackers, Ferenc Puskas and Sándor Kocsis, instead of one. They even swapped places quite often, which was unheard of at the time. The fact they wore the numbers 8 and 10, which were the traditional numbers for inside forwards, confused people even more. Shirt number 9 was worn by their centre forward, Nandór Hidegkuti, but instead of acting as a traditional target man Hidegkuti had his base in the midfield. From here he covered most of the field in a free role, which totally destabilised the English defence, which was based on man marking.

Matt Busby was one of the managers for whom Hungarian's flexible football style became a revelation. It was, according to Busby, of urgent necessity to set oneself up against the protectionist mentality that dominated the offices in the Football League's headquarters – a mentality that prevented the young English talents from pitting their abilities against European opponents and alternative styles. Manchester United's youth team had twice taken part in a European summer tournament. They had, in the presence of both Busby and Murphy, met central and southern European teams. One year the team completely outplayed Genoa's youth team, but still lost 1–0. The match had given the young Englishmen a taste of an alternative tactic based not on passion, ball possession and pace, but on cynicism, counter-attacking and composure.

In 1956 Busby got the full support of Manchester United's directors on the issue of Europe. The prestige was one motive, but another major reason for the club's endorsement of Busby's vision was the additional income the European Cup would provide. Busby then went to London to discuss the problem with representatives from the Eurosceptic Football League and the more pro-European Football Association. Here Busby succeeded and pushed through Manchester United's participation in the next season's competition. At the same time, however, it was stressed that the club's involvement in Europe in no way could interfere with the match schedule in the English league.

As Manchester United began their European adventure, English football lacked belief in itself after those defeats by the United States and Hungary. They either suffered from a paralysing awe or hid in pathetic isolation, nursing their wounded pride. Instead of England it was now the apparently unbeatable Hungarians and Real Madrid who led the game that England had taught the world to play. In this sense, Manchester United's European mission also resonated beyond the football world. It was also part of British society's quest for self-esteem and a country's attempt to recreate past greatness.

In the autumn of 1956, the club buzzed with expectation for the new pan-European tournament, which had been launched the year before on Gabriel Hanot's initiative. Hanot was a cosmopolitan French sports journalist and editor of *L'Équipe*. He was also the man behind the invention of the Ballon d'Or. Bobby Charlton talked in an interview about the expectations of the European matches: 'I can remember that everybody was really excited about the fact that we were going to play overseas. Because it was completely strange, there was no television, we didn't see Spanish football or French football or German football or whatever, so the only way you could find out was to play against them. It was just a great adventure.'

*   *   *

After eliminating Anderlecht from Belgium and Dortmund from Germany, Athletic Bilbao waited in the quarter-finals. The trip to Bilbao was met with great excitement among the players and the accompanying fans. The twentieth century was only just beginning to make air travel its defining development and air travel for its part was only just beginning to globalise the century. A flight to a foreign country was something completely new for the players and the fans. Initially, Bilbao and Spain created a picture of sun and heat to many, but in the Basque Country it snowed violently on 16 January 1957. As the *Dakota* with Manchester United's players approached the airport, the pilot couldn't see the runway. It turned out the airport had chosen to close down due to the snowstorm. The aircraft had circled Bilbao and the airport, which more or less consisted of a shed and a strip of asphalt, which had to be re-opened before the pilot could bring the players safely down.

During the match large quantities of snow fell and the pitch was slippery and muddy. The score stood at 5–2 to Athletic, but shortly before the end young Liam 'Billy' Whelan kept hopes of a semi-final alive. After an excellent solo run he hammered the ball up into the corner of the net to reduce the deficit. On the way home the pilot refused in the first place to fly from Bilbao airport, because the runway and the aircraft's wings were covered with snow and ice. The team, however, was forced to return home to England before the forthcoming Saturday match against Sheffield Wednesday in order to avoid penalties from the Football League. Several of the players were therefore equipped with shovel and broom to clear the runway and make the machine ready for take-off. The incident caused much laughter and fun at the time, but in hindsight the Bilbao comedy appears a fatal omen of the Munich tragedy.

The return match, as we already know, ended 3–0 to Manchester United, and in the semi-finals the giants from Real Madrid awaited. 'Los Blancos' were defending European champions and with world-class players such as the Argentine Alfredo Di Stefano, Frenchman Raymond Kopa, Ferenc Puskás from Hungary and the Spanish Francisco Gento, the club already back then symbolised cosmopolitanism and globalisation. To Matt Busby this double showdown was the ultimate litmus test to show how far his team had come.

On 11 April 1957 Manchester United played in front of the largest number of spectators in the club's history, with a total of 135,000 football enthusiasts turning up at the Santiago Bernabéu in Madrid. For almost an hour the Red Devils hold up firmly against 'the white football angels', but when Madrid score their first goal it is as if the next two goals follow logically from the first. Tommy Taylor reduces the deficit, however, and at the end of the match they lose 3–1. Manchester United are still alive in the European Cup. In the next day's edition of the *Daily Herald* the headline read 'Murder in Madrid', referring to the Spanish team's brutal behaviour in several situations in the course of the match. The English media were generally shocked and annoyed about Real Madrid's ruthless and unsportsmanlike playing style, but recognised the team's superlative offensive qualities.

On 25 April 1957, two weeks after 'the murder in Madrid', Manchester United play their first European match at Old Trafford. ITV Granada pays £2,500 for the rights, and millions of TV viewers join together with 65,000 enthusiastic spectators to witness another highly dramatic game. They also witness one of the most beautiful matches Old Trafford has ever seen, with the showdown ending all square at 2–2. But this match was to be the beginning of a wondrous series of fifty-eight games where Manchester United do not lose a single European/international match at home. This period would span 40 years.

When Real Madrid take a 2–0 lead there is no evidence Manchester's young lions can turn the tide. But, unaffected by adversity, they are still able to fight back and level with goals from Taylor and Charlton. In the next day's edition of the *Daily Mirror* Frank McGhee summarises the two matches: 'Brave failure. Fighting failure. Glorious failure. But that doesn't make it taste any better to those who cherished a proud illusion that in United England had the greatest football team in the world. They are not. Real Madrid are the real McCoy. They gave Matt Busby's league champions a lesson in the basic arts and crafts of the game. They had the edge in skill and stamina. And above all they had a man called Alfredo Di Stefano.' McGhee is right: Manchester United have met a superior team. But the Manchester team's average age of just twenty-two years, means the future belongs to them.

* * *

With the 1957 First Division championship in the bag Manchester United ensured participation in the European Cup for the second year in a row, and many thought them title aspirants yet again. In the domestic league the team had started the 1957/58 season with a number of great victories, and in the European Cup first round, against Shamrock Rovers, Manchester United continued their impressive goal run with victories of 6–0 and 3–2 respectively. In Ireland the majority of the 33,754 spectators were Irish Manchester United fans. Busby's Irish roots and his revolutionary impact on Manchester United since 1945 had not gone unnoticed in Ireland, Northern Ireland or Scotland. Many Irish people, Northern Irishmen and Scots felt a strong pull to Manchester and Manchester United. On one hand, Manchester represented a political–geographical alternative to the royal throne and the political power in London. On the other, Busby was, according to Wagg, perceived as an Irish–Scottish manager who in

Manchester United had introduced a form of football that expressed the poetry of the Celtic soul – and he not only did it in north-west England, where English professional football was invented, but also with mainly English players, and, on top of all this, in a city that historically was not only the city of the working class, the rebels and the maladjusted, but also the fortress of liberalism, non-conformist Protestantism and free trade.

If you look beyond the British Isles, there is no doubt Busby's Scottish and Irish origin was also a major factor in the globalisation of Manchester United's popularity. It really got under way in these years with the Babes, and with the club's participation in the European Cup. Irish immigration didn't limit itself to only Scotland or England. Thousands of Irish people crossed the Atlantic and took up residence in the United States and Canada. The Irish emigrated to Australia, New Zealand, Mexico, Argentina, South Africa and Europe. Around the world enclaves small and large exist with close cultural and family ties to Ireland, Manchester and the overall British footballing culture.

In close connection to the importance of the Irish diaspora, one can argue that Busby's vision of football – in addition to crossing national and cultural boundaries – appealed to many of those whom Frantz Fanon called 'the wretched of the earth'. Contributing to this appeal was Busby's own background in the Scottish coalmines, his youth policy (which had its social point of departure in Manchester's cobblestoned streets) and his Celtic stubbornness. The Celtic component in the United machine was also accompanied by an anti-sectarian component. One can therefore not single out Manchester United in the same way as, for example, the Catholic Celtic and Protestant Glasgow Rangers. Because of the anti-sectarian component Manchester United appealed to football followers in different countries, who would probably feel very uncomfortable if the club had a specific ethnic or sectarian affiliation.

Finally, it has been argued the Scots, more than any other people, even the Brazilians, elevated football to its proper status. It is possible the Scottish national team in our day do not embody a form of football that we might call the pinnacle of football's true nature. In this Brazil undeniably gets closest to this peak and has been there since 1958. It is also possible to say that Scotland these days have no world stars to show off. Here Brazil beats them again by several light years. But it does not necessarily mean the claim of the Scots' elevation of football to its proper status is incorrect. The concrete evidence may not be there, but the intent, spirit and soul very much are.

And it should be noted that in Busby's time, the Scottish national team had quite a different status than today. For example, when Busby grew up in Bellshill he could see up close three of the 'Wee Wembley Wizards' run around and show off their extraordinary skills. Jimmy McMullan, Alex James and Hughie Gallacher, who played in the all-time best Scottish national team, and who appeared in the famous 5–1 victory over England at Wembley in 1928, were all from Bellshill. For the young Matt Busby they represented the Celtic response to the more Calvinistic elements in Scottish and English football. The endurance, stubbornness and hard work for the collective were mixed with Celtic attributes, which put risk above security by emphasising the challenging and virtuoso elements of football. It was this Celtic poetry from Bellshill, represented by McMullan, James and Gallacher, that Busby took with him to Manchester United two decades later.

*　*　*

In the European Cup's quarter-final the strong Yugoslav team Red Star Belgrade awaited. On 14 January 1958, 60,000 spectators saw for the last time the Busby Babes in a European match at Old Trafford. Manchester United won a tough game 2–1, with Charlton and Colman scoring the goals. For United this meant a difficult, but not impossible task in Belgrade two weeks later. Just four days after the victory over Red Star the Babes won 7–2 against another one of the top domestic teams, Bolton Wanderers. Charlton, who scored a hat trick in the match, started to demand a regular place in the team because of his many goals and excellent performances. Scanlon had on his part begun to challenge Pegg on the left wing, but he also occasionally played on the right wing instead of Berry. Kenny Morgan, another of the new Babes, also challenged Berry on the right wing. In goal, the big Harry Gregg was often preferred instead of Ray Wood. The purchase of Gregg in December of 1957 was the club first since the signing of Tommy Taylor at the beginning of 1953.

The last match the Busby Babes play before Belgrade is legendary in British football history. Not only because the match is the team's last in England, but also because Manchester United win 5–4 at Highbury against Arsenal, and because the 63,578 spectators witness a fantastic football match with plenty of goals and drama. After just ten minutes Viollet passes the ball to an on-rushing Edwards, who hits the ball with such force it continues into the net in spite of Jack Kelsey's resolute attempt to keep it out. The goal is typically Edwards: only twenty-one years old, and yet feared and admired for his almost superhuman physical strength.

Spurred on by their fans, Arsenal fight back, and only a last-minute miracle save from Gregg prevents the Gunners from equalising. Gregg somehow gets his fingers on the ball as it is just below the crossbar and on its the way into the goal. But now this save leads to United's second goal. Gregg throws the ball out to Scanlon on the left wing, who runs the whole length of the field with the ball before he sends it into the penalty area. Here the ball meets Charlton, who with an unstoppable shot hits the ball into the net, and the Red Devils lead 2–0. Before halftime it's 3–0, when Scanlon once again terrorises Arsenal's right-hand side and sends the ball across the field to Morgan on United's right wing. Morgan tips the ball from here into the penalty area, where Taylor scores.

In the second half it takes fifteen minutes before David Herd (a future United player) reduces the deficit for Arsenal with a hard, well-placed shot. In the course of just two minutes Arsenal sensationally succeed in cancelling out United's comfortable lead. Highbury goes into ecstasy thanks to Arsenal's feat of strength, and any other team than the Busby Babes would certainly have collapsed after such a heroic comeback. But instead of just defending, Manchester United know attack is the best defence. With the assistance of Scanlon's speed and Charlton's technique, Viollet puts United back in front. Only a few minutes later, Colman finds Morgan on the wing with a precise delivery, which cuts Arsenal's defence right open with surgical precision. Morgan finds Taylor, who scores his second and United's fifth goal. The match is not over yet. Late in the match Arsenal's Derek Tapsfott breaks through an exhausted United defence and makes it 5–4, but the goal ends up being the last at Highbury on this incredible spine-tingling afternoon.

When the referee's whistle goes, the players almost drop into each other's arms. It is a gesture that clearly shows all twenty-two players are aware they have contributed to a historical match. In the stands even rival fans embrace each other as an impulsive reaction to the match's unsurpassed beauty and drama. The end result, and the course of the match's crystal-clear manifestation of the team's passion and creativity, stands to this day as a beautiful and emblematic monument of the Busby Babes.

*　*　*

It's simply called 'The last line-up': the photo of the eleven Manchester United players at Red Star's JNA Stadium on Wednesday, 5 April 1958. The picture shows them standing in a long row just before the match: 6. Edwards, 4. Colman, 5. Jones, 7. Morgan, 8. Charlton, 10. Viollet, 9. Taylor, 2. Foulkes, 1. Gregg, 11. Scanlon, 3. Byrne.

There was no adventurous or glamorous feeling at the prospect of playing in Belgrade. For the players it was a meeting with an unknown and dangerously mysterious world behind the Iron Curtain. Bobby Charlton has revealed all the players had a ton of sweets and chocolates in their suitcases because they were unsure of what food they would be getting in Belgrade. One player had even brought along a small gas oven as he was afraid he wouldn't get anything to eat. Yugoslavia was regarded as a hostile, Communist country, and the Busby Babes found themselves suddenly involved in the Cold War. Today, a trip to Belgrade would not be associated with anything out of the ordinary, but back then it was

'The last line-up'. The last photo of the Busby Babes before the Munich air disaster, from left: Duncan Edwards, Eddie Colman, Mark Jones, Kenny Morgan, Bobby Charlton, Dennis Viollet, Tommy Taylor, Bill Foulkes, Harry Gregg, Albert Scanlon, Roger Byrne.

not so easy to travel to Eastern bloc countries. Manchester United had decided to charter a private aircraft to Belgrade, partly because of uncoordinated timetables, partly as an attempt to avoid finding themselves in a similar situation to the year before, where the team had been close to missing a domestic game as a result of the airlines' erratic operation.

Several of the players expressed nervousness over having to fly to Eastern Europe. The evening before departure Colman admitted to his girlfriend he had no desire to go. Shortly before leaving, Ronnie Cope was notified he wasn't going to Belgrade after all as Byrne had suffered a minor injury, and Busby wanted Geoff Bent to come instead of Cope as back-up for Byrne. Cope's first reaction was disappointment and frustration at being left out; Bent's reaction, however, was pure anxiety. When Busby rang and informed Bent of his decision he told the new father he did not need to come if it was too difficult for his family. Bent's wife, who was slightly shocked at the news of her husband's impending departure, encouraged him to go with the team to Belgrade. On this ride into the unknown were also a number of the leading sports journalists in northern England.

Instead of defending their feeble one-goal lead from Old Trafford, Manchester United attack from the beginning. Both the Red Star and the 55,000 spectators are surprised at the English strategy, and after just ninety seconds Viollet puts Manchester United in front 1–0 with a beautiful shot. Just fifteen minutes later, Charlton has a goal disallowed for being offside. The match has now developed in a physical direction, and the Austrian referee Karl Kainer continuously interrupts the flow of the match with free kicks. Later in the half Charlton wins the ball from Kostic around the centre line, after which he makes one of his characteristic dribbles and irresistibly cuts past a few opponents, before he smashes the ball with his deadly left foot in the net, leaving the Yugoslav goalkeeper Beara with no chance of catching it. Just two minutes after the goal Charlton scores once again when, during some commotion in the penalty area, he just manages to direct the ball in the only direction that would lead to a goal.

But in the second half, the United players experience an uncomfortable déjà vu from Highbury just four days earlier, where they had jeopardised a 3–0 lead. In Belgrade, just two minutes into the second half Kostic reduces the score to 1–3. The Yugoslavians' comeback is helped further by the referee, who awards the home side a penalty. Tasic slips in United's penalty area and takes Foulkes with him in the fall. To the United players' surprise and great frustration, Kainer points to the spot. Tasic himself scores from the penalty. The Red Star players now show the self-confidence and commitment that they lacked in the first half. They dominate the match and United's defence works overtime in a heroic fight to stay ahead. The Red Devils regain their foothold, and a dazzling shot from Morgan hits the post. The equaliser doesn't come until two minutes before the end, when Kostic scores directly from a free kick, and the match ends all square at 3–3.

Manchester United have survived 'the Battle of Belgrade', as Henry Rose baptised the match in the *Daily Express*. For the second year in a row United go on to the semi-finals of the European Cup. Rose has only praise left for Manchester United's players: 'Heroes all. None greater than Billy Foulkes. None greater than Bobby Charlton, who has now scored twelve goals in the eleven games he has played since he went into the side as inside-right on 21 December. But all eleven played a noble part in this memorable battle.'

6 February 1958
The Munich tragedy

On Thursday, 6 February 1958 Manchester United ceased being just another football club among all the others. Until then, the team had mainly been a local phenomenon with some echoes proliferating on a national level. But on this day Manchester United was transformed into a worldwide phenomenon associated with something quasi-religious and mythic. These qualities still define the aura of the club today. Behind this transformation, however, was a tragedy of the deepest dimensions: a plane crash at Reim airport in Munich that wiped out the majority of Matt Busby's 'second generation', the famous Busby Babes. Admittedly, the club's reputation had already begun to spread in small waves across the world, first and foremost thanks to their semi-final qualification in the European Cup of 1957, but also because of Busby's three Championship triumphs, his revolutionary youth policy and his fluid attacking football. The tragedy in Munich, however, transformed the previous modest waves into a tsunami that washed across planet Earth and imprinted the name Manchester United in millions of people's consciousness. Not only neutral football enthusiasts, but also fans of some of their rival clubs in England and the supporters of many foreign clubs, as well as people who didn't normally have an interest in football, inevitably looked at Manchester United with sympathy.

But what happened on this Thursday afternoon in Munich, and why did it happen? On the way home to Manchester after their heroic 3–3 draw in the return match in Belgrade, Manchester United's private chartered British European Airways aircraft, *Lord Burghley*, made a stopover in Munich on the afternoon of 6 February to fill up with fuel. On board were forty-four people: twenty-one related to Manchester United (seventeen players and four coaches), eleven journalists, five crew members and seven other passengers. The weather was depressing and cold, and it was snowing heavily. The players had a hard and exhausting match from the previous day still in their systems. Some of them even were a little hung-over after the night's celebration in Belgrade, and with the prospect of a critical match against Wolverhampton at Old Trafford just two days later both Busby and the players were eager to get home to Manchester to rest. The prospect of the Football League's negative reaction and the possible sanctions if the team were to be home late for the match against Wolverhampton was another factor that weighed down heavily on Busby in the wintry Munich weather.

After a short break in the airport building for hot refreshments, the chilled and weary travellers boarded the aircraft ready for take-off. The two pilots, Captain Kenneth Rayment and Captain James Thain, registered a severe fluctuation in pressure. This meant the speed of the engines was too high. They therefore decided to abort take-off and run the aircraft back to the terminal to get the problem investigated. By the second attempted take-off the pilots again experienced an irregularity, and the same procedure was followed. After a longer service check the pilots decided to try a third time. This decision proved fatal. The passengers were asked to board again, but by now several of the players were anxious. Many of them switched seats just before take-off. For some, this meant survival, for others it meant death. As the aircraft began to take-off, Johnny Berry expressed his fear they would all be killed, and Billy Whelan confessed to Albert Scanlon that if this meant death, he was ready for it. During the third attempt to take-off at 15:04 hours it seemed the previous problems regarding over-acceleration had disappeared. But as the aircraft passed the point of no return, that is to say the point on the runway where it is no longer advisable to abort take-off, the pilots realised the aircraft was losing speed instead of accelerating. The aircraft just hadn't enough speed to be able to take-off, but on the other hand it also had too much speed to be able to stop before the end of the runway.

The pilots realised a disaster was in the offing. They responded by pulling up the landing gear to make the aircraft slide down the runway and out into some grass. They hoped this manoeuvre would slow down the aircraft to a stop before it reached the other side of the fence, which surrounded the outer reaches of the airport area. But this is not what happened. *Lord Burghley* continued to slide straight through the fence and across a road before one of its wings hit a house. The collision meant that the aircraft's one wing and its tail were torn off, and the house caught fire. The plane continued to slide forwards another 70 metres, and the cockpit hit a tree, while the aircraft fuselage hit a tree hut.

Out of the Manchester United delegation of twenty-one men, eleven people in total lost their lives. Eight were players of whom seven died instantly: Roger Byrne, twenty-eight; Eddie Colman, twenty-one; Mark Jones, twenty-four; Liam Whelan, twenty-two; Tommy Taylor, twenty-six; David Pegg, twenty-two; Geoff Bent, twenty-five. Fifteen days after the accident there was more bad news. The

Munich 1958

player who most believed to be the best of his generation and the symbol of Manchester United and the English national team's future died. Duncan Edwards was just twenty-one. Furthermore, Walter Crickmer died, a long-standing club secretary and manager before and during the war. Bert Whalley, head coach and responsible for United's youth work, and Tom Curry, who Busby saw as the best trainer in the UK, also perished. Johnny Berry, thirty-one, and Jackie Blanchflower, twenty-four, survived, but never played football again. Ray Wood, twenty-six, and Kenny Morgan, eighteen, survived too, but never regained their best form after the accident.

Out of the seventeen Busby Babes on board the *Lord Burghley*, only nine survived. But in reality, only five of those nine players would play a role in the future of Manchester United. One could indeed talk of the annihilation of an entire team – a team that many at the time and today agree would have dominated both the English and European game for the next decade. In Munich it was not only the present, but also very much the future, which was extinguished. It was a dream that died.

The five players who survived with no harm to their football ability came to play an important role for Manchester United in the years to come. Harry Gregg, twenty-four, showed considerable courage after the accident by returning to the burning aircraft, where he rescued several of the other passengers from death, including a little girl and her mother. Bill Foulkes, twenty-six, was also a mainstay of the team who at Wembley in 1968 finally helped United win the European Cup. Bobby Charlton, twenty, was one of the stars of the team in 1968 and, among others, scored two goals against Benfica. Albert Scanlon, twenty-two, scored a total of sixteen league goals in the season after the accident. Finally, Dennis Viollet, twenty-four, scored thirty-two league goals for Manchester United in the season 1959/60, which is still a club record. The last person from United's delegation who survived was Matt Busby, who miraculously overcame severe injuries. After having stayed seventy-one days at Rechts der Isar hospital in Munich, and after twice receiving the last rites, he returned to life, to Manchester and to Old Trafford.

Of the eleven journalists travelling, only Frank Taylor and the photographers Peter Howard and Ted Ellyard survived. Two of the seven other passengers died, one a Yugoslav travel agent, the other a close friend of Busby, the successful, local businessman Willie Satinoff. Of the five crew members, the captain Kenneth Rayment and airline flight attendant Tom Cable died. Two hostesses and Captain James Thain survived. Thain was initially criticised for not having de-iced the aircraft's wings, but the subsequent technical studies of the accident showed the aircraft's inability to accelerate was caused by snow and slush on the runway. The awful reality is twenty-three out of the forty-four persons who were on board the *Lord Burghley* died as a result of the accident.

*   *   *

The Munich accident is perhaps the most remembered disaster in the world of sports. As Stephen Wagg notes, the tragic event froze a very young and attacking team in its act of becoming. If the Busby Babes were a flower, which had given promises of unprecedented beauty and perfection, Munich was the ruthless pruner, cutting the stem at the very moment the flower was about to unfold in full bloom. The Busby Babes will therefore always remain what they might have been. Therein lies their enormous magnetism and mythic power, for there is nothing so conducive to the creation of myth as the combination of youth, death and unrealised potential.

Thus, it is youthfulness that separates the Busby Babes and the Munich Air Disaster from Il Grande Torino and the Superga accident. On 4 May 1949 a Fiat aircraft from Italy flew into the Superga church on a hill outside of Torino and crashed. On board the plane were the Italian champions Torino FC, known as 'Il Grande Torino'. All thirty-one people on board were killed. This included the legendary Valentino Mazzola, one of the all-time best Italian footballers. Il Grande Torino, whose squad counted no fewer than ten Italian internationals, were multiple Italian champions and without doubt one of the world's best teams in the late 1940s. But in contrast to the Busby Babes the team had peaked, and the average age of Il Grande Torino was more than thirty years. In terms of potential the Italians had already achieved everything they could. In 1958 the British, however, were still in the process of perfecting and widening the scope of the game's tactical and technical beauty. This brief survey of the differences between Munich 1958 and Superga 1949 should not be seen as an attempt to downgrade the Torino tragedy's painful extent, but it should be read as one of the explanations of the imbalanced mythology surrounding the two events.

Another reason for the mythological imbalance is undoubtedly the well-oiled northern English PR machine. In modern times, Manchester United have managed to integrate the Munich tragedy and the extinction of Busby Babes as one of the main components in the club's brand. Munich quite simply plays one of the leading roles in the club's efforts to market Manchester United as a unique club. The accident endowed Manchester United with a glow of mystery, and thus 'Munich' is transformed into a marketable product in the attempt to attract new fans from all over the world. Today the Munich disaster is a centrepiece of a steadily increasing memory industry, both in and outside the club, which helps to reinforce the mythology and mystery around the Busby Babes.

There are numerous websites, television documentaries and books about the Busby Babes and the Munich tragedy, as well as several biographies about some of the Babes. Most of these products are hagiographical and uncritical, but there are some critical voices. For example, Jeff Connor's thought-provoking *The Lost*

Babes (2006) blames Manchester United for spinning gold over the disaster and not taking proper care of the bereaved. There have been documentaries like the Granada-produced *The Busby Babes* as well as the BBC's *Surviving Disaster: Munich Air Crash* (2006), which reconstructs the events around the accident. In addition, there are songs written about the Busby Babes and the air crash. The most famous are The Spinners' 'The Flowers of Manchester', Morrissey's 'Munich Air Disaster 1958' and the Futureheads' 'News and Tributes'.

* * *

But let's turn our attention to 1958 again to have a closer look at the repercussions of the accident. The news about the air crash hit Old Trafford and Manchester hard. Jimmy Murphy had been in Wales to lead the Welsh national team and had therefore not been included in the trip to Belgrade. When he arrived at Old Trafford on Thursday afternoon he was told about the accident by one of the club's receptionists. At that time there was still some uncertainty at the extent of the disaster, but it was certain that there were deaths among United's delegation. Murphy managed, despite the initial shock, and the heartfelt sorrow for the loss of 'his boys', to get the club back on track. It is Jimmy Murphy who can be credited for the fact Manchester United in the months after 'Munich' sensationally reached the final of the FA Cup.

Manchester's inhabitants were deeply affected by the disaster, and the city was almost in collective shock. 'Anyone who was in Manchester in February 1958, particularly if they lived there, as I did, will remember forever the stunning impact on the city of the air crash at Munich airport which killed eight of Manchester United's players. The shock was followed, just as it is in particularly closely tied families after a death, by a lingering communal desolation. No other tragedy in sport has been as brutal or as affecting as this one', writes Arthur Hopcraft in *The Football Man*. The Busby Babes were in many ways 'the city's kids', and even though there was a rivalry between United and City, it is important to emphasise, as Gavin Mellor does in a few fine articles, that the rivalry then had a completely different nature than today. Mellor notes, for example, that the football culture in 1950s Manchester was marked by a greater mutual respect between the clubs and the fans. And also, by and large, the borders between City and United and their respective fan delegation were much more fluid than today. In the 1950s it was quite normal that City and United fans turned up at each other's grounds to support a team from Manchester, and the mutual respect and the fluid boundaries were very much a result of the common working-class roots.

The Munich accident also made good headlines in the media. These played a significant role in placing the accident as an essential part of Manchester United's history. On one hand, the media helped to consolidate the mythologisation of the accident, on the other they contributed to the polarisation between the supporters of Manchester United and those of the other English clubs. In the days after the accident there was naturally a comprehensive coverage of the disaster in both the local and national media. It is also very understandable the coverage was only sympathetic. But as the weeks and months passed, the media in Manchester were accused of overexposing the accident and thus Manchester United. The criticism came from nearby towns such as Burnley and Bolton, whose football clubs historically have competed with the Manchester clubs for being the leading club in Lancashire.

According to Mellor, the local media exposure gradually led to hateful comments from some of the Manchester City fans. This hatred was not only due to local media overexposure of the disaster, but also resulted from the fact that Manchester United, according to these City fans, used the emotional impact of the disaster for commercial gain. Today the criticism of Manchester United's commercial exploitation of the Munich incident is widespread among all the rival clubs' fans. Among them Manchester United's fans are simply referred to as 'Munichs'. In addition to criticising Manchester United's commercial exploitation of the Munich disaster, the accusation is that the club and its supporters constantly invoke the role of victims. The rival clubs' supporters argue that United, after all, have benefited more from the disaster than they actually have suffered pain and distress. On one hand, the Munich disaster has endowed the club with a mystery, myth and aura that no other English club can match. On the other, the club has managed to take advantage of the event's emotional force commercially, and that in a nauseating and distasteful way, according to the rival clubs' supporters.

'Munich' can therefore be said to have created as many enemies as friends. The antagonistic development between the rival clubs' supporters is a clear indication of the return of tribalism in our post-modern world. In the 1950s a greater mutual respect reflected a common class affiliation. But today it is no longer the industrialised society and modernity's class affiliations that make up the kit of the football clubs' supporters. In the post-modern world the identity-creating components are rather of a cultural nature, just as they are self-chosen. We no longer get our identity assigned through given components such as class affiliation and family. We choose our own identity by 'connecting' to symbolic values – symbolic values that can, for example, be associated with a football club.

In the 1950s, you could easily cheer on the home team at Old Trafford one week and the home team at Maine Road the next. The identity at that time was less rooted in the club than in the class. Today it is vice versa. The clubs have now increasingly become identity markers containing a number of symbolic values that people can connect to. In Manchester United's case this does not mean that traditional working-class values, such as solidarity and humility, have been rejected. On the contrary, Manchester United's PR machine takes working-class virtues and recycles them as symbolic values in the 'Manchester United' brand. Here they are placed next to a series of other values, such as glamour, cosmopolitanism and exclusivity.

* * *

If youth can partly explain the difference in the extent of mythologisation between Superga 1949 and Munich 1958, the loss of young and talented players cannot all by itself explain the mystery that surrounds the Busby Babes and 'Munich'. Another reason is that the Busby Babes were in fact heroes, not just budding celebrities. The term 'hero' derives from Greek, where it means half-god. In Ancient Greece a half-god was the offspring of a human and a god(dess), but a hero could also be a human being who through his exemplary deeds was raised to a status near the gods. In this sense the hero served as a moral example, such as Achilles, Perseus, Heracles and Oedipus.

Liam Whelan's last words to Albert Scanlon – 'If this means death, I'm ready for it' – are heroic and morally exemplary. These worlds reflect a bygone era, where the afterworld indeed was the place you would go after this mere transitory life. The Catholic Whelan's conscience was clean, and he was ready to meet his maker and receive his judgement. Another example: at the Rechts der Isar hospital, while he was seriously injured and struggling for his life, Duncan Edwards asked Jimmy Murphy to confirm that the kick-off on Saturday against Wolverhampton was at three o'clock. He fully intended to be there! Edwards would not, for everything in the world, miss that fight. Edwards's and Whelan's words bear witness to an incredible vitality, innocence and heroism. In addition, we have Harry Gregg's courageous efforts in the minutes after the accident, when he rescued a baby out of the burning aircraft and then got back into the wreck and rescued the child's mother out of flames. 'In our family he has always been treated as a hero', says Miss Lukic, the child who was saved, in *The Busby Babes: End of a Dream*.

But there is, as Stephen Wagg points out in 'The team that wouldn't die', something more about the Babes that endows them with this special aura and mystery. In addition to the hero status and youthful dynamism, it was also their position between two worlds that made them so fascinating. The Busby Babes had one leg planted in the past where the keywords were security, safety, family and community. They had another planted in a future world where freedom, social mobility, self-expression and sexual liberation were key concepts. On one hand, the Busby Babes belonged to the exhausted and austere post-war England, on the other they had begun to sense their celebrity status, just as they had begun to enjoy the freedom that was an essential part of that period's urbane and commercial popular culture.

As already mentioned, the Babes were the first non-musical megastars, and the media attention around Colman's clothing style and Pegg's hairstyle supports this claim. But this suggestion of post-modern commercialism and celebrity status were counterbalanced by the Babes' deep and undeniable roots in the working-class communities of the industrial north. The Babes were on the borderline of fame, but lived like anybody else and could be your neighbour's kid. Wayne Rooney has a little of this authentic aura about him. He could indeed be your neighbour's boy, but one thing is for sure, he no longer lives just around the corner. Back then the distance could be felt, but it was minimal; today it's gigantic. Colman was, for example, from Salford, the poor neighbourhood described by Robert Roberts as 'the classic slum' and also portrayed in Walter Greenwood's social-critical novel *Love on the Dole* (1933) and Shelagh Delaney's play *A Taste of Honey* (1958). Roberts, Greenwood and Delaney are all from Salford.

In addition, Mark Jones, Tommy Taylor, David Pegg and Geoff Bent were all sons of miners, and some of the players had even worked down the pit. When Bill Foulkes in 1955 made his debut for the English national team, legend tells us that he worked in the coalmine the same morning. Many of the players still lived in so-called 'digs', boarding houses run by older, trusted ladies. Even when the shy George Best in the mid-1960s was transformed into the pop icon 'Georgie', he still lived for some time with Mrs Fullaway. 'It's something normal to come back to if you've been off the rails a bit', said Best to Hopcraft.

The Busby Babes were frozen in the middle of their becoming. They were a bunch of boys who were on the way to becoming men. Photographs and movie clips show them as happy, uncomplicated and conscientious lads with a large appetite for life. They died at a time when they, as Wagg puts it, had just said goodbye to a world of outdoor loos and said hello to the dance hall's jive. To the nostalgics and romantics the Busby Babes represent the last true football heroes with working-class backgrounds, killed while they were still a part of 'the people'. To the children of pop culture they are the first non-musical megastars who were destroyed while at a peak only matched by the Beatles half a decade later. Here again we find the same elasticity as with the myth of Busby: on one hand, a touch of the modern, on the other a drop of traditionalism.

It may very well be that the Busby Babes symbolised the dawning teenage revolution and celebrity cult, but the key word here is 'dawning'. The Babes were a 1950s phenomenon with strong links to their local communities and working-class culture, and they only vaguely represented what was coming. Therefore, the contrast between Duncan Edwards and Eddie Colman on one hand, and George Best and David Beckham on the other, is also as great as the contrast between social realism and pop art (cf. Wagg). If the Busby Babes are *A Taste of Honey*, then Best and Beckham are more akin to a James Bond movie.

This, however, according to Wagg, makes 'Munich' even more important, since every company likes a story of humble origins. Manchester United's first 'birth' among Manchester's railway workers represent such a humble origin, but their 'rebirth' under Busby, and especially with the Busby Babes in the mid-1950s, is in many ways the club's true beginning, and it is surrounded by humility just like the one in 1878. To Manchester United the mythology and the global brand related to the constellation the Busby Babes, Munich is like an emblematic family photograph: it is like the sepia-toned image of an ancestor that hangs on the wall in many of our homes, peering over the descendants. It is the very prototype that subsequent United teams never can match.

And then we are back to the ambiguity and elasticity: to football's political left wingers, to its activists, traditionalists and sentimentalists, the Busby Babes and 'Munich' symbolises the world we have lost. To the post-modern entrepreneurs in the twenty-first century they represent the motive with which you must utilise commercially (cf. Wagg). The antagonism is perhaps too rigidly delineated, though, because the question is whether there has ever been a mythical past where football was not commercialised. Even in Billy Meredith's time clubs operated according to commercial guidelines and on the basis of the economic bottom line. The difference between then and today is rather the degree of complexity in relation to commercialisation, and one of the most important changes has to do with the leading role that sign, image and signal play.

*   *   *

After 'Munich', Jimmy Murphy was responsible for keeping the club afloat. It was a virtually impossible task, but Murphy managed to hold together the remaining pieces and was forced to add a few new ones. Manchester United's first match after the Munich tragedy was an FA Cup tie against Sheffield Wednesday. It was played at Old Trafford just thirteen days after the accident. The only two players left from Belgrade were Gregg and Foulkes, the latter taking up the role as the club's new captain. Charlton, Viollet and Scanlon were all unable to play. Murphy managed to purchase two experienced players to support the many new younger players from the academy. At Aston Villa he found Stan Crowther, while Ernie Taylor was purchased from Blackpool. It was indicative of Murphy's situation that the match programme only contained Sheffield Wednesday's team line-up. The section reserved for United's team line-up were empty, as Murphy to the last was uncertain about which eleven players he had available, and whether the club would get an exemption to use the otherwise cup-tied Crowther and Taylor.

The match was a strong emotional event, not just for Manchester United's players, but for the away team's players and the spectators as well. Shay Brennan scored two goals in his debut, while young Alex Dawson scored a single goal as United won 3–0. It was as if Manchester United simply couldn't lose. The team was carried forward by waves of sympathy from the 59,848 spectators, and the Sheffield Wednesday players wanted to be anywhere else but at Old Trafford. In many ways they couldn't win. In a place beyond this world seven former players and three coaches followed the match, and the match had to be won for them. The victory was the only correct response to the paralysing grief that had affected many thousands after the disaster, although victory was, of course, inadequate. Two days after the game, Duncan Edwards died.

The team's run in the FA Cup was nothing less than sensational. In the league United won only one match after the Munich disaster, while five ended in a draw and eight were lost. But a post-Munich spirit pushed the team on in the cup competitions. On 3 May 1958, a beautiful and sunny Saturday, Manchester United and Bolton met in the FA Cup final at Wembley. On the chest the team from Manchester bore a badge, a phoenix, a symbol of the club's ability to rise from the ashes. In United's case the FA Cup adventure was without a happy ending, though, as Bolton won 2–0.

The season was, however, far from over. The fight in Belgrade against Red Star had sent Manchester United into the semi-finals of this year's European Cup. Here the European football authorities showed real character by deliberately pairing Manchester United with the one of the three remaining teams they could visit easily by train or ship. Their opponents were AC Milan, and nobody expected the Red Devils to do well against the experienced and clever Italians. On 8 May Manchester United beat them 2–1 at Old Trafford, but in Milano the 'Rossoneri' left United chanceless and won 4–0.

* * *

The Munich accident wiped out Busby's 'second generation'. When Busby in 1945 arrived at the bombed Old Trafford, he had inherited, rather than shaped, his 'first generation'. This generation consisted of a bunch of players whose best football years had been used on the European battlefield in the war against Hitler. Busby was a young and inexperienced manager who may have possessed a strong charisma and a natural authority, but he was only a few years older than many of his players. Among them were very headstrong and determined types like Chilton, Rowley, Mitten and Morris. The image of Busby as the paternalistic figure therefore was only really established with the Busby Babes. Busby's 'first generation' was, in addition to their advanced age and partial high-handedness, best known for their floating passing game, where football was played from the back.

With the Busby Babes, Busby created a new team and a new style, where some of the classic Busby virtues were displayed. They were still focused on the fluid and attacking passing game, but this was combined with youthful energy and ease. In addition, the team was free of rebellious types like Mitten and Morris. The Busby Babes consisted of individualists who wreaked havoc on the pitch, but in relation to the 1948 team, the collective was better knit as a result of the players' strong friendships off the pitch.

14 January 1964
Champagne Louis and the butcher's boy

Matt Busby first met Louis Edwards in 1950 during one of Tommy Appleby's famous Monday soirées at the Manchester Opera House. Busby was at this time concerned about the board of directors, which consisted entirely of men on the wrong side of retirement age and he used Appleby's parties to search the ground for potential new board members among Manchester's industrious business-men. When James Gibson died in 1951, Harold Hardman took over the post as chairman of the board, while James Gibson's son Alan took over his father's seat on the board. Alan Gibson, however, was not a future chairman, because his health was weak. In fact, Gibson also admitted that he had never held any special interest in football.

When Busby met the Catholic Louis Edwards, who had Italian roots and, together with his brother Douglas, owned a slaughterhouse and meat enterprise in Manchester, he considered him to be a candidate for the post as United's future chairman of the board. Edwards was not, however, elected to the board until 1958 in the days immediately after the Munich accident. Edwards was a lively, overweight person with a taste for good food, champagne and big cigars. Edwards, who was born in 1914 in Salford just two kilometres from the then brand-new Old Trafford, claimed to have been a fan of Manchester United since childhood. He could also claim to be related to one of the club legends, as his sister was married to Louis Rocca's cousin.

The elegant, articulate and charismatic Willie Satinoff was, according to several sources, Busby's preferred candidate for the post as future chairman of the board. But since Satinoff had died in Munich, Busby was relying on Edwards. Just a few weeks before the accident Edwards had been on the agenda as a possible new member of the board, but George Whittaker had opposed the meat giant's membership. Had it not been for Whittaker's veto, then it was highly probable that Edwards would have flown with the team to Belgrade. Just five days before the Munich accident Whittaker died at a hotel in London, and his death was the main reason that the board met on the afternoon of 7 February 1958, the day after the Munich accident, in Alan Gibson's home in Bowdon, Cheshire. Here, Hardman, Petherbridge and Gibson decided unanimously to appoint Edwards as a new member of the board.

As we read in the thought-provoking *Manchester United: The Betrayal of a Legend* by Michael Crick and David Smith, the board issued ten shares with a value of £10 to Edwards immediately after the appointment. There existed at this time, according to Crick and Smith, 4,132 ordinary shares in the club, all of which had a value of £1, so Edwards owned only a small fraction of the total shareholding. Edwards quickly became the most active of the four board members. When in September 1958 Busby bought Albert Quixall from Sheffield Wednesday for a record-breaking amount of £45,000, he was in company with Edward. Three years later, when Denis Law was signed for £115,000, it was also with the assistance of Edwards. In Edwards, Busby had got what he wanted: a man who did not hesitate to pull the trigger in crucial situations, and who could bring the club further on in the quest for European success.

In the period from 1958 to 1961 Edwards supplemented his original ten shares with seven more. The rules were that any trade with club shares had to be approved by the board. And when shareholders sometimes offered to sell shares to the board, they were equally divided between the board members and bought for £1 each. In 1962 none of the 142 shareholders owned a majority stake in Manchester United. Anne Gibson, James Gibson's widow, owned 894 shares, while Alan Gibson owned 832 shares. Mabel Whittaker, George Whittaker's widow, owned 468 shares, and there were only five more people who owned more than a hundred shares. But in the next fifteen months, from October 1962 to January 1964, the allocation of the shares changed in Louis Edwards's favour. With a copy of the list of the 142 shareholders in his hand, Frank Farrington, one of Edwards' aides, visited the shareholders Edwards thought might be willing to sell. An elderly couple was offered £500 for their hundred shares, and as a thank you for the trade the couple received a few days later a few cutlets and some ground beef from Edwards's company. After a period of time Edwards decided to contact shareholders via letter. He had now increased his bid from £5 to £15 per share, an amount far exceeding the official price of £1. But as Edwards stated himself in the letter, the price reflected his ambition and commitment to Manchester United.

The first to accept Edwards's offer was ironically Mabel Whittaker, whose husband, just a few weeks before his death, had vetoed Edwards's entry on the board. Edwards bought 443 shares from Mabel Whittaker at a price of £12 each. On 16 October 1962 the board sanctioned the trade of the first 120 shares, which

Farrington had bought on Edwards's behalf. Early in December the Whittaker sale of 443 shares was approved, and later the same month an additional 300 shares in Edwards's name were approved. In just a few weeks Edwards became the holder of 880 shares. In January 1963, the board agreed to another trade, this time containing 155 shares, but with the condition no future deals involving Anne Gibson, Alan Gibson or Louis Edwards were to shift the balance of power between the three major shareholders.

The purchases ceased thereafter for a period. But in March 1963 Louis's brother Douglas and his brother-in-law Denzil Haroun began to buy additional shares. In May 1963 Haroun secured himself the greatest remaining share except for Gibson's, when he bought 160 shares of £15 each. The board approved the transaction. In July the board approved eight deals involving Douglas Edwards and a total of eighty-one shares, and in October an additional nineteen deals equalling 147 shares in total were approved. Eight of Douglas's new shares were in fact purchased from Winifred Meredith, Billy Meredith's daughter, for £200. And twenty shares were purchased for £500 from Clarence Hilditch, the former player and manager in the 1920s. In the course of a year, the price of the shares had increased from £5 to £25, but the official value was still £1.

The trade, which in theory secured Edwards control, occurred according to Crick and Smith in September 1963 when Alan Gibson agreed to sell 500 shares of £25 each. Gibson's acceptance symbolised the board's resignation to Edwards's project. On 8 October 1963 it was decided the previous decision, which did not allow a shift in the balance of power between Edwards, Anne Gibson and Alan Gibson, should be cancelled, and the trade between Edwards and Alan Gibson went through. Later that year, Denzil Haroun was elected to the board. Edwards now held 1,835 ordinary shares and 642 of the so-called 'preferred shares', which meant he effectively was sitting on 1,899 shares: 44 per cent. But Douglas Edwards's and Denzil Haroun's shares meant Louis Edwards and his family actually owned the majority of the stakes in Manchester United FC Ltd. On 14 January 1964 Louis Edwards purchased 238 shares from his brother Douglas Edwards and 150 from his brother-in-law Denzil Haroun. Manchester United was now owned by Louis Edwards. In December 1964 Edwards was appointed to vice-chair of the board, and when the eighty-three-year-old Harold Hardman died in June 1965, Edwards was the inevitable choice for the chairman of the board.

Louis Edwards had managed to buy Manchester United for a remarkably small sum of money. It is estimated he had only paid between £31,000 and £41,000 for the club, perhaps a considerable sum of money at the time for just one man, but a sum Edwards could afford after his meat company in 1962 had been listed as one of the UK's most successful businesses. The purchase price seems modest when it is compared to Manchester United's revenues from tickets for the season 1963/64, which were £172,000, or when you look at Denis Law's signing in 1962, which had cost the club £115,000. This means that Louis Edwards had bought the entire club for one-fifth of a single season's ticket revenues, or for a third of Denis Law's value. Edwards's acquisition of shares also turned out to be a great investment in the long run, because when his son Martin Edwards began to sell off his shareholding in the course of the 1990s, the £40,000 Louis Edwards had bought the club for had transformed into a staggering £93 million.

But in 1964 the investment didn't make Louis Edwards rich, since the annual return of the shares was extremely modest. Edwards had, however, without a doubt purchased one of the world's most popular and glamorous football clubs for a sum that was considerably smaller than the club was really worth, also at that time. It had been straightforward, and he had done it without a lot of show and in a very sly, irresistible and, sometimes, shady way. Edwards's plan only succeeded, however, because the board ultimately allowed it to happen. Alan Gibson, the only one with enough power to stop Edwards, was not strong enough or motivated enough to withstand the meat giant, and Harold Hardman, who feared Edwards' takeover of the club, had neither the power nor energy to stop him. Matt Busby, who himself had been the man behind Edwards's introduction to the club, followed the development with deep scepticism.

*　*　*

Louis and Douglas Edwards's butcher company flourished in the post-war years by selling low-quality meat to homes and schools. Success however, was also the alleged consequence of dubious practices such as bribery documented in Granada Television's *World in Action* in the programme 'The man who bought United', shown on 28 January 1980. When the brothers in 1962 chose to register their company on the London Stock Exchange they became extremely wealthy, and Louis Edwards used some of the money to buy the majority stake in Manchester United.

But in the mid-1970s, both the company and the football club were in crisis, the former economically and the latter sportingly. As a consequence of the company's financial problems, Louis Edwards tried to make Manchester United more profitable, and in 1973 he allied himself with Roland Smith, a marketing professor from Manchester University. Smith told Edwards there was a huge economic potential in Manchester United and proposed to him a plan to launch shares that, without undermining Edwards's control of the club, would raise money to purchase more players and for Edwards himself. In September 1976 Louis Edwards and Roland Smith, along with Alan Gibson and Matt Busby, travelled to London to discuss the possibility of a new share placing with the financial experts at Kleinwort Benson. It was a plan that would reinforce the business aspect of the football club and at the same time ensure that the Edwards family kept control of the club well into the future. But the plan meant the ties between Busby and Edwards would be irrevocably broken.

Roland Smith and Kleinwort Benson subsequently made a proposal to Edwards that not only included increasing the total number of United shares, but also raising £1,000,000, which could, among other things, be earmarked for buying players. The new shares would only be offered to already existing shareholders, and it was decided the shareholders would be allowed to buy 208 new shares for each share they owned in advance. The original 4,644 shares were thus transformed into 965,952 shares, and at a price of £1 a piece it would put £1,000,000 into the club's piggy bank. While these discussions were going on internally between Smith, Kleinwort Benson and the board of Manchester United, the Edwards family commenced a new raid against the remaining shares, which were still in circulation. Since spring 1963 there was no noticeable change in the distribution of the shares. The board had gone through a few changes with the inclusion of Louis's son Martin Edwards in 1970 and Matt Busby in 1971. That same year, Alan Gibson, who earlier had sold a high proportion of his shares to Edwards, inherited his mother's 894 shares. It was only Busby, who had received 500 shares when he joined the board, who also owned a considerable share.

In 1977 it was decided at the annual general meeting that the fixed price system of the shares should be lifted. Again the Edwards family began to offer people a price they could not refuse. The Edwards family targeted the three remaining major shareholders besides Busby. In November 1977 Beryl Norman, daughter of Walter Crickmer, sold 51 shares at £200 each to Roger Edwards, Louis's second son. In December 1977 Elizabeth Hardman, daughter of Harold Hardman, sold 71 shares at £200 each to Louis Edwards's wife, Muriel. The final pieces of the plan were carried out in February 1978 when Alan Gibson sold 1,138 shares worth £172.70 each to Martin Edwards, and in order to fund the acquisition, Martin Edwards borrowed £200,000 from the bank. The Edwards family had raised their shareholding in the company from 47 per cent to 74 per cent of the 4,644 shares in Manchester United. This meant Busby's 500 shares had proportionally fallen to less than half. Both the Norman and Hardman deals took place at a time when the shareholders could not know anything about the impending share expansion plans, a scheme which would of course add a considerable value to their shares. What the Edwards family carried out in other words was 'insider trading'. They took advantage of their knowledge of the impending plans to increase the value of the already existing shares. At this time, such actions were not illegal, but they were considered to be unethical. The Edwards family was therefore aware of the fact that the more of the original 4,644 shares they could manage to buy, the easier it would be to retain the majority stake and also make a large profit selling the excess shares.

When the share expansion was first on the agenda of a board meeting in September of 1978, Louis Edwards easily obtained a majority vote for the proposal. Both Alan Gibson and Bill Young, a new board member since 1960 and Gibson's friend, expressed reservations about the plans but ended up voting for it. Denzil Haroun and Martin Edwards also voted for it, and Martin Edwards justified himself by saying the club would need £350,000 to buy a new goalkeeper. Only Busby was strongly opposed to the proposal. He pointed out the club had no need to raise money in this way both because more than 50,000 spectators showed up at Old Trafford each weekend and because the club was in possession of £425,000, which was money accumulated on the so-called Development Association account.

When the plans were published, many experienced businessmen and financiers thought a bank loan or a share expansion, in which the public could buy shares, would be preferable. Even the London Stock Exchange expressed their surprise. Edwards responded by saying a bank loan would mean high interest charges and debt, and a public share expansion would mean he and his family would lose control of the club. To maintain control of the club the family were willing to pay around £740,000 for the new shares, which they would be eligible for after the increase. But there were very few who didn't see the plan simply as a money-making machine for the Edwards family. First, the abolition of the fixed price system meant Edwards would be likely to get about £4 for each of the shares he himself had paid £1 for; second and (the worst-case scenario), it meant the annual dividends could rise from £600 to £150,000.

Busby was worried and appalled over the changes. He even went to London where he met with an equally worried FA in order to examine whether the plans could be stopped. He even considered resigning from the board. The relationship between Edwards and Busby further soured when Edwards refused to comply with the agreement they made for both of their sons to be given a place on the board. Martin Edwards had already been elected in 1970, but Matt Busby had never succeeded in getting Sandy Busby elected onto Manchester United's board of directors. In several internal – and very brave – letters, Les Olive, Walter Crickmer's successor and the club's long-time secretary, warned Louis Edwards of the plan's consequences; for example, bad publicity and the high return from shares. He also pointed out the plans could not be justified from an economic perspective as Manchester United had a healthy financial base. Also protesting against the share expansion was local millionaire and United fan John Fletcher. Fletcher formed Manchester United Action Group '78, and suggested a public share expansion of 1 million shares at a price of £2 each to exploit the enormous goodwill among the club's fans. The board refused, however, to meet with Fletcher and said the club had no need of £2 million. Fletcher went to the Supreme Court, who ruled in Edwards's favour.

With Fletcher defeated, Busby resigned to the deal and Olive ignored, the share expansion was confirmed at Manchester United's extraordinary general meeting on 18 December 1978. Martin Edwards, who with almost 400,000 shares was now the largest shareholder in the club, took out another mortgage and now had a debt of around £600,000. The bank stipulated that Martin Edwards's shares were to be traded on the free market and therefore not subject to pricing restrictions, and the board no longer had to approve all trades. In the beginning, the shares didn't reach the £8 Martin Edwards had hoped for. At first they made between £4.50 and £5, but the price quickly fell to between £1.50 and £2.75.

According to Martin Edwards, the one million pounds that the share expansion brought the club was initially supposed to be spent on buying a new goalkeeper. But in 1978 Manchester United bought Gary Bailey for just £5,000 from Witts University in South Africa. Most of the money went instead towards the purchase of Ray Wilkins, who in August 1979 was brought to the club from Chelsea for £700,000. However, in the wake of the Wilkins transfer, Dave Sexton (United manager at the time) was told to sell players and to balance the books. This meant that Stuart Pearson was sold to West Ham for £200,000, David McCreery to QPR for £170,000 and Brian Greenhoff to Leeds for £350,000. Sexton gained a transfer surplus of £15,000, so the capital increase of 1 million pounds cannot be said to have been spent on new players, as the club had earlier been reporting.

On 28 January 1980 Granada Television aired the programme 'The man who bought United'. The journalists behind the programme had spent the previous two years gathering evidence of the Edwards family's corrupt practices and illegal transactions. The burden of proof was solid, and in addition it claimed that Manchester United had for years paid the parents of the talented sons they were scouting money under the table to get them to sign a contract with the club. According to Granada, a secret account existed, which was used in connection with such deals. Just four weeks after the TV show Louis Edwards died of a heart attack. According to Martin Edwards his death was a direct consequence of the Granada programme.

*   *   *

On 22 March 1980 the thirty-four-year-old Martin Edwards was elected as Manchester United's new chairman. Busby, who had now become more and more disillusioned with the way the club was run, announced he did not want to be considered for the post of chairman. Instead he was appointed as the club's president, a position that had been vacant since James Gibson's death in 1951. In November 1981 Edwards voted for the FA's proposal that professional football clubs could have one paid executive, and in January 1982 Manchester United's board appointed him to be one of the first full-time directors in British football.

Edwards's initial wage was £30,000 a year, and just half a year later his annual salary increased to £40,000. Only four players at this time earned more than Edwards. According to Denzil Haroun, the salary should be seen as recognition of the fact that Edwards had been the architect behind several lucrative contracts, for example, the sponsorship from the electronics company Sharp, which brought the club £500,000. Edwards set out to transform Manchester United into a football club run along business lines. He optimised the legal, administrative and economic strands of the organisation, and the club's activities were subdivided in separate departments: administration, business, football and catering services. Edwards also implemented a procedure in which player contracts were negotiated by himself and the player or his agent.

At the annual general meeting in 1979 it was agreed to pay a return of 5 per cent of the share value, which was the maximum permitted. The year before the pay-out had been £312, but in 1979 the amount had increased to £50,419, and the same amounts were paid out in both 1980 and 1981. In three years Martin Edwards received more than £80,000 in return for his Manchester United shares, and, according to Crick and Smith, it was money he badly needed to pay off his loans, which still amounted to £600,000. In 1981 Edwards was joined by his brother Roger on the board. A few years earlier corporate executive James Gulliver, who had bought the Edwards family's company in the late 1970s and had transformed it into the success story Argyll Foods, also became a board member. In his attempt to make the board more modern and commercially oriented, Martin Edwards also tried to get Mike Edelson on board, and he succeeded in the autumn 1982. In August the same year, the now seventy-three-year-old Matt Busby announced he would resign from the board due to health reasons. Two years later Edwards succeeded in convincing Alan Gibson, who had been on the board since 1948, and Bill Young, who had been a member since 1960, to withdraw. As replacements for Gibson and Young, Edwards recruited the lawyer Maurice Watkins and Bobby Charlton. In the now professionalised, commercially oriented board Charlton would work as a consultant in football-related matters, just as he was to be the public face of the club in the same way as Busby had been.

Martin Edwards was soon involved in national football matters and together with the chairmen of the major clubs he pushed for initiatives to make football more commercial. First of all they wanted a league with fewer clubs in order to avoid the small clubs sponging off the large. Second, they suggested gate revenues should go to the home team for the same reasons. Next they attempted to reduce the voting percentage needed (75 per cent) to get a proposal adopted at the Football League's meetings. Finally they wanted better television contracts.

Manchester United did not pay out any dividends in 1982 and 1983, and Edwards therefore had to find alternative options to pay his personal expenses. In 1983 he followed with great interest how Tottenham became the first English club to register themselves on the London Stock Exchange, where the club was valued at the staggering sum of £9 million. Edwards and Watkins once again contacted Kleinwort Benson, and they estimated Manchester United to a value of between £6 and £8 million, a disappointing amount to Edwards. Edwards could, if the value came to £8 million, get around £500,000 released and still retain the majority stake in the club. Before he got any further with the plans, in January 1984 he was contacted by Andrew McHutchon, who told him the media mogul Robert Maxwell was interested in buying Manchester United. An amount of £10 million was bandied about in the media as Maxwell's offer, but this amount cannot be confirmed. Edwards was said to have offered Maxwell his shares of £15 each and thus a total price on Manchester United of £15 million.

What took place between Edwards and Maxwell is still unclear to this day, but fortunately for Manchester United the trade didn't take place. The FA raised the return limit from 5 to 15 per cent. In 1984 Manchester United came out of the financial year with a record profit of more than £1.7 million, and after two non-profitable years Manchester United paid the maximum 15 per cent of the company's share value, £151,284 in total. To Martin Edwards the sum amounted to £77,319. When Michael Knighton, under a great fanfare, in 1989, offered £20 million for Manchester United, Martin Edwards decided to say yes. This was partly to help the club in its efforts to return to the top of English football, and partly in order to meet his personal debt and realise his father's investment of twenty-five years earlier. The trade, however, collapsed as some of Knighton's investors suddenly withdrew. The Knighton and Maxwell affairs were without doubt a major reason for the board's decision to register Manchester United as a public limited company on the London Stock Exchange in 1991. The decision was an attempt to prevent similar possible 'hostile' acquisitions in the future, boost Edwards's private finances, as well as giving United some much-needed resources.

The club was assessed to be worth £47 million, and with this stock listing and the capital expansion the club was well equipped for the boom football experienced during the 1990s. In 1998 Rupert Murdoch and BSkyB tried to buy Manchester United, and Martin Edwards reportedly accepted a bid of £98 million for his shares, while the total value of the sale amounted to £623.4 million. The trade was prevented by the United Kingdom's Monopolies Commission. In the course of the 1990s, Martin Edwards sold off his shares and ended up earning in total of £93 million. In 2000 he handed over the post of chief executive to Peter Kenyon, and in 2002 the butcher's boy was forced to resign as chairman after accusations he used prostitutes on club travels and allegations of spying on women in public toilets.

29 May 1968
The quest for the Holy Grail

In the month after the Munich accident, racked with guilt and in physical pain, Matt Busby was seriously considering retiring as manager of Manchester United. When Busby, after much consideration, decided to follow his wife's advice to continue, he returned to Old Trafford with a dream bordering on obsession: the dream of creating a third team capable of winning the European Cup. To Busby, a European triumph was the only way in which he and the club could atone for their guilt and honour the deceased. To abandon or fail this mission would mean his Babes died in vain.

A place in the final of the FA Cup in 1958 had given the first indication the club had a future. At Wembley, the phoenix on the players' shirts symbolised Manchester United's unique ability to rise from the ashes. The cup adventure had, however, been more a result of emotions and superhuman performances rather than real football-like strength. The food chain in Manchester United was absolutely the most powerful in the country, but to replace stars such as Edwards, Taylor, Byrne and Whelan all at the same time put too much pressure on the young reserve players. United collapsed to ninth in the league. Immediate reinforcements therefore seemed an imperative necessity, but Busby maintained faith in his new brood of young talents and only invested in Albert Quixall up to the 1958/59 season.

In this first season after Munich, Murphy and later Busby managed to bring Manchester United up to an impressive second place in the league. The team consisted of the few survivors from Munich, Quixall, and a large group of new faces well known to people close to the club. In short: talent from the academy. Many of the players were new, but the style was the same. The next season saw United reach a respectable seventh place. In addition the 1960s extensive improvements of Old Trafford started with the Stretford End being covered. But the season will be best remembered for Dennis Viollet's thirty-two goals in thirty-six league matches, which at the time of writing remains a club record. In Munich, Viollet had been admitted to the Rechts der Isar hospital with severe damage to the head, and his life and his career had been in danger. Just two years later, he was named as the league's top scorer. In 1960/61 the team yet again reached seventh spot. The next season saw them fall to 15th place, the lowest since relegation in 1937.

In 1962 Busby broke his principle of not buying his way to success. The team still consisted of a core of players developed at the academy, but the previous year's difficulty in finding the right formula for success made Busby act. In the summer of 1962 as a replacement for Viollett he signed the twenty-two-year-old Scottish striker Denis Law from Turin for the astronomical sum of £115,000. Six months later, Busby boosted the midfield with Pat Crerand, who was purchased from Celtic for £56,000. But with only a few matches left the club was deeply involved in the fight to avoid relegation.

* * *

Sometimes a single goal can change football history. It happens on Saturday 25 May 1963 in the FA Cup final between Leicester City and Manchester United. 100,000 spectators are in place at Wembley, and they witness a first half of intense Leicester pressure on David Gaskell's goal. It seems only a matter of time before Gaskell and the other Red Devils must buckle. For many years Manchester United has only been a shadow of the club that dominated English football in the 1950s and, judging from the first half, the mediocrity is here to stay. That Manchester United again will symbolise confidence, elegance and vitality seems unlikely.

But then something magical happens. A Crerand pass from the left wing lands at the feet of the genius Law, who has his back to Leicester's goal and is marked by two opponents. But Law manages to create microscopic space around himself so he can turn and thunder the ball past Gordon Banks into Leicester's goal. The goal galvanises Manchester United. Gone is the hesitation and uncertainty that had impeded the team in the league throughout the season, and instead Law's goal seems to give the players a glimpse of what they could achieve if they just play with the bold style of their past. In the second half United extend their lead after Gordon Banks blocks Charlton's projectile. The ball lands at the feet of Herd and the former Arsenal striker quickly slips the ball into the empty goal. Busby's brave men switch to a higher gear and Herd closes the match with his second goal after another lovely piece of attacking football.

The victory proves Manchester United have survived, but not forgotten, 'Munich'. The final had, until Law's goal, been a microcosm of the club's last five years: forced to its knees and vain attempts to rise again, mediocrity and a loss of belief. With Law's goal it all turns around, and the rest of the match provides a foretaste of the next five years in the club's history: arrogance, entertainment and success. The bleakness since the Munich accident that had threatened to engulf the club fades away with the triumph at Wembley. The time has come for Manchester United to move out of the harsh 1950s and bid hello to the hedonistic 1960s. Goodbye social realism; welcome pop art.

With the Wembley triumph as a springboard Manchester United stormed to runners-up spot the very next season, only outdone by rivals Liverpool. Law's total of forty-six goals this season remains a club record. 'The Lawman' or 'The King of Old Trafford', as Law was called, is one of the most natural goal-scorers to have worn the famous red shirt, along with Ruud van Nistelrooy years later. Both possessed astonishing finishing skills and were born to score goals on a football field. In addition to Law's goal instinct, it was Law's swiftness in thought as well as action that made him lethal in the penalty area. He also possessed the temperament of a predator. On the pitch he was inexorably ruthless and aggressive. He gave the opponents a taste of their own medicine, but off the field he was as meek as a lamb. After his forty-six goals, many of them spectacular, and after a string of notable performances, Denis Law was the first player in Manchester United's history to be named Europe's best footballer, in 1964.

The 1963/64 season is not only memorable because of the silver medal, the reunion with European football (Cup Winners' Cup), Denis Law's Ballon d'Or and a general face lift to Old Trafford. The season is also historic, because on 14 September 1963 the seventeen-year-old Irish wonder boy George Best made his debut for Manchester United in front of 50,453 spectators at Old Trafford. In *The Football Man*, Arthur Hopcraft claims Best's first match was one of the two most memorable debuts in the league's history. With his challenging play Best brought the concept of 'dribbling' back to life, after it for many years had been non-existent in the football journalist's dictionary. Already after his first season it was clear to everyone Manchester United was in the possession of a unique talent.

*   *   *

It is the autumn of 1962, the year after George Best arrived in Manchester, and the year before the Beatles recorded their first singles 'Love me do' and 'Please please me'. Their first television appearance is on Granada Television in Manchester. The accelerating 'Beatlemania' also hits George Best. However, this is not until 1966, when he, with his flamboyant football, his long dark hair, and his hypnotic eyes, captivate millions of TV viewers and thousands of young Portuguese women during a UEFA Cup match against Benfica in Lisbon. After this achievement George Best is named 'El Beatle'.

1962 is also the year of Andy Warhol's famous work 'Campbell soup cans', a recording of and tribute to American mass culture and consumerism. In the cinema you can see Stanley Kubrick's adaptation of Vladimir Nabokov's novel *Lolita*, John Ford's western classic *The Man Who Shot Liberty Valance*, and *Dr No*, the first James Bond film. Anthony Burgess, the English writer from Manchester, publishes *A Clockwork Orange*, and Rachel Carson's *Silent Spring* kick-starts the modern environmental movement.

At the Marquee Club in London the Rolling Stones go on stage for the first time, thus ensuring the Cold War's bipolar mindset is transferred to the world of music. 'Do you prefer Stones or Beatles?' is the epoch's most asked question. As for George Best, he prefers the Stones' more interesting sound. In Israel Adolf Eichmann is executed, and Algeria achieves independence from France. In Los Angeles Marilyn Monroe is found dead in her home, and the first black student is enrolled at Mississippi University. At the end of the year the whole globe is holding its breath for several weeks because of the Cuba crisis. This is the world in snapshots, the year after George Best arrives in Manchester, and the year before his debut at Old Trafford.

In George Best's second season, Manchester United regained the English Championship and reached the final of the Fairs Cup. They did it with style, but not without hard competition from Don Revie's no-nonsense Leeds United. Throughout the season they ran a sometimes ruthless race with Busby's Red Devils. The Championship was won not only because Busby had the best and most talented players, but also because the 1965 championship team was characterised by a tactical sophistication, where flow and flexibility time after time checkmated the opposing team's rigid organisation. In particular, the six offensive players practised kaleidoscopic patterns of movement, which proved to be impossible to stem with traditional man marking.

In a time, where wing play seemed to be losing its appeal Busby maintained speed and challenge on the flanks with Best and John Connelly. The attacking duo Law and Herd complimented each other superbly. Herd was usually the stationary target man, Law the moving forward, who created havoc by falling back and finding the duty free zones between the opposing team's defence and midfield. In midfield Crerand and Charlton were at work and added creativity, perseverance, and slick passing. Law's mobility opened up the opportunity for forward thrusts and goals, not least from Charlton, just as it paved the way for Best's terrorising raids down the middle of the field. The team's strength was obviously its attacking options and there were many strings to play. Best was a strong header and had a good long shot as well as mesmerising dribbling abilities. Law was an unmatched finisher in the penalty area and also deadly with his head, and both Herd and Charlton were notorious for powerful long-range shots.

With the redemptive championship seven years after the Munich accident Busby had again the prospect of participation in the tournament, which more than anything else drove him on: the European Cup. The overriding goal for 1965/66 was success in this tournament, as United at this time was far from being guaranteed a place in the tournament each year. Unlike today, it was only the champions of each league who took part, and not the three or four best teams from the big leagues. It's worth noting that the English league at this time was not always a race between the same two or three clubs, which has been very much the case since 1996. In the course of the nineteen years from the end of the Second World War to 1965, ten different clubs won the Championship: Manchester United (4), Wolverhampton (3), Liverpool (2), Arsenal (2), Portsmouth (2), Tottenham (2), Chelsea, Burnley, Ipswich and Everton all won one each.

Therefore, in the years after the war both the football power and the money was far from concentrated in a few clubs, which is the case today where the English championship for many years to come seems to be a rivalry between Manchester United, Chelsea and Manchester City. The old system had its charm, mainly because of its unpredictability, but as already mentioned the flat hierarchy was also the English club's Achilles' heel when it came to success in Europe. It was only with the abolition of the maximum wage in 1961 that English football began the long and bumpy road towards today's sedimentation of top and bottom, but simultaneously also towards European success.

To Busby the participation in the European Cup of 1965/66 was the chance he had been waiting for since the Munich disaster. It was the chance to exorcise guilt, to honour the dead, to justify his international vision and complete his European mission. In the quarter-finals Manchester United faced Benfica with the great Eusébio in the team. United won 3–2 at Old Trafford. Benfica had been finalists in four of the previous five years, and had won twice. At home at Estadio da Luz the team had never lost a European match. The Portuguese 'Eagles' were therefore favourites to go on to the semi-finals. Led by a bubbly Best, Manchester United shocked the spoiled home audience and the many million TV viewers across Europe with a fantastic achievement, winning 5–1 in Lisbon in one of the club's best ever performances.

As fate would have it, Busby was to face a bittersweet reunion with Belgrade, the city where his heroic Babes eight years earlier had secured themselves a spot in the semi-finals of the European Cup, and the city from which they departed on their last journey before Munich. Back then the opponent was called Red Star, but in 1966 they were called Partizan. The reunion clearly didn't suit United, as they lost 2–0, and after a drowsy effort at Old Trafford they only managed to win 1–0 with a goal by Stiles. 'Now we shall never win the European Cup', said a disappointed Matt Busby after the match, and there was a real chance that Busby had missed his last chance of European triumph.

Busby's resigned attitude was understandable, as Manchester United apparently had a bad habit of losing semi-finals. The defeat to Partizan was Manchester United's fourth defeat in as many European semi-finals (Real Madrid 1957, Milan 1958, Ferencvaros 1965, Partizan Belgrade 1966). And in the FA Cup, the team for the fifth year running reached the semi-finals, but lost for the fourth time.

To Stiles and Charlton however, the season, was not over. The disappointment of the two semi-final defeats and fourth place in the league was partly compensated by the gold medal they won at Wembley when England's national team won 4–2 against West Germany in the World Cup final. In addition, Charlton attained the honour of being named Europe's best footballer of 1966.

*　*　*

Bobby Charlton is a legend in Manchester United's history. A true 'company man' in the same category as Ryan Giggs and Paolo Maldini from AC Milan, Charlton symbolises the duality of continuity and rupture that characterises United's long history. He is a survivor, just like Manchester United. With his 758 games, a record that was only surpassed by Ryan Giggs in the Champions League final of 2008, he is simply the embodiment of loyalty and continuity. He is the historic link from the Busby Babes to the triumph at Wembley in 1968 and into the post-Busby era. Charlton's role as link is only reinforced by the fact that today he is a member of the club's board of directors and earlier served as the official ambassador for the club. But as a survivor of Munich and as a 'survivor' following Busby's retirement, he also experienced two of the most violent fractures of the club's red thread and therefore represents Manchester United's tragic dimension. As son of a miner he is the classic working-class hero, who through his football skills ascended from the coalmines, a bit shy and astonished, to take centre stage at Old Trafford.

On the field Bobby Charlton's athletic body radiated both power and grace. He was the type of player who could get the spectators to hold their breath in anticipation of whatever the next moment would bring. He was one of the few players who could cause the temporal continuity to be 'out of joint' so that both time and the match took an unexpected direction. Charlton primarily possessed this ability through his shots and passes. A shot from Charlton, particularly from long range and executed while running, represented of the game's most beautiful actions, not only because the shot possessed monstrous power, but precisely because this power was rooted in athletic and graceful elegance. Charlton was thus never awkward or panicky in his movements. The ball seemed to obey him and find the goal almost before he hit it. When it came to passing he was totally precise, like David Beckham later on, even if his passes spanned half the length of the pitch. What was special about Charlton was that with a single move, often a combination of acceleration and quick footwork, he managed to convert defence into attack. It is this suddenness that makes football so dramatic and fascinating, and Bobby Charlton was a true master in this 'Ästhetik der Plötzlichkeit' (cf. Bohrer).

Charlton furthermore had his very own style when it came to dribbling. In contrast to Best, who dribbled by letting the ball ping-pong between his feet, Charlton flipped the ball. It looked a little bit like the Argentinian dribbling technique, 'el toque', where the ball is flipped with the outside of the foot. Charlton also seemed to strike the ball as if it was a guitar. With his striking the chord and his instrument he invited the opposing team and the spectators to a dance. After a Charlton flip the ball rolled before him along the ground, even quite often far ahead of him, and then he sprinted after it. Charlton's contact with the ball was like a series of stop overs or intermediate stations that was quickly abandoned on his explosive ride forward, but as a result of his acceleration the defenders time and again came too late with their challenges. When Charlton received the ball and got ready for such a run, the soundscape of the stadium suddenly transformed itself, the formless murmur turned into an expectant buzz, Arthur Hopcraft notes. Should he decide that the moment wasn't right, the soundscape immediately changed again, now into a mass sigh of disappointment.

Charlton embodied the poetic style and Corinthian ideals. He was the essence of courtliness on the football field, a modern version of Sir Gawain, King Arthur's famous nephew. But Charlton would not have been the same to either Manchester United nor England without his 'twin' and antithesis: Nobby Stiles. Stiles is the essence of the prosaic element in football, and the Corinthian ideals meant nothing to this terrier who would do anything to win. If Charlton's strength first and foremost was his creative actions in the opponent's half, then Stiles's strength was the destructive 'karate chop', which he handed up to his opponents' creative prima donnas.

* * *

The Championship of 1965 had been the culmination of a great season with plenty of entertaining football, and the match in Lisbon in 1966 against Benfica was the team's peak of performance. The question was whether the players could repeat that performance. Busby sensed the team was close to having peaked, but only made minimal changes, and it proved to be a wise decision. As the team boarded the train to London to meet West Ham in the second to last match of the 1966/67 season, the players were aware of the fact that victory would be enough to ensure the Championship. Manchester United won 6–1. 'My greatest ambition now is to bring home the European Cup', said Matt Busby to the *Sunday Mirror* after the match. The way the Championship in 1967 was secured convinced Busby his team was strong enough.

May 1967. The Championship is brought home with a 6–1 win over West Ham. It is United's fifth Championship since the Second World War. From left: Bobby Charlton, Denis Law, George Best and Billy Foulkes.

The 1968 European Cup Final against Benfica, with a dancing Bobby Charlton.

In 1967/68 Busby again made only a few changes. As some of the key players were injured, particularly Law, Herd and Stiles, it opened up for new academy talents, who were given the chance to prove their worth. This included the local Brian Kidd, an eighteen-year-old attacker. In Europe, Manchester United were among a number of big clubs. Real Madrid, Juventus and Benfica were the southern European challengers, but also Ajax and Dynamo Kiev, together with Celtic and Manchester United, were regarded as serious contenders for the title of Europe's best team. After hard duels against Sarajevo and Gornik Zabrze, United faced Real Madrid in the semi-finals. The role as underdogs suited United very well. On 24 April 1968 they defeated 'Los Blancos' at Old Trafford with a 1–0 win thanks to a fantastic volley from Best. At the Bernabéu on 15 May 1968 Madrid pushed the English back throughout the entire first half, and when Pirri after half an hour scored a magical goal to level the aggregate score it looked ominous for United. The next fifteen minutes saw a continuous bombardment of Stepney's goal. Franscisco Gento put Real further in front 2–0, but before Amancio scored Madrid's third goal, United were so lucky to reduce the scoreline with a sloppy own goal from Zoco.

Busby told his disoriented and discouraged players at half time that they were all great footballers, but that they had not played football in the first half. He told them they should go back out and *play* football and that they would win the fight. A combination of United's new-found belief in their own skills and Real Madrid's touch of arrogance meant that for the first time in the match the Red Devils began to dominate. The Spanish seemed satisfied to let the British keep possession of the ball, but this tactic quickly proved to be fatal. Shortly after the beginning of the second half Best delivered a pass to Sadler's head and he beautifully despatched it into Madrid's net to level the aggregate score. Real didn't manage to rediscover their rhythm and rarely visited United's half as Best once again shined on the wing and sent a flat pass backwards in the penalty area to an oncoming Foulkes, who then equalised. It was 3–3. It seemed almost predestined that it was Foulkes, the survivor from Munich, who scored the historic goal that sent Manchester United to the final for the first time ever.

Foulkes's goal was not the only sign indicating 1968 would be Manchester United's European year. The final was to be played at Wembley and would thus ensure the best support. In addition, Benfica had beaten Juventus in the other semi-final, and with the 5–1 victory in Lisbon two years earlier fresh in their minds, Busby and his players were convinced the trophy, which had become the Scottish manager's holy grail, was within reach.

*   *   *

On 29 May 1968 at Wembley, Matt Busby lines up the following flexible 4–4–2 formation:

Stiles is assigned to shadow Eusébio while the versatile Sadler, who in addition to being a striker also could be used in central defence and in midfield, is positioned up front next to Kidd. But if it proves necessary he is to fall back and assist Crerand and Charlton in central midfield. With Sadler falling back, Aston and especially Best are then given a better opportunity to attack.

On this hot evening in late May, 100,000 spectators witness a match that is characterised by anxiety and a lot of free kicks. But it is also an example of how an ugly game can still be beautiful. Beautiful, because the victory first and foremost is a symbolic memorial plaque on which the names of all the Busby Babes are engraved, but also because it is a tribute to and legitimisation of Busby's international vision back in 1956.

I have watched the match on DVD and it is more 'touch and go' than the result of 4–1 suggests. Today most people only remember the winner and perhaps the end result. Many have forgotten that the regular match actually ended 1–1, and it was only during extra time that Benfica were broken. Many people have also forgotten that Eusébio, with the score at 1–1, spurned two great chances against Alex Stepney.

In a goal-free first half tempers are about to boil over, and for Manchester United it's as if the expectation of victory bears down on their play. It seems that all of the United Kingdom and the vast majority of the football world requires 'poetic justice', and the legacy of Munich and the Busby Babes seem to weigh down the English players. Instead of playing in their normal passing style Manchester United are too keen on producing goal opportunities and lose too many balls going forward.

After Busby during half time repeats some of his fundamental principles – to keep the ball and patiently let it do the work – it does not take long before the team's reawakened composure bears fruit. In the fifty-second minute Charlton jumps up high, and with his forehead he unfamiliarly, but resolutely, directs a Sadler cross from the left into the right-hand side of Henrique's goal. The goal gives rise to excessive United domination, and Aston in particular plays the match of his life on the left wing. But, in spite of a number of opportunities, Manchester United can't kill the game off. With ten minutes remaining, Torres finally manages to win a head dual against Foulkes, from which Benfica's Graca equalises.

Now Benfica dominate the game. In the minutes following Benfica's equaliser Eusébio – for once without Stiles at his heels – plays a one-two with Torres and rips up United's defence with an explosive move, but he shoots straight at Stepney. With the clock ticking down, Eusébio suddenly chases a through ball and wedges in between Foulkes and Dunne. Now the Portuguese finds himself alone with Stepney. His technique and nerve usually guarantees a goal in such crucial moments. Busby has already turned his face away when Eusébio gets ready to pull the trigger. The Scot cannot bear seeing his dream shatter so close to the finish line. But this evening Eusébio makes a wrong choice. Instead of placing the ball to one of the sides, he instead chooses a powerful instep kick, and the consequence is that Stepney, with a reflex save, makes one of the best and most important saves in Manchester United's history. In the seconds after this decisive moment, there is the unforgettable sight of Eusébio applauding Stepney's save. A historic moment and a warm gesture of acknowledgement in the middle of a cynical and commercial football world.

As Foulkes's goal in Madrid, Eusébio's miss seems to contribute to a complex mythic constellation that began with Busby's European vision and a historic rebellion against the insular Football League. It continued with the Babes' heroic accomplishments against Athletic Bilbao, Real Madrid and Red Star, only to reach a temporary (but, in a mythological context, also a 'necessary') nadir with their tragic deaths in Munich. Now, ten years later and with Foulkes's Bernabéu heroics and Eusébio's Wembley miss as fated narrative components, it seems on its way to completion.

Eusébio's gesture simply underlines the football drama's close tie with destiny. In addition to recognising Stepney's abilities, Eusébio's gesture is also an emphatic demonstration of his own powerlessness in much the same way as in the ancient theatre, in which the dialogue and masks, as Roland Barthes expresses it in *Mythologies*, 'concurred in the exaggeratedly visible explanation of a necessity. The gesture of the vanquished [Eusébio] signifying to the world a defeat that, far from disguising, he emphasizes and holds like a pause in music, corresponds to the mask of antiquity meant to signify the tragic mode of the spectacle.' Eusébio's gesture is simply poetic justice expressed through mime and gesture.

The oppressive heat has eaten into both teams and an exhausted set of players prepares for extra time. But one man still has some energy left and this turns out to be the difference between United and Benfica this evening: that man is George Best. Just a few minutes into extra time Kidd skilfully flicks on a ball from Stepney with his head. Best times his run perfectly as he has done so many times before, so that he – in terms of both direction and speed – 'melts together' with the ball as it approaches the ground. When Best's run and the ball's curve converge in an epiphanic form – in a form suddenly emerging against all expectation – Best, with an elegant dribble, leaves the nearest defender behind on his way towards Benefica's goal, after which he finds himself face to face with Henrique. Best takes advantage of his speed and feints a shot that leaves Benfica's goalkeeper to one side, after which he pulls sharply to the other and puts United back in front 2–1 by rolling the ball into an empty net. The goal has a demoralising effect on Benfica, but works as a shot of adrenalin for Manchester United. Just one minute later Kidd, on his nineteenth birthday, scores, and United's fourth goal is scored by Charlton from an assist by the excellent Kidd.

As the final whistle sounds the Manchester United players' reaction is atypical. Instead of euphoric cheering and hugging of the nearest teammate, what we see is more like a series of inverted, individual redemptions, as well as an unconscious and immediate gesture to Matt Busby, who is the first to be congratulated by the players. Bobby Charlton breaks out in tears as the referee's whistle sounds, and when he later raises the trophy Busby also breaks into tears: 'The moment that Bobby Charlton took the European Cup, it, well, cleansed me. It eased the pain of guilt I had of taking the club into Europe. It was my justification', Busby later said.

*　*　*

In addition to excellent performances from Aston and Kidd it was George Best who stood out at Wembley. The Irish supernova was at his very best in 1968 and won the title of Europe's best footballer, four years after Law and two after Charlton.

Outside the world of football, 1968 is the year when Czechoslovakia both experience the Prague Spring and the invasion by the Soviet Union. The Vietnam War is now raging into its third year. In Folsom Prison, Johnny Cash gives a legendary concert, and Martin Luther King is murdered in Memphis, Tennessee. 1968 is also the year in which Stanley Kubrick's *2001: A Space Odyssey*, Sergio Leone's *Once Upon a Time in the West* and Mike Nichols's *The Graduate* are released in the cinemas. Italy wins the European Championship in football, but

111

1968 is also the year in which their former manager, the legendary Vittorio Pozzo, passes away, aged eighty-two. The Beatles release *The White Album*, and the Rolling Stones follow suit with *Beggar's Banquet* and 'Sympathy for the Devil'.

In the middle of these beautiful and tragic, sad and joyful, divine and demonic events, Georgie's light radiated stronger than ever before. Just a week before the final at Wembley Best turned twenty-two, and the game against Benfica was his 225th for Manchester United. Seven years had passed since Bob Bishop discovered Best in Belfast and immediately afterwards sent a telegram to Busby, in which he wrote: 'I think I've found you a genius.' The subsequent thirteen years showed Bishop was right in his prediction, but they also showed the flipside of the genius. The story of George Best is the story of a shy, and not particularly articulate boy from Belfast, who was transformed into 'Georgie', the pop-culture icon and confident city slicker. It is the story of how the fragile and exceptionally talented apprentice was transformed into the strong but fiery-tempered professional. It is the story of how Mrs Fullaway's boarding house and public transport were replaced with an endless series of mink-clad models, as architect-designed villa and a white Jaguar. It is also the story of how snooker evenings in the company of David Sadler were turned into visits to nightclubs in the company of gorgeous women. And it is the story of how abstinence is transformed into addiction.

It was precisely the urge for alcohol and the flashlights of fame that began to eclipse Best's footballing radiance in the late 1960s and early 1970s. And the flashlights of the sixties were undeniably sharper and more dazzling than the ones pointed at the Busby Babes in the fifties. Their fame was characterised by a necessary, but at the same time also minimal distance to the common people. Some of them still lived at boarding houses or at home with their parents, and they earned no more than the ordinary skilled worker. When George Best made his debut for Manchester United in 1963, the maximum wage in English football had been abolished two years earlier. The top footballers of the mid-1960s inevitably, therefore, had quite a different status to those from an earlier decade.

During the 1960s Best gained an image of being both arrogant and extravagant, but he was basically just a young and popular guy and based on lower middle-class standards, he was also rich. However, it was only because it was just a few years since footballers and workers earned the same money that Best and some of his contemporaries seemed so wealthy and swashbuckling. Best's extravagance was thus a relative phenomenon and partly the result of the time in which he lived. His decadent lifestyle, which began to escalate in the early 1970s, was also partly the result of the new times characterised by the dialectics between more powerful flashlights and the abolishment of the wage limit. This dialectics certainly created superstars, but it also created victims. Of course these external circumstances do not explain the entire reason for Georgie's fall, but they are essential for understanding the contrast between the Busby's Babes and Busby's Best.

George Best.

George Best plays his last match for Manchester United on 1 January 1974, at only twenty-seven. In the quantitative sense it may indeed look like Best's brilliant light burnt out too quickly, but behind the supernova theory, statistics also tell the story of a player who actually played in 470 matches and scored 179 goals for Manchester United. His career also contains thirty-seven international matches, two English championships, a European Cup winner's medal and a Ballon d'Or.

Best's career cannot only be summarised quantitatively and statistically, though. It is the qualitative impression that is left behind: the impression of George Best as an artist; as football's answer to a painter. In the same way a painter uses paintbrush and paint to create shapes and patterns on a canvas, Best created figures and patterns on the turf using football boots and a ball. When I see Best perform his ping-pong dribbles, his long diagonal runs and score his courageous goals using his head, I come to think of one of abstract expressionism's front men, the American Jackson Pollock and his 'action painting'.

Pollock had the habit of stretching out his often enormous canvases on the floor, and he painted by dripping and pouring paint onto the canvas, while he himself walked around on top of it. Pollock literally moved around on his canvases as a football player moves around on a football field.

Pollock's bodily interaction with the canvas underlines the actual physical event 'to paint' as an important part of the finished work of art. In football it's the same. The match is really nothing else than a series of physical actions and events. To see the finished product, the result, in the newspaper or on the computer screen may have an affective effect, for example joy or disappointment. But without the actions and epiphanic forms that made up the actual match, without the bodily events and intensities that preceded the result, the majority of people, except perhaps the addicted gambler, would find the result a dead product.

However, it would be wrong to call Pollock's finished paintings 'dead'. They are different from football matches in the sense that the canvas actually contains visible traces of the creation. The turf is, however, empty after the match. A football match is, in an absolute sense, a singular event, irreversible and impossible to repeat. It may well be stored, either materially as a recording that makes it possible to review it or immaterially in our memory as beautiful and completely useless memories, but the forms that emerge in the course of a match as a result of movements between bodies and between body and ball are characterised by the fact that they dissolve in the same moment as they appear. In this sense they are epiphanic, a sort of revelation, and they don't last physically as Pollock's traces after the creation do.

But there is more to Pollock's art and his unique method that brings you to think about football. On Pollock's canvases you don't see representations of recognisable motifs. His art is what we call non-figurative. Pollock saw the canvas as an arena in and on which something should be created, performed and acted. Rather than to *re*-present a motif, the canvas presents an *event*, namely the traces of Pollock's movements across the surface of the canvas. It is the event of the creation and not the creation you see. Pollock paints 'to paint'. The finished painting is simply a physical manifestation or a remnant of the real work of art, namely the specific process of creation.

To the footballer and spectator, the turf is an arena in a Pollockian sense: it doesn't represent anything but is instead a space and surface, in and on which one acts and creates. The footballer's movements with and without a ball across the turf are similar to Pollock's patterns and lines in that they represent nothing. They don't refer to an object, but point back at themselves as an event. They are nothing more than formally articulated traces of the event, which created them. As the Peruvian writer Mario Vargas Llosa writes: 'To admire a footballer is to admire something very close to pure poetry or abstract painting. It is to admire form for form's sake, without any rationally identifiable object.' Vargas Llosa further writes: 'Sport, for those who enjoy it, is the love of form, a spectacle which does not transcend the physical, the sensory, the instant emotion.' The same can be said about Jackson Pollock's artwork.

Elegance is perhaps what comes to mind first and foremost when you think of George Best. But when I saw old clips of Best, it struck me he had an extremely energetic style and quite simply thrived on action, two often neglected elements in his style. Energy and action are at least as important characteristics as elegance, which is why Best is to football what Jackson Pollock and his energetic 'action painting' is for painting. George Best's energetic style is especially expressed in dribbles, long runs without a ball and goals from headers.

Best was best when surrounded by a horde of opponents, and his dribbles marked lines of flight from the entrapment (just like the black splashes in Pollock's 'Number one') often by uniting his unique technical ability with the tackles from his opponents and making both equal partners in his dribbles. The confrontation was actually often something he often sought out voluntarily, which only emphasises his need for action.

Best also possessed unmatched timing and precision in his long, often diagonal, runs. He thereby managed to find exactly the right spot, where long high balls from his fellow players would land. And there is nothing as beautiful as the form that emerges, when you see such a run by Best (with the ball behind him) suddenly converging with the path of the ball (much like the long thin lines in Pollock's 'Convergence', which meet and together become thicker and more powerful), in particular because the form often culminates in a goal.

Finally, Best's courage is admirable when in a cluster of teammates and opponents he fearlessly goes for the ball and with his head directs it into the opposition's goal. Such moments constitute particularly intensive spots on the canvas (like the red spots in Pollock's 'Number one'), because the unfolding comes close to pure energy.

In other words: destabilising line of flight, powerful convergence and spotwise intensity are the three specific characteristics that Pollock and Best share. On a more general level, it is the delicate balance between control and contingency that epitomise both Best and Pollock. What characterised their 'artistic' practice is the balance between split second decisions and coincidence, choreography and contingency. Best's energetic action style was, like Pollock's energetic 'action painting', an exploration of the borderland between chaos and form, where intuition functioned as GPS. In both cases we can speak of a 'performance' that emphasised physical expressivity and each performance was a unique, spontaneous and non-repeatable event. Pollock's paintings cannot be imitated, they cannot be copied, and in this sense they are inextricably linked to their own unique act of creation. The same applies to Best's actions on the field, which by definition disappeared in the exact same moment in which they occurred. It is the process that counts, not the product.

Of course, there were also many differences between Pollock and Best. But these differences are primarily to do with things outside the 'arena'. As to public image, Pollock was closely associated with the 1950s; Best the 1960s. Pollock was typically 'working class' with fag, jeans and chequered shirt; Best was the fur-clad pop star. Pollock had a touch of the '50s rebel over him à la James Dean and Marlon Brando; Best's rebel gene rather made him related to Mick Jagger and his 'Sympathy for the Devil'. So yes, Pollock and Best also had rebellion in common. And the demons too. Alcohol killed Jackson Pollock and destroyed George Best's career. Both were supernovas of the twentieth century, one the most important American painter, the other the best British footballer.

21 May 1977
The years of instability

All of Matt Busby's work through the previous twenty-three years culminated with the triumph at Wembley on 29 May 1968. European success, together with the youth policy and a football philosophy based on entertainment, had been the overriding vision for Manchester United since the Second World War, and Busby had been the man behind them. After Wembley in 1968 it was as if both the will and purpose slowly began to leave the club.

It had been the same scenario in the years just after the Munich tragedy, where Busby at times had found it hard to find the motivation. The team no longer solely consisted of Busby's 'golden apples', all of whom were created in his image and where any rotten apples were discarded very early. The combination of Busby's tending resignation and players with their own strong opinions about things meant that anarchy sometimes reigned in Manchester United's dressing room in the early 1960s. A player like Noel Cantwell, for a while club captain, led a fraction of players who wanted to modernise Busby's paternal methods and tactical dispositions.

Charlton and Foulkes were Busby's loyal squires, while Law and Best may have had prima donna ideas, but basically they were loyal to the boss. In this sense the 1968 team also represented a different style than both the 1948 team and the Babes. In Best, Law and Charlton the team had the kind of individualists that, in order to work, required a solid counter balance that was provided by hard workers like Stiles, Crerand and Foulkes. The Babes were perhaps a stronger collective, but with the 1968 team the English spectators witnessed a form of football that had never been seen before. The entertainment, the individual virtuosity, the flexibility, and the madness were more extreme, but the results on the other hand were also much more inconsistent. The road from the sublime to the miserable was not long.

On 14 January 1969, during the difficult post-Wembley season, Busby announced he would step down as manager of Manchester United at the end of season. The big question was who would, or perhaps could, succeed him. There was much speculation in the British media, and names like Wilf McGuinness, Don Revie and Dave Sexton were mentioned as favourites. According to Busby, who was to take on the position as 'general manager' in the club, the new 'team manager' would be given full control, just as he himself had demanded and was given back in 1945: 'There will be no interference from me', said Busby to the *Daily Mirror*. 'I will be there to give advice and help if it is asked for, but he will have full control of all team matters, buying and selling.' Busby also stressed the new manager would be guaranteed a large dose of patience from both himself and the club's additional management.

Busby had the final say when the choice of the new manager had to be made. He decided continuity was best secured by selecting internally in the 'company', and the choice fell on the thirty-one-year-old Wilf McGuinness, who in the 1950s had been one of the Busby Babes, but because of an injury had not gone to Belgrade in 1958. McGuinness's career came to an abrupt end when he fractured his leg in December of 1959, but in the 1960s he had with great success served as coach for the club's reserve and youth team.

With the title 'head coach' McGuinness was, however, not given full control. Both Busby and McGuinness were aware of the fact the team needed renewal, but it was Busby from his office chair who made whichever transfers he thought necessary. Whether McGuinness didn't have the authority to rebuild Manchester United, or whether he never really got the chance to prove that he could, is difficult to answer today. One thing is for sure: the solution with McGuinness as head coach and Busby as a kind of sports director didn't work.

McGuinness got off to a bad start, with three draws and three defeats. He omitted in turns some of the old stars such as Charlton, Foulkes, Law and Dunne in order to provoke a reaction. 'When I dropped Bobby Charlton and Denis Law, when I left them out of the team, I thought I had dropped the atom bomb. People said I would have dropped George Best if I could have found him', McGuinness says. His problem was not a lack of courage but rather that he had difficulty finding replacements for the old pioneers. McGuinness had a clear idea about the players he wanted as reinforcements, but when he wanted his wishes transformed into action, he lacked the necessary support from both Busby and the board.

After one year's trial period, in August 1970 McGuinness was given the title as manager. But the season started poorly and attendances kept falling as a result. In December after a 3–1 defeat at home to Arsenal, McGuinness was degraded to his former position as head coach of the reserve team. The demotion understandably was too much for McGuinness, who left the club in February

1971. When McGuinness reluctantly stepped down, Busby reluctantly stepped up again.

In the summer of 1971 Manchester United sold Nobby Stiles to Middlesbrough, and Pat Crerand retired from playing to become a coach at the club. But there was no longer a new generation of ambitious and talented players from the academy, who were ready to be Old Trafford's new stars. However, two years earlier Matt Busby had invested in a player, who has also been called the last Babe. From Belfast, following in the footsteps of George Best, Sammy McIlroy had arrived on 2 August 1969 on his fifteenth birthday. As for Best, he was rarely seen on the training grounds. Feebleness and pointlessness had slowly but surely infected Manchester United in 1971.

The club's main priority was to find a new manager. Jock Stein, who in 1967 had led Celtic to European triumph, was favourite. Chelsea's Dave Sexton and Leicester's Frank O'Farrell were also on Busby's and Manchester United's wish list. Busby met in secret with Stein and according to Busby they agreed on the terms of Stein's employment. However, Stein ended up not taking the job due to family commitments. Busby was subsequently very bitter, and when his next name on the list, Dave Sexton, seemed unwilling to move north from London, Manchester United tried their luck with Frank O'Farrell, who had impressed by winning the Second Division with Leicester. O'Farrell accepted the challenge and determinedly placed himself in his office chair – but only after he had persuaded Busby to exchange offices. As O'Farrell arrived at Old Trafford and was shown around by Busby, he realised his own office was much smaller than Busby's. He pointed out to Busby that this was not acceptable, as it would look awkward if the new manager did not have an office that matched his position. Busby agreed, perhaps a little shocked over O'Farrell's forthrightness, but also, perhaps deep down, understanding of his demand for authority. Rather than take on the role as 'general manager' with responsibility for administrative affairs as originally planned, Busby in fact decided to hand over these responsibilities and become a board member.

O'Farrell was faced with an almost endless amount of challenges. In addition to the power struggle with Busby, which he initially seemed to have won, he was faced with a bunch of players, who had won everything and whose best football years lay behind them. To add to his frustrations, the directors were impatient and George Best seemed to be running his own solo show. Finally, the youth academy needed a complete overhaul. But O'Farrell succeeded in bringing both the team and the club back to life. Manchester United started 1971/72 with lightning and thunder, looking impressive in a new 4-3-3 formation with Alan Gowling, Willie Morgan and Bobby Charlton in midfield, and Best, Law and Kidd in attack. By New Year they led the First Division by 5 points.

119

But 1972 started disastrously with seven defeats in a row. Manchester United's match against Leeds at Elland Road on 19 February 1972 is by many commentators regarded to be the endgame of the club's first period of greatness in the post-war era. The Red Devils lost 5–1, and on this day passionate and entertaining red was replaced by clinical and boring white. Leeds's tough and methodical style set a new standard for English football in the subsequent years.

In spite of repeated no-shows at training George Best still managed to play forty league matches and score eighteen goals. For the first time Best admitted publicly his drinking was out of control. After staying away from an international match in May 1972 he fled to Spain over the summer. The pictures from his voluntary exile no longer show a slim dribbler but an overweight hedonist. Best, who was only twenty-six years old, insisted he would end his career immediately, but after two weeks in the southern sun he returned home to Manchester.

Manchester United experienced a disastrous start in the 1972/73 season when they didn't manage to collect a win in the first nine matches and languished with only 4 points. McGuinness was given 18 months to prove himself and O'Farrell was given the same. After the 5–0 defeat against Crystal Palace on 16 December 1972, perhaps the worst United performance in the post-war era, O'Farrell was sacked. He left Old Trafford bitterly disappointed at the lack of support that made it impossible for him to exercise his authority.

O'Farrell had been the quiet type, bordering on the self-effacing. He had an academic approach to football and could spend hours at the tactical board. It had been new to the players, and most of them had acted dismissively. The successor to O'Farrell was his antithesis, Tommy Docherty. He was a confident type, who could be both harsh and uncompromising, but his straightforward nature won him many loyal supporters, including the hard-core Stretford End fans. 'There were lots of big names there long past their sell-by date and the rot had set in. A lot of it was down to Sir Matt staying on too long. . . . Even by the time I arrived Sir Matt was still there, still with a big influence on the players. . . . They called him "the old boss". That kind of thing isn't good for the stability of a club or for discipline. You can only have one boss.'

Docherty saved Manchester United from relegation in 1973, but the season was generally one of pure misery. As Manchester United met Chelsea at Stamford Bridge on 28 April 1973 in the season's last match it was also Bobby Charlton's last match out of 758 appearances for the Red Devils. Denis Law also left the club to join neighbours City, where he had played a single season before he came to Old Trafford (via Torino) eleven years earlier. On 1 January 1974, George Best played his last match for Manchester United.

Docherty was convinced the club and the team were back on track. He had bought good players, said the necessary goodbyes to some of the old, and he had modernised the youth policy. But waiting up ahead was another downturn:

relegation to the Second Division. As the saying goes, sometimes things have to get worse before they get better, and Manchester had to reach the bottom before the climb back could start. The second to last match of the season was against Manchester City at Old Trafford, and here 56,996 spectators watched a ghost of the past come back to haunt them. Shortly before the final whistle the result was still 0–0, and time was running out for Manchester United, but suddenly Denis Law appeared in United's penalty area and instinctively back-heeled a pass from Francis Lee. Law's strike went into the goal and symbolically sealed Manchester United's relegation.

'It was a good job, because when we got relegated it was devastation, but when we came back it started to mean the rebirth of United again.' The words come from Sammy McIlroy, and underline the club's ability to rise from the ashes like a phoenix. Docherty responded positively, as he spent the next season building an attack-minded team with the right balance of youth and experience, flair and brawn. Docherty reinstated the 4–4–2 system and, as their opponents were no longer named Liverpool and Leeds but Leyton Orient and Oxford United, he could, without the normal pressure and in peace, let his offensive tactics with emphasis on wing play settle in the players' mind.

Manchester United led the Second Division from start to finish. More than 48,000 spectators on average watched the home matches, and in away matches, the team was supported by many thousands of travelling fans. It was in these years hooliganism seriously began to show its ugly face, both inside and outside the English football stadiums, and Manchester United's Red Army was the largest and most feared tribe. It was this aggressive fanaticism that for many years occupied the void emerging after religious fervour, political passion and burning patriotism had declined.

In 1975/76 Doc's vibrant boys took the position as teacher's pet right from the start. Five victories and a draw saw them storm to the top of the First Division, and with the purchase of Gordon Hill on the left wing Docherty seemed to have created a powerful United team that played entertaining and offensive football in the spirit of Matt Busby. The emphasis was on wing play, because as Doc said himself, he always had two weaknesses in life, 'wingers and women, but not necessarily in that order'. Throughout the season Docherty stuck to his offensive style, and Manchester United kept pace with both Queens Park Rangers and Liverpool, but ended up in third place.

In the FA Cup, United showed the same strong form, reaching the semi-final. They drew Derby County from the First Division, while the other semi-final was played between Southampton from the Second Division and Crystal Palace from the Third. The cocky Docherty said: 'This is the first time that the FA Cup final will be played at Hillsborough. The other semi-final is a bit of a joke really.' Manchester United, lead by a sparkling Gordon Hill, swept aside Derby and now Southampton awaited them in the final at Wembley. On this day, 1 May 1976, Manchester United was one of the strongest favourites in FA Cup history. They were a top tier team and had throughout the season fascinated people with their attacking style while Southampton was somewhere in the middle of the Second Division. In addition, Southampton were a bunch of old men, in contrast to the relatively young United team.

Towards the end of ninety minutes the result was still 0–0 and Docherty's arrogant remark returned to haunt Manchester United, but they were also haunted by an old friend when the former United player Jim McCalliog sent Bobby Stokes on a run towards goal. Stokes, who was close to being offside, scored for Southampton, and it sensationally won them the cup.

A year later, however, Manchester United reached the final of the FA Cup again, but in contrast to the previous year's final they themselves were underdogs. Their opponent was Bob Paisley's Liverpool, who had just regained the Championship and who were also to meet Borussia Mönchengladbach in the European Cup final, just four days after Wembley.

Liverpool were in other words on the trail of a historic Treble, but a surprising 2–1 victory for United foiled their rival's record dreams. The team on 21 May 1977 was as follows:

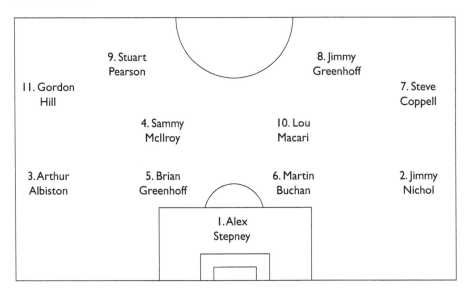

The first goal of the match fell five minutes after the break, when Stuart Pearson set Manchester United on a winning course. The assist came from Jimmy Greenhoff, when he lobbed the ball over Emlyn Hughes in Liverpool's defence. Under normal circumstances, a goalkeeper of Ray Clemence's calibre would have saved Pearson's hard shot, but Clemence let the ball slide under him. A few minutes afterwards Jimmy Case equalised for Liverpool, but just five minutes after the game's first goal Lou Macari and Jimmy Greenhoff jointly put Manchester United on in front. Macari came through on the right wing, but his shot was on the way out into the stands as it hit Greenhoff in the chest and tricked Clemence.

What nobody could know at the time was that the 2–1 win was Tommy Docherty's greatest moment as a manager. Just six weeks later he was fired. His weakness for wingers had brought him success with Manchester United, but his other weakness (women) was now – together with the treatment of certain players and dubious economic transactions – responsible for his dismissal. Ten days previously, Docherty publicly announced he was leaving his wife to live with the wife of Manchester United's physiotherapist. Many other clubs would probably have forgiven Docherty, especially after his successful attempt to rehabilitate a fallen great club, but at this time United was still a club full of Busby's religious principles and family ethos. Docherty's affair with a staff member's wife, true love or not, was a breach of the internal cohesion, and the club was forced to let him go. In Docherty, Manchester United had, for once, a manager whose mentality seemed to be strong enough to be the front figure of England's most successful club, and his frank nature and lippy manner had furthermore washed away the dull mood from the lustreless years 1969–1974. With the FA Cup triumph in 1977 Docherty seemed ready to take the team a step further and challenge Liverpool, English football's new dominant team. But this was not to be.

* * *

Manchester United now turned their binoculars toward London and someone who had earlier attracted their interest, namely Dave Sexton, a completely different character to Docherty. Sexton had started his coaching career at Stamford Bridge in 1962 when Docherty included him in his coaching team. Docherty led Chelsea from 1962 to 1967, and Dave Sexton took over until 1974. In 1977 Sexton therefore succeeded the Doc for the second time. At Chelsea, Sexton won the FA Cup in 1970 and the Cup Winners' Cup the year after, and in a relatively conservative and narrow-minded era he was absorbed by tactical subtleties and could even be found changing formation during the match in order to confuse his opponents. Besides, his Chelsea team had been a fine mix of defensive solidity and offensive virtuosity. Before his arrival at Old Trafford in 1977 Sexton had even led Queens Park Rangers to their best league position in 1976: runner-up in the title race. Only a Liverpool goal in the very last seconds of their match against Wolverhampton prevented Sexton sensationally winning the championship with QPR.

Docherty's strengths were not on the tactical level. He was a superb motivator, who also had an excellent eye for young talent. His managerial career had been a long series of controversies, and this, together with his rebellious attitude and his love for wingers and women, had immediately made him a popular figure with the Stretford End. In Sexton, Manchester United got a completely different personality and manager. Sexton was the reflective type, a tactician, who loved to read philosophy and poetry in his spare time. On his bedside table you could find Ludwig Wittgenstein, John Stuart Mill and Robert Frost. But this fine cultural and press-shy side of him didn't endear him to the Stretford End. Sexton's relationship with Manchester United's supporters was never good. At Old Trafford, it seems as if the fans prefer Scottish managers, usually from Glasgow and the surrounding county's working class, rather than academic types from London.

Sexton generally didn't manage to transfer the shine from his time at Chelsea and QPR to Manchester United. He had a scientific approach to the play, and one of his first moves in the course of the summer of 1977 was to buy a video camera and a projector, so players could watch and analyse their matches. Under Docherty, training had mostly consisted of five-a-side, now it mainly consisted of tactical exercises and personal coaching. In a way Sexton was ahead of his time, because today training methods are very similar. But English players in 1977 were, for the most part, not ready for his style of coaching.

Dave Sexton, on his arrival, immediately redefined the equal relationship between *agon* and *arête*, which otherwise characterised Manchester United: 'I want to see the team winning and playing attractively. Which comes first? It must be winning.' It is not that Sexton opposed the principle to entertain, but any aesthetic enjoyment that his team could produce was simply a by-product of any possible victories. Sexton downplayed the obligation to entertain, which had, since Busby, been an integral part of the club's self-image.

Tommy Docherty had perhaps been, of Busby's successors, the one most committed to the footballing philosophy of Sir Matt, but on the moral level he failed badly. For many United fans the Sexton years symbolised what Eduardo Galeano in his book *Soccer in Sun and Shadow* characterised as the sad journey from love to obligation in the history of football: 'When the sport became an industry, the beauty that blossoms from the joy of play got torn out by its very roots.' Play is replaced with work, improvisation is prevented, and freedom controlled. The game has been turned into an act, Galeano says, and the act at Old Trafford, which had Dave Sexton as instructor, was not staged in order to be acted out as a play, but rather to prevent playing during the game. Docherty's adventurous 4–2–4 was converted to Sexton's boring 4–4–2, and the players who were most affected by this transformation were the two wingers, Steve Coppell and Gordon Hill. Arthur Albiston, who during the period 1974–1988 played 485 matches for the club as left back, has admitted Sexton's approach came as a shock to most of the players, but at the same time Albiston underlines that he enjoyed playing under Sexton: 'He was a deep thinker about the game and I liked that about him.'

During the first few years as manager of Manchester United, Sexton began to rearrange the team he had inherited from Docherty. After thirteen years and 539 matches, the goalie Alex Stepney was replaced by Paddy Roche, while Stuart Pearson and Alex Forsyth were sold. But the most traumatic transfer for United's devoted followers was Sexton's sale of Gordon Hill to Tommy Docherty's Derby County. If any, Hill was the one who symbolised Manchester United's revival under Docherty.

As Galeano writes: 'Luckily, on the field you can still see, even if only once in a long while, some insolent rascal who sets aside the script and commits the blunder of dribbling past the entire opposing side, the referee and the crowd in the stands, all for the carnal delight of embracing the forbidden adventure of freedom.' Gordon Hill was just such an 'insolent rascal'. His defensive laziness, which at times could irritate his teammates, was also the prerequisite for his offensive opportunism, and the fans loved him. He brought the team shine, speed and a devil-may-care power after a series of sterile years. Under Docherty, Hill had 'licence to kill and thrill', an uninhibited freedom for adventurous football, but on Sexton's tactical board there was little room for luxury players such as Hill. Sexton's sale of Hill was, however, doubly expensive: first, the sale of the spectator's favourite made it impossible for Sexton to gain a good relationship with the fans; second, he never managed to find Hill's many goals in any other player.

As compensation for the sold players, Sexton went to Leeds in search of a goal-scorer; there he set the British transfer record by signing Joe Jordan for £300,000 in January of 1978, and repeated his stunt a month later, when centre-half Gordon McQueen followed Jordan over the Pennines, but this time the amount was £495,000. To McQueen it was a dream come true: 'Ask all the players in the country which club they would like to join and 99 per cent would say Manchester United. The other one per cent would be liars.' This kind of statement immediately made McQueen a hero at the Stretford End.

* * *

Sexton's first two seasons produced ninth and tenth place finishes. In the league and in Europe it was still Brian Clough's Nottingham Forest and Bob Paisley's Liverpool who set the standard. In the course of the 1970s Liverpool won the championship in 1973, 1976, 1977, 1979 and 1980, while Nottingham Forest won it in 1978. After Ajax from 1971 to 1973 and Bayern Munich from 1974 to 1976 had each scored their European hat trick, it was the English teams' turn to dominate. From 1977 to 1982 Liverpool won the European Cup three times, while Nottingham Forest won it twice and Aston Villa once. Liverpool then won it again in 1984, after Hamburg in 1983 had interfered with the English hegemony.

Manchester United had to rely on sporadic success in the cup competitions. After the defeat in the FA Cup final of 1976 and the victory in 1977 United once again faced Paisley's men in 1979, this time, however, in the semi-finals. At Maine Road in Manchester the two giants played out a 2-2 draw in a blistering match.

Manchester United started the game with lightning and thunder, but Kenny Dalglish put Liverpool in front with a brilliant goal, where he outsmarted United's defence and coolly sent the ball past young Gary Bailey. Just two minutes later Jimmy Greenhoff crossed into Liverpool's penalty area, where Joe Jordan took advantage of the defence's hesitation and equalised. Just before the break Terry McDermott spurned a penalty kick for Liverpool, and in the second half United continued to dominate the match. Brian Greenhoff put United in front 2-1, and now it was Liverpool's turn to push for a goal. It came shortly before the final whistle sounded, as Alan Hansen intercepted a loose ball in the penalty area and shot past Bailey. In the re-match at Goodison Park in Liverpool both teams kept hitting the post, and the busiest players were Ray Clemence and Gary Bailey. The score was still 0-0, with only ten minutes remaining of the match, but finally Jimmy Greenhoff managed to score the liberating goal for United to send the club on to the FA Cup final for the third time in four years.

* * *

In the final Manchester United face Arsenal. If the first semi-final against Liverpool had inscribed itself in the tournament's annals as one of the best matches ever, the match at Wembley on 12 May 1979 was one of the tournament's best finals. With only four minutes remaining of the match, Manchester United are 2-0 behind. A free kick in the right-hand side from Coppell lands right in front of Jordan, who sends it into McQueen, who scores. And just two minutes later McIlroy equalises after a few nifty moves in the penalty area. In just two minutes Manchester United have turned 0-2 into 2-2, and Arsenal's players seem paralysed. The most likely winner, if not in the regular match then at least in extra time, is now Manchester United. And the most incredible scenario actually happens: the third goal is scored in just four minutes. However, to Manchester United's heartbreak it is Arsenal's Alan Sunderland who scores it. It ends 3-2 to Arsenal in a historical final with three goals in the last four minutes.

In the summer of 1979, Manchester United bought Ray Wilkins from Chelsea for £700,000. Sexton had been Wilkins's mentor when he was a young player and believed Wilkins could bring Manchester United the creativity needed to push for the title. He seemed to be right. United challenged Liverpool throughout the season, but ultimately had to settle for second place. The season didn't only offer a silver medal, but also deaths. After an away match on 12 January 1980 against Middlesbrough, two of the home team's supporters died when a wall collapsed at Ayresome Park, and the Red Army was involved in the tragedy. A month later Manchester United's chairman of the board Louis Edwards died of a heart attack.

In the stands, the air was full of dissatisfaction, despite the runners-up spot. If goals are to be compared with football's orgasm, as Eduardo Galeano claims, then the attitude at the Stretford End was that Sexton's tactics represented the soul of frigidity. The team perhaps won most matches, but in spite of the purchase of Wilkins the team was missing players who could seduce and bewitch the fans with technical beauty and dramatic unpredictability. Martin Edwards congratulated Dave Sexton and his assistant Tommy Cavanagh with the silver medal and rewarded them both with new three-year contracts, and a salary increase of 50 per cent. But in the next season the relationship between Edwards and Sexton changed for the worse.

As a consequence of an unfulfilled attacking department Sexton purchased Garry Birtles from Nottingham Forest for £1.25 million in October 1980. But instead of seducing the Stretford End with erotic sporting delights from football's *Kama Sutra*, Birtles turned out to be impotent, and this impotence led indirectly to Sexton's castration. In the twenty-five league matches Birtles played for Manchester United that season, he scored zero goals, just as he didn't find the goal in the first four games of season 1981/82. In three matches in the FA Cup he scored one single goal. The result: thirty-two matches, one goal.

Birtles, however, was not solely responsible for Manchester United's anaemic efforts in 1980/81. The midfield struggled to feed the attackers, and the team suffered from the absence of Ray Wilkins, who had a long-term injury. When Wilkins returned to the team at the end of the season, Manchester United won the last seven matches. The score tally however was not goals galore at 18–8, but 10–2 and it depicts the story of *agon's* (hard work's) victory over *arête* (excellence), and shows a triumph of frigidity over orgasm. The number of spectators turning up at Old Trafford tells the same story. A week after the season ended Sexton was sacked.

Martin Edwards had long been concerned about Sexton's results, his unattractive playing style, his lack of desire to promote the club positively in the media and his inability to communicate with the fans. Sexton's season finish of seven victories embarrassed Edwards, who was obviously planning a change, but his dismissal fell anyway. 'I felt we'd gone backwards. It was having an effect on gates', said Edwards. 'We want a good publicist who can communicate with our supporters – a man with very special qualities.' McGuinness and O'Farrell had been fired because of poor results and Docherty had been fired because of his affair and his unethical behaviour in relation to the team, coaching staff and certain financial transactions. Sexton, however, had the honour of being the first manager after the war fired for commercial purposes.

In the course of the summer of 1981, a number of Manchester United's preferred candidates thanked United for their interest but ultimately said 'no thanks' to the challenge of lifting the legacy after Busby. Lawrie McMenemy from Southampton refused, as did Bobby Robson, who had worked miracles by transforming obscure Ipswich to cup winners and championship candidates. The third person who rejected United's overtures was Aston Villa's taciturn Ron Saunders. Manchester United, however, succeeded in attracting another and far more outspoken and flamboyant Ron.

30 December 1978
The birth of fascination: an autobiographical fantasy

It is Saturday afternoon. 1978 is slowly drawing to a close, and in three days I will be seven years old. *Sports Saturday*, which Denmark's radio presenters Claus Borre and Jørgen Steen Nielsen has recently launched, starts soon. In today's televised match Manchester United meets West Bromwich Albion at Old Trafford. In spite of the aforementioned uneven performances in both this and the previous season, the club's aura cannot be denied, and thousands of Danish men with sideburns and boys in brown corduroy trousers look forward to seeing the mighty Manchester United. But West Bromwich Albion's eager attacking style under a certain Ron Atkinson and, not least, the team's significant – and at this time unusual – Afro-Caribbean stars (Brendon Batson, Cyrille Regis and Laurie Cunningham) also endow West Bromwich Albion with a genuine appeal and exoticism. This Saturday afternoon, in the hessian-wallpapered living rooms of Denmark, the expectations are understandably very high.

When I think back on Batson, Regis and Cunningham in 1978 and the years that followed, I can (despite the obvious differences) see parallels with the black athletes during the 1936 Olympic Games in Hitler's Berlin. Those carefully orchestrated Olympic Games were to be Hitler's demonstration of Aryan racial superiority. This demonstration was, for example, to be displayed through aesthetic constructions that showed the contemporary Aryan's similarity to the Greek ideal body. The crown examples are, of course, Leni Riefenstahl's films *Olympia 1: Fest der Völker* and *Olympia 2: Fest der Schönheit* from 1938, which are at the same time aesthetically fascinating and propagandistically nauseating. Hitler's master plan failed since it is the impressive performances by a number of black athletes – not least Jesse Owens's four gold medals in both track and field – that have stuck in people's minds. One of the highlights in Berlin was the German Luz Long's warm embrace of Jesse

Owens in front of the leading Nazis after Owens had outclassed Long in the long jump.

West Bromwich Albion was the first English club to have three black players on the team. Batson, Regis and Cunningham symbolised a revolution in English football, first by opening the fans' eyes to these players' qualities, and second by challenging the prevailing racism within the football environment, and thus paving the way for thousands of other black and Asian players to be able to pursue a career as professional footballers.

However, there is also a more straightforward parallel between the brilliant Laurie Cunningham's run with the ball and Jesse Owens's gracious style of running. Both of them make me think of Heinrich von Kleist's famous text 'On the Marionette Theatre' (1810) in which Kleist praises the gracious movements of puppets. When one sees Owens and Cunningham run it is as if they float across the surface of the earth. The force of gravity seems to be suspended and the inertia of matter overcome. Or perhaps it is more as if both of them – like the puppets – are in complete harmony with the laws of mechanics and nature, and have found the perfect centre of gravity. The soul is in the elbow, as Kleist claims. By this he means that the awkwardness that sometimes, if not always, sneaks into the movements of humans as soon as they become aware of themselves and their bodies does not exist in the mechanical puppets. Neither does it exist in Owens or in Cunningham, or in the never awkward Bobby Charlton and the sliding Ryan Giggs for that matter.

Laurie Cunningham was not just the first black player to represent England, he was also the first British player at Real Madrid. After he left Real Madrid in 1983, he was actually for a brief moment lent to Ron Atkinson's Manchester United, but without much success. Laurie Cunningham sadly died at the age of just thirty-three years old when, on the morning of 15 July 1989, he was killed in a car accident in Madrid.

* * *

In 1978 I am in the first grade at Lindum school. Lindum is a small village with about 200 inhabitants. During break time we boys play football in the schoolyard on the rough asphalt. In gym classes it is also always football. It is what you do in the countryside if you are boy. You form two equal teams and there are dribbles, kicks and falls, resulting in bloody scrapes on the knees. From the breaks I particularly remember Knud Erik's green rubber ball the size of a handball. It is perfect for schoolyard football. Lindum school only teaches children from pre-school age to third grade and there are only eighty of us in total. Today it is closed, just like many other of Lindum's public institutions and private businesses. The two banks, the curtain store, the mechanic, the grocer, the petrol station and the nursery from my childhood, all are gone. There is a blacksmith and a forest day care centre left. 'But we are close to the motorway,' as they say in Lindum.

My parents still live there. In the late 1970s and early 1980s my father is the call out man at the local bingo hall at Lindum's local meeting house. Each Saturday evening young and (especially) old flock to Lindum from the neighbouring villages to satisfy their inner ludomaniac and to chain smoke in company with other chain-smoking ludomaniacs. In the lead-up to the night's festivities I go with my mother, father and younger sister each Saturday morning to Føtex, a big grocery store in Hobro, to pick up the prizes for the bingo game: coffee, schnapps, chicks, ducks and quarter pigs. And while in the big city we also do our own grocery shopping. That part the local grocer in Lindum doesn't understand. Often we bring Alfred. He is the farmhand on the big courtyard next to our newly built detached house and has worked there since the war. He smokes Prince and is a keen bingo player. If Alfred comes with us to Hobro, and he often does, he always buys us hot dogs at Grillhytten before we drive home in our light blue Volvo 142. The hot dogs have become a ritual.

In the course of autumn 1978 it also becomes a ritual for Alfred, my father and me to watch *Sports Saturday* on our new colour TV when we get home from Hobro. Alfred is not only a bingo fanatic, he is also a football enthusiast, just like me. On this cold and dark afternoon the high expectations to match of the day are fully met. Manchester United v. West Bromwich Albion is for many Danish spectators still imprinted in their memory as one of the best live matches ever as West Bromwich Albion, aspirants to the title, defeat mighty Manchester United 5–3. It is simply a match that has been instilled in the collective consciousness. The majority of those who saw the match can fairly accurately remember where they were when they watched it. In this sense, the match is a kind of positive contrast to negative events such as the air crash in Munich in 1958, the murder of JFK in 1963 or 9/11 in 2001.

In a literal sense, I'm fascinated by the two teams. I am bewitched. It is as if my eyes are glued to the screen as a result of an inexplicable magic. Like Odysseus drawn to the sirens' seductive song, I'm allured in an irresistible way by the match at Old Trafford. But contrary to the story of the Greek mythical hero, there is no mast in our living room that I can tie myself to. I don't have any wax with which to block my ears. I willingly let myself be seduced. Manchester United v. West Bromwich Albion is the match that awakens the soon-to-be seven-year-old boy's interest in English football and Manchester United. Admittedly, in the following years I oscillate between Manchester United and West Bromwich Albion. In the end, however, the Red Devils take the strongest hold on me. Even though Manchester United lose the match against WBA, the club's history, stadium and aura cannot be denied.

At school all of my classmates swear their allegiance to the 'wrong' reds, that is, Liverpool and Arsenal, so my choice of Manchester United may also have something to do with marking out my individuality. This is no longer the case if you are a fan of the Devils, though. My nephew, who is ten years old, has not been pulled into Manchester United's irresistible orbit as a result of a televised match, but rather as a result of the club's omnipresence in the form of merchandise, hype and star quality.

*   *   *

On a warm summer's afternoon in 1977, more than a year before the match between United and WBA, Svend comes to visit me for the first time. Svend, who is one year older than me (and still one of my best friends), comes walking up the Firkløvervej in Lindum's new single-family house neighbourhood, where I live. On his head he wears an American baseball cap, which was quite unusual at the time. At least in Lindum. What is more, *Star Wars* is written on it. Svend is, by the way, also the first person I ever saw with a 7Up in his hand. He is a living proof of the fact that American popular culture's entry into Denmark in the years after the Second World War doesn't reach Lindum until the late 1970s. Svend is also wearing football shorts and sports shoes this summer afternoon. But what catches my eye the most is the ball that he has in his hands, and occasionally bounces onto the ground. It is dark brown. I can see that it is not a normal leather ball. Judging from the muffled sound it makes when it hits the asphalt, it is a rubber ball. 'Do you want to play?' he says, and I answer affirmatively. He throws the ball to me, and I notice its perfect mix of softness and hardness and its ideal weight.

We run down to the football field and do not return until years later. Okay, we do dash home on Saturday to watch *Sports Saturday* on TV and to get renewed inspiration for our endeavours at Lindum Stadium. After the match between Manchester United and West Bromwich Albion, these two English clubs are the constant sources of inspiration to our football play. We know all the names by heart. And of course, we have all the players in our football card collection: Regis, Cunningham, Bryan Robson, Peter Barnes; McIlroy, Bailey, McQueen, Coppell. After the summer's World Cup in Argentina, Mario Kempes is also high on my hero list. It's not until many years later I hear rumours of Argentinian amphetamines. The World Cup in 1978 is, by the way, the first sporting event I remember having seen on TV. In colour, mind you, since we get our first colour television just before the finals – strong in my memory are also the orange shirts of the Dutch. In my room I have a poster on the wall of Kempes. Next to Kempes hangs a poster of Ronnie Peterson, the Swedish Formula 1 world star, who died after an accident at the Monza racetrack on 11 September 1978. Ole Olsen, the Danish speedway driver, also hangs there.

The match between Manchester United and WBA is not only remembered because of the many excellent goals, but because of the special English magic Old Trafford radiates on this cold afternoon. In Denmark it is winter, and the domestic league is on a break. In England it is also winter, but there they play football all year round in shorts and T-shirts. 45,091 spectators are huddled together at Old Trafford this December afternoon and they experience, along with millions of TV viewers, a condensation of everything captivating about the English league. In addition to the many excellent goals, there's a heroic fight until the last whistle, stunning individual performances, two eager attack-minded teams and all the drama you could wish for. The cold and damp December weather in Manchester only contributes to the magic and evokes memories of the old Vikings.

I imagine Manchester United's fans leave Old Trafford this afternoon with a bittersweet taste in the mouth. On one hand, depressed about the defeat, a mood to which the city's damp cold only contribute. On the other, exhilarated about having been present at this historical match, saturated with moments of distinctive English beauty. Distinctive because of the mud, the cold and the pale legs mixed with a splash of dark elegance personified by Laurie Cunningham. The perfect way to extend this bittersweet mood must have been to go to see Joy Division at the Russell Club in Hulme just east of Old Trafford, where Tony Wilson had organised concerts under the name of The Factory. Here one could have experienced Joy Division at a time before Ian Curtis's suicide in May 1980 endowed the group's *oeuvre* with a tragic glow, where the band's live performance and their music as a whole still sounded the way they actually were: courageous, innovative, ferocious and energetic – although perhaps already imbued with a certain aura of apocalypse and sadness about them. In the same way as the match at Old Trafford, the Joy Division concert would leave the spectator/listener in a peculiar state of sad happiness. The form in both cases means the historical event and the awareness of having experienced something extraordinary makes you happy. The content, that is, Manchester United's defeat and the agonising loneliness and the damp, cold melancholy that is the signature of Joy Division, makes you sad.

Unknown Pleasures, Joy Division's amazing first album from 1979, suggests through its soundscapes the city of Manchester in the late 1970s. The album *is* simply Manchester in 1979. It's in a sense also Manchester United in 1979. The songs are haunted by splintered glass and industrial noise, of hiss and hum from traffic passing by in the rain on one of Manchester's big roads, illuminated by the yellow light of the sodium lamps. You sense the city's dim and dark places and its empty factory grounds, the ruinous remnants from the nineteenth century's industrial hot spot in the middle of 1970s Manchester. In Michael Winterbottom's movie *24 Hour Party People* (2002) you also see how the brilliant and mad producer

Martin Hannett indeed records some of the soundtracks to the album on the spot in Manchester's daily life. And in Anton Corbijn's *Control* (2007) there is a fascinating personal portrait of Curtis, Joy Division and Manchester at this time.

* * *

No such thoughts on mood similarities between The Factory and Old Trafford on this Saturday afternoon in 1978, though. I have no idea who Joy Division are. I am also not reflective, on the contrary I'm immersed and totally mesmerised. The fireworks start with Brian Greenhoff's projectile of a volley. After a corner from McIlroy the ball drops down just outside the WBA's penalty area. Greenhoff, who stands just outside the area, manages to take a few steps backwards and to the left. United's number two has calculated the ball's curve perfectly. He balances on just one leg, the left, and as his arms point to each side, Greenhoff now moves his right leg backwards. It looks like a cocked pistol with the thumb pulled backwards. Greenhoff starts to swing the right leg forward (and the pistol cock with furious speed approaches the cartridge), with his arms outstretched he ensures that his centre of gravity remains perfect. Just before the ball hits the ground, he hits the leather with a mixture of instep and the outside of his foot and the ball enters the goal in the top-right corner. The goal, which is an impeccable conglomerate of balance, precision and power, is so spectacular that Danish television chooses to run it in the lead-up to *Sports Saturday* for a long time to come.

West Bromwich soon turns the tide of the match, first with a beautiful first timer from Tony Brown from the edge of the penalty area. The pass comes from Cunningham on the left wing, while United's spectators are busy booing him because of his skin colour. Cunningham's foot is also involved in WBA's second goal. With an elegance and sharpness, reminiscent of today's Cristiano Ronaldo, Cunningham leaves several opponents sprawling in vain on the ground, and he passes the ball to Regis. WBA's centre forward finds Len Cantello with a stunning backheel pass, and Cantello hammers the ball into the nearest corner of the goal. Cantello's goal is not inferior to Greenhoff's volley. Shortly afterwards the big Gordon McQueen equalises for Manchester United, when relatively untroubled he jumps up and heads the ball in behind Albion's goalkeeper after a free kick from the left side of the field. And it becomes even worse for WBA, as McIlroy with a few nifty moves in the penalty area finds the target at the near post. 3–2 to Manchester United.

In the Greek tragedy, according to Aristotle, there was only one 'peripeteia', one crucial reversal in the action. The tragedies that Aeschylus, Sophocles and Euripides wrote for the Dionysia in Athens more than two thousand years ago were characterised by a rigorous narrative economy. The match between

Manchester United and West Bromwich Albion is, on the contrary, characterised by its narrative extravagance. It has already seen two reversals. First, WBA turn 0–1 into 2–1 and then Manchester United turn 1–2 into 3–2. However, it doesn't stop here. The third reversal of this modern football drama also becomes the final and most decisive peripeteia. First, Tony Brown equalises shortly before the break when he penetrates United's defence and taps the ball under Bailey into the United goal. Then a goal kick from WBA's goalkeeper flies over the Red Devils' defence, and Cunningham gets a free run, which results in a fourth West Brom goal. The match's last goal, and the culmination of the dramatic crescendo, is a true pearl of counter-attacking. Cunningham floatingly runs and runningly floats half the length of the field with the ball, before passing to Alistair Brown. Brown makes a perfect pass in between two United defenders to an oncoming Regis, who slams the ball over a defenceless Bailey and into the net. 5–3 to West Brom.

Gary Bailey has also made a big contribution to making the match an all-time classic by having made two world-class saves. One in particular, from a fantastic volley by Regis with his left foot, I still vividly remember today. Bailey's posture is a classic goalkeeper motif: lying horizontally in the air he saves the volley from Regis out by the far post, and even manages to hold onto it with both hands.

There are a number of similarities between Gary Bailey and Peter Schmeichel, which may explain why Bailey was a big idol for Schmeichel. They were both easily recognisable because of their bright hair, and they were both tall and physically imposing. But in addition to this external similarity, which can hardly explain Schmeichel's great respect for Bailey, they both arrived at Manchester United as a relatively blank slate and quickly made the number one jersey their own. Gary Bailey came from a university in South Africa in 1977; Schmeichel came from Brøndby in 1991. In addition, they both possessed a great faith in their own abilities and an unshakable self-confidence, which spread to the rest of the team. Finally, both Bailey and Schmeichel were eminent communicators on the field. For Bailey's part, his career, unfortunately, ended all too soon, as in 1986 he was injured while away on duties with his national team, and in the spring of 1987 he had to give up playing at just twenty-nine years of age.

3 October 1981
Captain Marvel and Don Ron

On Saturday, 3 October 1981, Bryan Robson signs a contract with Manchester United. Two days earlier it had been revealed that the Red Devils had purchased the strong midfielder from West Bromwich Albion for £1.5 million, a record amount for a British club. The actual signing of the contract is carried out on Old Trafford's turf in front of 46,837 excited fans. They have turned up to inspect the club's new titan and, immediately after the contract signing, to see Manchester United beat Wolverhampton 5–0 with a hat trick from Sammy McIlroy.

The very same day, in McIlroy's home country Northern Ireland, the hunger strike in the Maze prison ends. It's been going on for seven months and cost ten prisoners from IRA and the Irish Liberation Army their lives. Earlier this year Gro Harlem Brundtland becomes Norway's new prime minister, and in France François Mitterand takes over the presidency. To the delight of the British Prime Minister Margaret Thatcher, there is also a change of power in the US, where Ronald Reagan succeeds Jimmy Carter as president. In Los Angeles they discover the first cases of what later is known as AIDS, and in London Prince Charles marries Diana Spencer. The music channel MTV is aired for the first time. Elias Canetti wins the Nobel Prize in literature, while Salman Rushdie wins the Booker prize for his breakthrough novel *Midnight's Children*.

In the film world *The Ironman* by the Polish director Andrzej Wajda wins the Golden Palm Award. In 1981 Harrison Ford plays Indiana Jones for the first time, and this year's James Bond is played by Roger Moore in *For Your Eyes Only*. Depeche Mode release their first album *Speak and Spell*, while Kraftwerk's *Computer World* and U2's *October* also can be purchased in the stores. Soft Cell hits the top of the charts with 'Tainted Love', and 1981 is also the year for The Cure's beautiful 'Charlotte Sometimes'.

On 7 October 1981 Bryan Robson makes his debut for Manchester United. Robson, who went under the nickname Captain Marvel, was by many seen as a genuine one-man army. Rather than a mere midfielder he was a veritable force of nature. He was several players in one: defensive bulwark, creative pivot and frequent goal-scorer. He possessed all of football's most significant qualities. The short pass, the long pass, the tackle, the shot and the header, and in addition he could seemingly run for ever. As captain, Robson was the team's omnipresent driving force and an inspiration to his fellow players in the same way as Eric Cantona and Roy Keane would be later. There was passion, attitude and intensity in his play and as a player he was brave and uncompromising bordering on ruthlessness. He neither spared himself, nor his teammates or opponents.

'I told Martin Edwards that when you sign Bryan Robson [for £1.5 million] it's not even a risk. I said, "He is solid gold."' The words come from Manchester United's new manager, Ron Atkinson, who was convinced Bryan Robson was going to be the new Duncan Edwards. From 1978 to 1981 Atkinson had transformed West Bromwich Albion into one of the most watchable teams in England, and he had a reputation of wanting his team to play attractive and entertaining football. Admittedly, he had only been Manchester United's fourth choice after McMenemy, Robson and Saunders, but as Martin Edwards later revealed, Atkinson showed an insatiable desire to become the club's manager.

Atkinson was more Docherty than Sexton, outgoing and fond of glitz and glamour. Evidently, he also possessed a charisma able to match Manchester United's magic. In relations with the media he was comfortable as a fish in water, and he knew what buttons to press when it came to the fans. From day one he promised them action and drama, and he also spoke about the Old Trafford's historical commitment to entertainment. However, according to Arthur Albiston a big part of Ron Atkinson's manner was a façade blurring the fact that he actually was similar to Dave Sexton in many ways: 'Ron projected this flash image that he lived up to, with all the champagne and the gold jewellery, but that was all nonsense. In reality he was like Dave, a serious thinker about the game. And he had an amazing memory for players and matches that he could call on. He was so knowledgeable about the game.' With Edwards's blessing, Atkinson decided immediately to invest heavily in the team. His intention was to create a powerful unit to be the team's backbone in the years to come. Joe Jordan and Jimmy Greenhoff had already been sold, so Atkinson was desperately in need of an attacker. He was able to buy a new number 9, namely Frank Stapleton, who was purchased from Arsenal for £900,000. In addition to Bryan Robson he also signed Remi Moses for £500,000 from his old club, and with the purchases of Robson and Moses, United were now in possession of brand-new engine room.

* * *

After a third place finish in his first season Ron Atkinson hoped to strengthen the team even further with the aim of taking on Liverpool. He secured the elegant Dutch left winger Arnold Mühren from Ipswich on a free transfer, and also signed the young defensive talent of Paul McGrath from St Patrick's Athletic in Ireland. Also a young Northern Irishman from Belfast broke through into Manchester United's first team. His name was Norman Whiteside. The new Northern Irish wonderboy was the youngest player since Duncan Edwards to make his debut in the red shirt. It happened on 24 April 1982, when, at the age of just sixteen and 352 days, he contributed to the 1–0 victory away at Brighton. 'Norman was never sixteen, Norman was twenty-five, I guess, when he was born. Norman was born a man', said Atkinson later.

United finished third again, but the distance between the champions from Liverpool was increased. In two fast-paced League Cup semi-finals Manchester United defeated Arsenal 6–3 on aggregate. Norman Whiteside scored in the final and thus became the youngest goal-scorer in a League Cup final. The goal was pure class: McQueen sent a high ball up towards Liverpool's penalty area and there Whiteside brought the ball under control with his chest. He had his back to the goal and was closely marked. When the ball hit the ground slightly to the right of him, Whiteside turned to the right, which also made his marker, Alan Hansen, take a step to the right. But Whiteside's turn was not 90 or 180 degrees, but more like 225 degrees. His right turn thus didn't end with a move to the right, but with an angle backwards and to the left, which confused a dazed Hansen. Subsequently, Whiteside took the ball with him with his left leg, and in spite of Hansen still clinging on to Whiteside's leg, the seventeen-year-old Whiteside managed to hammer the ball past Bruce Grobbelaar in Liverpool's goal. Manchester United, however, lost the League Cup final 2–1.

On Saturday, 21 May 1983 Manchester United play at Wembley for the second time this season. This time their opponents are Brighton, who have just been relegated after finishing their campaign at the bottom of the table. It's the FA Cup final. Manchester United are favourites, but fifteen minutes into the match Gordon Smith puts Brighton on a winning course. Early in the second half Stapleton equalises for United, and twenty minutes before time Mühren finds Wilkins with a visionary pass, and Wilkins elegantly puts the favourites in front. However, Gary Stevens equalises in the closing minutes and the match goes into extra time,.

In the dying seconds of extra time Gordon Smith is suddenly very much alone with Gary Bailey, but the miracle fails to happen, as his weak shot hits United's goalkeeper on the leg. In the re-match on 26 May Manchester United quickly take charge, and with a victory of 4–0 the team ensures the club's first trophy since 1977. Robson gets a brace of goals, Mühren converts a penalty kick and

Whiteside also becomes the youngest goal-scorer ever in an FA Cup final when he scores United's second goal.

*   *   *

With two third places, a place in the League Cup final and an FA Cup triumph, in two years as manager Atkinson had brought stability and self-confidence back to Old Trafford. The time had now come to make a serious tilt at Liverpool's throne. The only new player in the team in 1983/84 was a Welsh attacker from United's academy by the name of Mark Hughes. Manchester United managed to keep up with Liverpool until the season's final phase. In the rivals showdown at Old Trafford United won 1–0, at Anfield they drew 1–1, and in the Charity Shield United won 2–0. But despite this impressive record, Atkinson's men only finished in fourth place, six points behind Liverpool. The big encouragement came in the Cup Winners' Cup, where Manchester United, for the first time in fifteen years, reached a European semi-final. Prior to the semi-final Old Trafford hosted one of the very best matches in the arena's history.

On 21 March 1984, Manchester United face the challenge of overcoming a two-goal deficit after having suffered a 2–0 defeat in the Nou Camp against Barcelona two weeks earlier. In Spain, with players like Diego Maradona and Bernd Schuster in the side, the Catalans outplayed the British, and only a few people still believe the Red Devils have a chance in the return match. But the unlikely happens on an evening when the atmosphere at Old Trafford starts as euphoric and ends up being ecstatic. On a typically cool and damp March evening in Manchester the rocking of the stands spread right down to the pitch. The northern English weather doesn't fit with the Spanish players very well, and they clearly cannot get a foothold on the rocking turf. This evening Old Trafford shuts everything else out; only the temple exists. 'In this sacred place, the only religion without atheists puts its divinities on display', writes Eduardo Galeano about the stadium, the game, the fans and the players. In particular one Englishman seems to be divinely inspired this evening. In a symbiotic interaction with the 58,547 believers, the god Bryan Robson is playing games with the Spanish players as if they were merely a bunch of human-like and thus imperfect and fragile creatures.

Robson ruthlessly destroys each initiative to a Spanish attack even before it begins to take shape, and at the same time he orchestrates, irresistibly, his own team's offensive scheme as an endless bombardment of Barcelona's goal. It is Robson himself who gives the home side the lead when he heads the ball into the net after Graeme Hogg, United's centre-back, has flicked on a corner kick. It is also Robson who equalises Barca's initial 2–0 lead when he is the first to react after a shot from Wilkins is dropped by the nervous Barcelona goalkeeper. Just two minutes after Robson's second goal, a hard cross from Albiston lands at the rear post where a flying Whiteside heads the ball across to Stapleton, who then scores to make it 3–0 to Manchester United. The euphoria is now superseded by ecstasy. The performance this evening in March 1984 makes Atkinson and his team immortal, and this despite the fact they lose the semi-final against Juventus 3–2 on aggregate.

Off the pitch, rumours spread about a takeover of Manchester United. The potential buyer is the media mogul Robert Maxwell, who had identified the football world as the next golden calf. The trade, however – fortunately for Manchester United and the club's fans – did not succeed, and Maxwell instead ended up buying Derby County. Posterity has proven that the suspicions of fraud that were already surrounding Maxwell when he was alive were true. He had (among other things) illegally used several billion dollars from pension funds to help with his corporate debt, and many thousands of his employees had lost their pensions. When Maxwell Companies was declared bankrupt in 1992, a year after his mysterious drowning, his two accomplice sons were left with a debt of £4 billion.

*　*　*

Manchester United's fight back against Barcelona demonstrated that the team, on a good day, could match the best teams in Europe. The three showdowns against Liverpool supported this. The puzzle Atkinson had not yet been able to solve was how to stabilise the team enough to sustain the threat to Liverpool's title dominance. During the 1984/85 season, Manchester United said goodbye to two midfield players, Macari and Wilkins. However, in Alex Ferguson's Aberdeen, Atkinson bought the Scottish midfielder Gordon Strachan for £600,000, and from Ajax he signed Jesper Olsen for £800,000. But for the second year in a row Atkinson had to be satisfied with fourth place, as Manchester United finished fourteen points adrift of champions Everton.

Manchester United once again had to make do with a place in the UEFA Cup. The team gave way to Hungary's Videoton in the quarter-finals, and in the FA Cup semi-final the giants from Liverpool awaited at Everton's Goodison Park. In a hectic and fast-paced match, which swung back and forth, it was Robson who broke the deadlock after seventy minutes with an unruly shot, which was grazed on by Hughes and tricked its way past Grobbelaar. Just as the United players and fans thought victory and a place in the final was secured, Ronnie Whelan equalised with just two minutes left. In extra time Stapleton scored to put United up 2–1 just before the break, but once again Liverpool managed to come back, as Paul Walsh equalised in the dying seconds of the match. The re-match was played at Maine Road, and now it was United's turn to come back after falling behind. Shortly before the break McGrath scored an own goal, but immediately after the beginning of the second half Robson lead the way. Impossible to rein in, he stormed forward and then thundered an unstoppable shot past a chanceless Grobbelaar. After an hour of the game Strachan sent Hughes on his way toward Liverpool's goal after a wonderful pass, and the Welshman didn't fail: 2–1 to Manchester United.

Atkinson is now, for the second time in three years, in an FA Cup final at Wembley, and the opponents are Everton, the newly announced English champions and winners of the UEFA Cup. In 1977 Manchester United prevented the red side of Merseyside from winning a historic treble, but can they do it again? Atkinson decides upon the following team on this Saturday, 18 May 1985:

Jesper Olsen, who has had an excellent debut season (fifty-one games, six goals), is the first Danish player in to play in an FA Cup final. Because of his stature and his ability to avoid tackles by dancing, bouncing and twisting, Olsen was quickly given the nicknames of 'the Flea' and 'the Untouchable' when he arrived in Amsterdam. In the young Ajax troupe, with his exceptional technical and tactical skills he was considered to be one of the most talented players by their coach Kurt Linder.

When Olsen arrives at Old Trafford, no one questions this assessment, but there are many who doubt whether he can physically go the distance in the English league, and whether his playing style is compatible with Manchester United's. The scepticism is only exacerbated when Gordon Strachan, another dimensionally diminutive player, arrives at the same time as Olsen. But both Olsen and Strachan are excellent for Manchester United, and with Bryan Robson and Norman Whiteside as their physical antithesis they provide the team with lightness, grace and creativity just as their presence contributes to bringing the ball down on the floor.

Jesper Olsen in the FA Cup final against Everton.

At Wembley against the favourites and double winners Everton, the Merseyside team's odds become even better when, after seventy-eight minutes, United's Kevin Moran is the first player ever to be given a red card in an FA Cup final. But the sending off only makes the United players come even closer together. They don't just hold Everton off in the remaining twelve minutes of regular playing time, they are also the most attacking team, and this continues in extra time. In particular, Olsen is a constant source of worry for Everton's defence with his tireless and unstoppable raids forward and with the ball glued to his left foot.

It is, however, not Olsen but another of Manchester United's wingers who settles the final. Five minutes into extra time Hughes sends a ball out towards the right and a tired Whiteside intercepts the ball, almost reluctantly. He drives the ball forward out wide and is not particularly disturbed by Everton's Pat van den Hauwe, but there does not seem to be any immediate danger. When Whiteside reaches the penalty area, he hesitates, but suddenly with a step-over dribble creates just enough space to get a shot in with his left foot. This first bends Van den Hauwe and then Neville Southall's fingertips, before it sneaks into the goal by the opposite post. With this ballistic masterstroke Whiteside ensures Manchester United's sixth FA Cup triumph, and he is still only twenty years old.

* * *

On 29 May 1985, ten days after Manchester United's triumph at Wembley, Liverpool played against Juventus with the triple winner of the Ballon d'Or Michel Platini in the team. The match, which is the final of the European Cup, was played at the Heysel Stadium in Brussels. Before and during the match thirty-nine spectators died, mainly Italians, when they were crushed as a result of pressure from English hooligans. The Heysel tragedy resulted in all English teams being banned from European tournaments for an indefinite period. In Liverpool's case the suspension was abolished in 1993 after eight years of island isolation, while Manchester United and the other English clubs were granted access to the continent in 1990, after five years in exile.

Therefore, in spite of the cup victory at Wembley over Everton, there was no European football in store for Old Trafford's devoted followers. But instead they could rejoice in a record haul of victories at the start of the following season. This meant the Manchester United players were already looking like champions around Christmas time, and the way they were playing it would have been foolish to bet against them. The departure of both Mühren and McQueen didn't seem to have much influence on Atkinson's tightly knit group when they crushed Aston Villa 4–0 in the season's first match at Old Trafford. There, 49,743 spectators saw an effervescent Hughes score two goals, while Olsen and Whiteside also contributed to the party. The carnival and attacking play continued in the next nine matches, all of which ended with three points. There were several victories of 3–0 in the record haul, but the icing on the cake was, without a doubt, an away performance to savour against Atkinson's former club WBA, which Manchester United won 5–1.

But the spring of 1986 saw a downturn for Manchester United, who slowly saw their large lead decrease. Amazingly, Atkinson's boys ended in a disappointing fourth place, 12 points behind Liverpool. One of the main reasons for the team's dive was the reoccurrence of Robson's injuries, which began mid-season. Another reason was the transformation the young Hughes underwent after New Year. Hughes had been United's sharpest before Christmas, but when it was announced after New Year that Hughes had been sold to Barcelona in the forthcoming summer, it unsettled his form and he found it hard to stay focused.

Barcelona's English manager Terry Venables was hoping Hughes would be the ideal attacking partner for Gary Lineker. It later came to light that Mark Hughes never wanted to leave Manchester United, but it was the club who choose to complete the deal. Hughes wasn't a success at Barcelona, and after just one season at the club he was loaned to Bayern Munich before Alex Ferguson later brought him back to Old Trafford after two years of unwilling exile in both Spain and Germany.

In spite of the freefall in the spring of 1986, Atkinson was still able to show acceptable statistics. In his five seasons at the club he had twice led the team to third place, three times to fourth place, and also to a European semi-final, a League Cup final and two FA Cup triumphs. The big question, however, was whether he was able to take the club onto the next level. His actions in the transfer market in 1986 didn't point to it. They seemed arbitrary and gave the impression Atkinson lacked a master plan. This was probably a key factor in the club's decision to sack him on 5 November 1986. That Manchester United had lost 4–1 to Southampton in the League Cup after a horrible performance two days earlier probably also helped to make the board's decision easier, and the same could be said of the fact that the team stood in nineteenth place after the first thirteen matches.

That same month, November 1986, the board appointed the manager who would go on to oversee Manchester United's dominance of football for the next twenty-five years and counting: Alex Ferguson.

7 January 1990
The spark that ignites the return

I have said it before and I say it again: there are goals that constitute the epicentre of such extraordinary seismic vibrations that they rearrange the football landscape. One such goal takes place on Sunday 7 January 1990, and the goal-scorer is Mark Robins of Manchester United. In the third round of the FA Cup the Red Devils meet Brian Clough's talented Nottingham Forest at the City Ground in Nottingham, and they win 1–0. It's not because there is anything spectacular about Robins's scoring, but the goal inscribes itself as the first and epoch-making letter in the prologue on Manchester United's return and subsequent heyday under Alex Ferguson. Steve Bruce: 'That was the start of the comeback right there. We needed a spark to ignite the whole thing and get the club going, and that FA Cup run in 1990 was exactly what we needed. You can trace everything that followed, all the titles and the trophies, the European Cup and the Treble, back to Mark Robins' goal on that afternoon in Nottingham, because from that came the Cup run and our first trophy under Alex, and from then on we added success after success.'

What Bruce actually says is: Without Mark Robins there would have been no Treble. Bruce is of course talking in the clear light of hindsight, where it's always easy to identify epoch-making moments. But Bruce and other players have also subsequently spoken about the knock-on effect Robins's goal created – *hic et nunc* while the masks were still fluttering from Robins's goal – among the United players, who each immediately sensed future scenarios consisting of podiums, medals and the popping of champagne corks. Legend also has it that the goal not only heralds Manchester United's forthcoming heyday, but also rescues Alex Ferguson from the sack.

Ferguson and Martin Edwards have both ruled out that side of the story, however. Ferguson later revealed he was called into Edwards's office before the

City Ground clash because of the recent disappointing results and speculation in the media about the Scot's early dismissal. Ferguson was at first worried about what the meeting would bring, but Edwards had simply summoned Ferguson to give him his full support, regardless of the outcome in Nottingham the next day. Edwards has repeatedly reaffirmed Ferguson's version, but their stories do not mean a defeat against Nottingham Forest couldn't have triggered Ferguson's dismissal notice anyway.

To understand the importance of Robins's goal, it is necessary to understand the situation in which United and Ferguson found themselves in January 1990. In the summer of 1989 Ferguson spent more than £8 million on new players, an astronomical sum at that time, on players like Paul Ince, Gary Pallister, Neil Webb, Danny Wallace and Mike Phelan, and expectations were naturally very high. As Manchester United in November began a run of eleven games without victory, the media, as well as fractions of the club's own fan base, began to sharpen the knives and began to shout for Ferguson's departure. The situation wasn't improved by the stadium attendances at Old Trafford, which, for the most part, remained below 40,000, and the fact Ferguson's expensive purchases were falling flat.

Mark Robins's goal against Nottingham Forest ignited a cup adventure lasting all the way to Wembley's podium. But during this time the line between failure and success was extremely thin. On Saturday 12 May 1990 the Red Devils returned to Wembley after an absence of five years, and the opponent was this time Steve Coppell's Crystal Palace. In the league, United had finished in a disappointing thirteenth place with Palace just two places below. The final didn't seem much different from United's previous six when it came to drama and tension. Shortly before the break Bryan Robson equalised Palace's lead, and in the second half Mark Hughes put Ferguson's team on a winning course. With ten minutes left Coppell sent out his young rocket Ian Wright and his first contact with the ball resulted in an equaliser for Palace. During extra time Wright scored yet again, and it all pointed in the direction of a Palace win, until Mark Hughes in the very last minute ensured Manchester United a replay via a fantastic volley.

Ferguson was not satisfied with Jim Leighton's performance in goal, and in a highly controversial move, he chose to bench the goalkeeper he himself had brought with him from Aberdeen. In the replay, Les Sealey would keep goal for United, and in a team consisting of veritable star warriors such as Bruce, Pallister, Ince, Robson and Hughes it was surprisingly the young and unheeded left back Lee Martin who secured Ferguson his first trophy as manager of Manchester United. A precise pass from Neil Webb sent Martin free in the space behind the Palace defence, and from a position on the left side of the penalty area he cannoned the ball up into the roof of the net, leaving Nigel Martyn in the Palace goal with little chance.

* * *

The day after the dismissal of Ron Atkinson, Alex Ferguson arrived at Old Trafford. It was 6 November 1986. The impetuous Scot had made the trip south from Aberdeen, where in eight years he had won an incredible ten trophies, including three championships and one European Cup Winners' cup against the mighty Real Madrid. Ferguson's CV spoke for itself and, in contrast to the previous recruitment, the Scot was the club's first choice. If Manchester United's compass couldn't avoid pointing in the direction of Ferguson, then Ferguson couldn't resist Manchester United's magnetism. An indirect cause was an old ghost from United's cabinet of regrets, namely Jock Stein, who in his time ended up saying no to the job. Ferguson said: 'Jock Stein once told me that he turned down the job with United and he regretted it all his life. I am determined not to miss the chance.'

The club was completely aware of what Ferguson represented. He was a manager who with Aberdeen had broken the Celtic/Rangers monopoly in Scotland by not only transforming Aberdeen into the country's best club, but also leading them to European success. He was a manager who had valuable international experience from his role as the Scottish national coach during the World Cup in Mexico in 1986. And with Alex Ferguson, the players knew what to expect. Ferguson had created a reputation as a tough and authoritarian manager who required total sacrifice of his players, not only on the field but also in their private life. Atkinson had been the players' man, a jovial cosy buddy, who allowed the players a great degree of freedom and responsibility. Ferguson, however, maintained a relatively large distance to the players, and he started slowly but surely a reform of the club's ethos that Atkinson had let slide. In particular, Ferguson tried to change the players' diet and drinking habits, but Manchester United appeared in general as a club in crisis, where everything from the youth team to the first team, and from washerwoman to vice-president, was in need of an overhaul.

Ferguson's immediate task was to save the club from relegation, and without money for reinforcements Ferguson was driven to create the necessary results from the team Atkinson passed on to him. The training was harder, and Ferguson also tried to imbue his players with a strong work ethic and team spirit, which has always been a fundamental component in his football philosophy. With the available material Ferguson succeeded in lifting Manchester United up to eleventh place, the club's worst finish since the relegation of 1974, but given the circumstances, a very encouraging performance. After his first six months in the club Ferguson had a clear idea of who Manchester United's future was to be built on. Peter Barnes, John Sivebæk, Frank Stapleton and Terry Gibson left the club, but on the other hand, Ferguson invested in three players who in the following years came to play a leading role in the club's advancement toward English football's peak. Central defence was strengthened with Steve Bruce, who arrived from Norwich for £825,000, while Celtic's king of goals Brian McClair was bought for £850,000, and finally Ferguson signed the English national team's full back Viv Anderson from Nottingham Forest for £250,000.

The purchases, in conjunction with Ferguson's new methods, immediately paid off in 1987/88, when Manchester United finished runners-up to Liverpool. The team's offensive clicked, and for the second season in a row United didn't lose against Liverpool. In addition, United completed the season with eight wins and two draws. There were thus reasons for optimism, but before the new season began, there were also a few concerns. The first was the position next to McClair in attack, as Peter Davenport had only contributed five league goals. The next was the distance to Liverpool: 'Sure, we finished second, and that was encouraging, but we weren't kidding ourselves', said Steve Bruce. 'We were a million miles away from challenging for the title. It had been twenty years since the club had won it and it seemed like it might be another twenty years before we won it again.'

In Ferguson's first year at Old Trafford, Liverpool had for him developed into an obsession similar to the one Matt Busby had regarding the European Cup after the Munich tragedy. With their national and international dominance right up through the 1970s and 1980s, Liverpool was the club Manchester United first and foremost were trying to beat. They had set the standard, as Manchester United had in the 1950s and 1960s, only in an even more astounding way. The result at Anfield in April of 1988 bore witness of Ferguson's resolute mission to challenge and destroy Liverpool's dominance. Manchester United, who were 3–1 down and with only ten men on the field in the last half hour still managed to fight back for a 3–3 draw.

Steve Bruce's words about yet another twenty years despite silver medals seemed to be confirmed in 1988/89, when Manchester United finished in a disappointing eleventh place. Instead of Manchester United, surprisingly it was George Graham's Arsenal who challenged Liverpool, and the championship was decided by a now historic game at Anfield when Arsenal sensationally triumphed dramatically 2–0. The crucial goal, which levelled both points and goal difference and guaranteed the championship to Arsenal on the rule of most scored goals, was scored by Arsenal's Michael Thomas in the dying seconds of the drama. Just a month earlier, on 15 April 1989, English football had been hit by yet another tragedy just four years after Heysel. Yet again Liverpool was involved, this time, however, as a victim. Fans were crushed as barriers collapsed at Hillsborough during the FA Cup semi-final between Liverpool and Nottingham Forest. In total, ninety-six Liverpool fans died as a result of the accident, and more than three hundred were injured.

* * *

Apart from that, how does the world look in 1989? At the beginning of the year George Bush is sworn in as America's forty-first president when he replaces Ronald Reagan. In Iran Ayatollah Khomeini issues a so called fatwa against Salman Rushdie because of the novel *The Satanic Verses*. In the Soviet Union the first free elections are held and the Communist Party doesn't get a majority. In Tiananmen Square in Beijing, the Chinese regime brutally suppresses demonstrating students, and in Poland Solidarity wins the parliamentary elections and thus ignites a series of anti-communist 'revolutions' in Eastern Europe, which includes the Velvet Revolution in Czechoslovakia, Erich Honecker's fall, and the election of Vaclav Havel as president. George Bush and Mikhail Gorbachev meet in Malta and announce the Cold War is coming to a close.

1989 is also the year in which Salvador Dalí, Sergio Leone and Samuel Beckett die. Tim Burton's *Batman* and the Bond movie *Licence to Kill* are premiered, and other notable films are Oliver Stone's *Born on the 4th of July* and Giuseppe Tornatore's *Cinema Paradiso*. Madonna hits the charts with the old Busby-mantra 'Express yourself', and who can forget Roxette's 'The look', Midnight Oil's 'Beds are burning' and 'Fool's gold' by the Manchester band The Stone Roses.

The results of 1988/89 led to Ferguson once again bringing out the large wallet. As already mentioned, he signed players such as Ince, Pallister, Webb, Wallace and Phelan. In exchange, Ferguson let Paul McGrath go to Aston Villa and Norman Whiteside left the club for Everton after being plagued by a series of injuries during the last few seasons and because of a difficulty adapting to Ferguson's discipline. The season was saved by Mark Robins's goal against Forest in January 1990 eventually resulting in a final victory of 1–0 over Crystal Palace in the FA Cup, but in the league Manchester United disappointed again with a miserable thirteenth place.

With the purchase of Denis Irwin from Oldham in the summer of 1990 for £625,000, Ferguson's reconstruction of the team was nearly complete. The backbone of the team which three years later secured the club the first championship in twenty-six years, was in place. There were, however, just two future legends missing a Dane, a Frenchman and two flying wingers, one an enduring legendary Welshman, the other a more short-lived Ukrainian. In a season where Ferguson succeeded in lifting the team to sixth place, the great encouragements were Mark Hughes being crowned by his peers as the Player of the Year (the second crowning in three years) and two cup finals, one domestic and the other European.

In the League Cup Manchester United reached Wembley, but surprisingly lost 1–0 to Ron Atkinson's Sheffield Wednesday. Manchester United also took part in the UEFA Cup, having been suspended from the European game for five years. On their way to the final the Red Devils showed their backbone by winning all four away games. The victory of 2–0 in Montpellier, after a 1–1 draw at Old Trafford in the first leg, demonstrated Ferguson had created a team with a winning instinct and warrior-like mentality. It was precisely these attributes that the team brought with them when entering the De Kuip Stadium in Rotterdam on 15 May 1991 where their opponents were FC Barcelona that had both Michael Laudrup and Ronald Koeman in their armoury.

Barcelona were favourites because Johan Cruyff had come a long way in his efforts to transform the Catalan megaclub into the future Dream Team, but also because the English team and the English league had suffered during their European exile. The English insularity, which Busby in 1956 had challenged with his Scottish stubbornness and with his vision for Manchester United as Europe's best team, and which he with the victory against Benfica in 1968 had emphatically overcome, had in the wake of the Heysel tragedy been re-awakened, although involuntarily of course. Isolated from Europe, the English league had simply lost its magnetism and no foreign stars could be found in the English clubs. Without the input of foreign impulses, the league and the English clubs had stagnated, which only reduced their magnetism even more. However, Alex Ferguson, Mark Hughes and Manchester United were determined to break this vicious circle in Rotterdam. Hughes was on a personal mission: he wanted to show the Spanish club, its players and its 'aficionados' that they were wrong about him when they after just one season sent him out on loan and subsequently returned him to Manchester. Not that Hughes regretted his return (on the contrary) but no professional footballer likes to be discarded.

After a goal-less first half Bryan Robson sends a free kick into the Barcelona box to Steve Bruce, who gets his head to it. Mark Hughes helps the ball the last bit across the goal line by slamming it into the net with his left leg. Just five minutes later Hughes goes on a counter-attack, but is being forced out near the edge of the field on the right-hand side. What first looked like a giant opportunity for a goal now appears to have ended in nothing. However, Hughes speeds up and gets free of his marker, and with an opportunistic kick with the outside of his right foot cannons the ball into the net from a very tight angle. The goal simply galvanises Mark Hughes's Manchester United career. Besides opportunism, it also contains power and brashness, acceleration and agonistic aggression.

When you watch the 163 goals Hughes managed to score in 467 matches in a United shirt, the general characteristic about many of them is that they quite simply slammed into the net. I guess only Alan Shearer could measure up to Mark Hughes in this respect. There was simply no restraint in Hughes's finishes, they were all executed with an enormous power, whether they were headed or kicked, whether it was from close range or far range. When you look at Mark Hughes, you understand where the enormous strength comes from: his thighs are like two thick logs, and inevitably they make you think of Duncan Edwards. In situations where most attackers would have chosen a more restrained finish in fear of hitting the ball out into the stands, Hughes never hesitated for one split second but just hammered onto the ball as if it had to be punished – and many times the hammering resulted in goals, and often spectacular goals.

Hughes was not only important for Manchester United because of his goals, though, but also because he radiated a commanding presence on the field. With his powerful body Hughes had the ability to cover the ball which he was capable of more or less absorbing, regardless of whether it hit his feet, stomach, chest, or head. This absorbency required a high level of technical skill, and Hughes's stays in Barcelona and Bayern Munich clearly had a positive impact on his technique and first touches. Hence, Mark Hughes was not the flamboyant dribbler who produced tricks and magic. What he embodied instead was the team's eternal and reliable gravitational force, ensuring that the magicians and sorcerers never catapulted into the Earth's atmosphere in pure aesthetic escapism but would remain in artistic circuit inside Old Trafford.

The dribbler's game is endowed with an immanent perversion in a Freudian sense as it by definition involves the risk of useless manoeuvres in the hunt for creating goal opportunities on the pitch. The dribbler has sex (football) without necessarily having reproduction (points) as his exclusive and highest purpose; not even an orgasm (the goal) always seems to appeal to him. The dribbler is most of the time located in the foreplay phase, in that purest of the purest aesthetic sphere where beauty is not contaminated by ecstatic utilitarianism and purposefulness, but instead is oriented toward the disinterested and intense pleasure. Mark Hughes was not a dribbler, but he facilitated and reinforced the dribbler's aesthetic potential, on the one hand by ensuring a space of expression for him, on the other hand by preventing the dribbler from ending up in the blind alley that the eternal foreplay inevitably must feel like for the spectators.

You rarely saw Hughes perform tricks. He was never without purpose in his game. Hughes always skipped the foreplay, leaving it to others. He was the champion of orgasms, the guarantor of climax and points on the board. But, we might ask, were his goals then pure and simple usefulness, devoid of any aesthetic element whatsoever? Were they not, spectacular as they often were, aesthetic and covered with useless glaze? Yes they were, but the uselessly spectacular was by Hughes an aesthetic by-product. It was not as by the dribbler a foreplay, but an afterplay; it was not as by the dribbler the most important thing, but a bonus. It was not the result of a desire to entertain the spectators, but simply the repercussions of Hughes's instinctive aggression and raw power.

At De Kuip in Rotterdam Mark Hughes's brashness and foreplay-neglecting style secured Manchester United a 2-1 win over Barcelona, and for the second time Ferguson had won the European Cup Winners Cup. 'We can use this as a platform. Having experienced this tonight, you need it all the time now. It becomes like a drug.'

In an effort to secure the necessary future fix , in the summer of 1991 Martin Edwards and the other directors on the Manchester United board chose to register the club on the London Stock Exchange. In total 2,597,404 shares were put on sale at a unit price of £3.85, and Manchester United's total value was set at £47 million. Alex Ferguson purchased the full back Paul Parker with some of the resources the registration on the stock market brought the club. In Brøndby he also captured a great Dane named Peter Schmeichel, for the modest sum of £500,000, a purchase Ferguson later called 'the transfer of the century'. In the last weeks of the previous season Ferguson had also introduced two new players: the Ukrainian Andrei Kanchelskis and a seventeen-year-old Welshman from the club's own youth academy, Ryan Giggs.

Manchester United's squad was now really strong and the club were, together with Arsenal and Liverpool, favourites for the title. In goal, the young Peter Schmeichel impressed in his first season by keeping clean sheets in the first four matches and by conceding just three goals in his first thirteen matches. For the first time since Big Ron's 1985/86 side United opened with ten victories in a row. United finally seemed capable of breaking the now twenty-five-year-old failure to win the English Championship. But an old friend wanted it otherwise. On the other side of the Pennines Gordon Strachan who had transferred from Manchester United, did his utmost to ensure Leeds constantly breathed down the Red Devils' necks.

In April of 1992 the Championship still seemed set for Old Trafford, but the combination of an unusually tight match schedule for Manchester United, and Eric Cantona's arrival at Leeds, tilted the tables and against Manchester during the last few games. The season, however, didn't end without titles for Ferguson and United, as at Old Trafford they won the European Super Cup with a 1–0 victory over Red Star from Belgrade. Later in the season the club also won their first League Cup trophy, as Manchester United defeated Nottingham Forest 1–0 at Wembley.

1991/92 was not only interesting because of the intense dual between Leeds and Manchester United. It was also the season in which Football Association and Football League fought a battle, which in fact was all about power and about the TV money from the new satellite channels, who wanted to continually show live football matches. The Football League wanted a balanced distribution of money among all ninety-two clubs, but the leading clubs understandably wanted a larger share of the cake since it was them the TV audience wanted to see. The largest and best-supported clubs threatened to break out of the Football League and form their own league, and the solution was a compromise where the English structure of divisions was retained while the best clubs were given the largest portion of the money. The agreement was one of the main reasons for the subsequent entrenchment of the English league's top and bottom. It has formed a seemingly unalterable unit at the top of the Premier League consisting of Manchester United, Arsenal, Chelsea, Tottenham, Liverpool and more recently Manchester City.

26 November 1992
The magic of coincidence and the French alchemist

The story goes that at some point in November 1992, Leeds's manager Howard Wilkinson calls Alex Ferguson to enquire about the possibility of buying Denis Irwin, but Ferguson promptly rejects Wilkinson's query. In a moment of intuitive and sudden inspiration Ferguson turns the conversation upside down and asks Wilkinson if he is willing to sell Eric Cantona, Leeds United's Gallic (but also eccentric) genius. To Ferguson's great surprise Wilkinson answers affirmatively.

From the meeting between Eric Cantona and Manchester United radiates the magic of coincidence. Had Wilkinson not made contact with Ferguson, and had Ferguson not 'seized the moment', then Eric Cantona might never have ended up at Old Trafford. In a few days the transfer is completed, and on 26 November 1992 Manchester United present their new French acquisition. The date symbolises nothing less than the Red Devils' transformation from reliable iron to pure gold, and Cantona is the alchemist who catalyses the alloy's transformation. Manchester United pays Leeds £1.2 million for the Frenchman, making it, in retrospect, one of the club's best purchases ever.

In the weeks after the surprising purchase of Cantona both sports journalists and Manchester United's own fans question Ferguson's judgement. In his previous career Cantona had been a troublemaker who had fallen out with coaches, spectators, teammates, opponents and even football's administrators. In 1991, Cantona decided to end his career after a controversy with the French football federation, but Michel Platini persuaded him to reconsider the decision and, in consultation with Gérard Houllier, they proposed a switch to English football. Platini first tried to sell the problem child to Liverpool, but Graeme Souness rejected the idea on the grounds he did not want unrest in the team. Then Houllier arranged a trial for Cantona at Sheffield Wednesday. As Trevor Francis was not prepared to offer Cantona a contract after one week, but instead

The French magician, Eric Cantona.

wanted the trial extended by another week, the proud Frenchman snorted at the humiliating treatment, pulled up his collar and left the club with his head held high (and perhaps also with smoke pouring out of his ears and eyes flashing red). At Leeds, Wilkinson immediately accepted him and the Frenchman played a crucial role for the club in their championship year.

The purchase of Eric Cantona is by many considered to be the triggering factor in the Red Devils' renaissance in the early 1990s and in recapturing the English throne after twenty-six championship-free years. The Frenchman was simply Ferguson's talisman, the team's creative and mental centre of gravity, who in the course of his five years at the club won four championships and two FA Cups. Had it not been for Cantona's suspension in 1995, it would most likely have been five championships in a row for United.

For many football experts, Wilkinson's decision to sell Cantona still to this day seems to be completely incomprehensible. In fact, behind the decision was a growing unrest in the Leeds team, as well as an increasingly problematic relationship between Wilkinson and Cantona. Seen in this light, and seen with 1992 glasses, Ferguson's decision to buy the feisty and unruly Frenchman indeed seem to be a gamble. But as Ferguson mentioned himself after the purchase of Cantona, the biggest gamble in football is to buy bad players, and Cantona didn't fit into this category. During his short stay at Leeds he was already recognised as the most talented and technically brilliant player the English league had ever housed.

The problem was the football genius went hand in hand with a destructive and uncontrollable behaviour both on and off the field. Like Faust, Alex Ferguson chose to make a pact with the demonic side of Cantona, because he considered the Frenchman the missing piece of the jigsaw puzzle called the English championship. The Scot was willing to take risks with Cantona, and perhaps even occasionally turn a blind eye to his excesses, because the Frenchman's huge talent was so undeniable. The Faustian pact was very well expressed when Cantona in 1995 served his long suspension for his kung-fu kick on the jeering Palace supporter Matthew Simmons. A discussion that was to be expected on Cantona's behaviour and his future followed in the wake of the Selhurst Park incident, but Ferguson's position was clear: 'The league needs him! The club needs him! I bloody need him.'

In what way can Cantona's arrival be said to have catalysed Manchester United's success? What did he specifically bring the club? First, he brought to United's attack an unfamiliar creative and technical ability, which for British teams in this period was unheard of. With Cantona in the team, United's attacking play took off into the sphere of beauty and, occasionally, even into the sphere of sublimity. Eric Cantona, Manchester United's number 7, was simply the Dionysian element in a predominantly Apollonian machine: a touch of divine genius, madness and creativity that Old Trafford had not seen since George Best ran around with the number 7 on his back twenty to thirty years earlier.

Second, Cantona possessed and radiated presence on an extreme level. Both teammates, opponents and spectators constantly sensed Cantona's presence on the field. Presence is not only dependent on physical size or strength, it also has something to do with tactical intelligence, technical gifts, mental strength and authority. The personal charisma that Cantona radiated on a field raised in the same way as his creative talent Manchester United to a higher level in that it had a spill-over effect on his fellow players at the same time that it had a demoralising effect on his opponents. It says something about Cantona's presence and motivating ability that he also on a mental level could lift a side containing strong-willed warriors such as Schmeichel, Robson, Ince, Keane, Bruce, Pallister and Hughes.

Third, and very much linked with his presence on the field, Cantona was also highly influential on the training ground and in the locker room. This influence was also dictated by his presence and charisma, and Cantona's role as role model for the famous 'Class of '92' consisting of Gary and Phil Neville, Nicky Butt, Paul Scholes and David Beckham cannot be overestimated. Schmeichel points this out in his book *The Great Peter*: 'It is my contention that Eric Cantona's importance for Manchester United mustn't only be measured by his efforts on the field, but just as much by the inspiration and experimental initiative that he quite naturally passed on.'

The experimental initiative, which Schmeichel mentions, may be illustrated by an anecdote. On Cantona's first training day – at a time when most of United's players were sceptical about the Frenchman because of his reputation as troublemaker and individualist – he lined up (probably with his collar turned up, and chest heaving forward) to kick the ball against a wall. Cantona juggled with the ball in a way that simply left the rest of the team open-mouthed. Young players like Paul Scholes and David Beckham, who at this time were merely periphery players, got a glimpse, by the sight of the lone and aristocratic juggler, of football's highest sphere, and the event marked them for life.

* * *

The 1992/93 season got off to an extremely volatile start. The striker Dion Dublin – purchased as an indirect consequence of Ferguson's failed attempt to get Alan Shearer – fractured his leg after only seven matches in the red shirt. Dublin's injury was a serious step backwards in United's Championship endeavour, but eventually it also paved the way for Cantona's arrival. Cantona made his debut in the 2–1 home victory over Manchester City on 6 December 1992, and in the remaining twenty-five matches of the season United only lost two games. This irresistible march meant Manchester United won the league by 10 points – Aston Villa being their nearest challengers. The Championship was already secured on 2 May 1993 on a day when United didn't even play. Alex Ferguson was on the golf course when a passer-by told him that Aston Villa had lost to Oldham, and Manchester United had won the English championship for the first time in twenty-six years. The day after, Manchester United celebrated the championship by defeating Blackburn 3–1 at Old Trafford in the presence of a delighted Sir Matt Busby. As was the case for Busby, Ferguson also had to wait seven years for his first championship.

In the summer of 1993 Alex Ferguson bought a player who would have a tremendous influence on Manchester United's success in the next twelve years, the twenty-two-year-old Irish midfielder Roy Keane, who was purchased from Nottingham Forest for £3.75 million. Keane's transfer was controversial, as it awakened an old dispute between two Scottish combatants. Back in 1992, Keane had talked to Kenny Dalglish about the possibility of him coming to Dalglish's progressive Blackburn, and Arsenal had also reported their interest in the Irish dynamo. In the summer of 1993, Blackburn and Forest formally agreed on a transfer of £4 million just as Keane and Dalglish reached an agreement on Keane's personal terms. The day before the contract was to be signed, Ferguson called Keane to see if he was interested in joining Manchester United instead. Keane wasn't hard to convince, and two weeks later he had signed for Manchester United. Dalglish was furious and Ferguson had, in his own way, thanked him for the time Dalglish had humiliated him in front of television cameras after United's 3–3 draw at Anfield in 1988.

Roy Keane made his debut for Manchester United on 7 August 1993, when the club won the Charity Shield against Arsenal, and in his first appearance at Old Trafford in the season's second league match Keane treated his new home audience with two goals. In the Premier League, United immediately headed towards the Championship, and after fifteen matches, the Red Devils had won thirteen, drew one and lost one. The next fourteen matches ended with seven wins and seven draws. One of the draws was at Anfield on 4 January 1994, where Liverpool and Manchester United repeated the result from 1988: 3–3. The match was interesting, because it could easily have been Peter Schmeichel's last for Manchester United.

After the match Ferguson had one of his infamous tantrums in the locker room, because Manchester United had thrown away a 3–0 lead. Schmeichel had been without fault in Liverpool's goals, but the impetuous Scot blamed, rather absurdly, the proud Dane's wretched goal kicks as the cause of United's downturn. Schmeichel refused to take the blame for the loss of points and answered Ferguson back in no uncertain terms. On the next training day Ferguson called the Danish goalkeeper into his office, where he told him he had to get rid of him. As manager, Ferguson could not accept someone speaking to him like that in the presence of the players and he had to act so that he didn't lose authority. Schmeichel apologised for what he had said, but agreed to Ferguson's decision. Later in the locker room the Dane also apologised for his behaviour in the presence of his teammates. Ferguson happened to overhear Schmeichel's apology, which rescued the great Dane's career at Old Trafford.

With 92 points, Manchester United regained the Championship with an eight-point lead over Dalglish's Blackburn. Cantona was the club's top scorer with twenty-five goals. On 8 May 1994, Bryan Robson led his team out at Old Trafford for the last time in his career. In spite of injury problems and the arrival of younger players, the United legend had once again played a large enough role to receive a championship medal and thus secure an appropriate end to a glorious career.

In the League Cup, Manchester United reached the final where their opponents were Aston Villa. Villa's manager was now Ron Atkinson, and his sabotage against his old club continued as Villa won the final 3–1. In the FA Cup, Manchester United also reached Wembley, and on 14 May 1994 they faced Chelsea. 79,634 spectators were witnesses to Chelsea dominance in the first half, but with half an hour left of the match Manchester United were awarded a penalty kick. Eric Cantona nonchalantly sent Dmitri Kharine to the wrong side and put the Red Devils in front. Just five minutes later Cantona repeated the act and put United two goals up. Mark Hughes scored to make it 3–0 minutes later, and finally McClair scored to make it 4–0.

The result was misleading, but it showed very well what this Manchester United team was made of: 'We were confident and that final against Chelsea was typical of our attitude', Brian McClair said. In spite of not always dominating in the first half the team often defeated their opponents in the final stages of the game. Schmeichel's brilliant goalkeeping often kept them in the match in the first half, and Cantona's coolness settled the match in Manchester United's favour in the second half. This set-up happened again and again. After winning the Championship in 1992 and 1993 respectively with Leeds and Manchester United, and the double with Manchester United in 1994, Cantona was that year named the PFA Player of the Year by his colleagues.

As a result of the FA Cup final victory against Chelsea, Alex Ferguson had achieved something that not even Matt Busby managed with his Babes or his world stars in the 1960s, namely to win the club's first league and FA Cup double. If 1993 had been a year of redemption, then 1994 was the year that Manchester United consolidated their status as Premier League's kings. On the international scene, though, there was still a long way to go. In the newly formed Champions League (like the Premier League, started in 1992/93) Manchester United faced Turkish side Galatasaray from Istanbul in the first round. At Old Trafford the

Turks surprisingly earned a 3–3 draw, and as the return match ended 0–0, Galatasaray went on to the group stages on away goals.

Sir Matt Busby supervised Manchester United's return to the European scene, but he failed to see the club win the double. Matt Busby died on 20 January 1994 at the age of eighty-four. Two days later a lone piper led the players from Manchester United and Everton onto Old Trafford's pitch in front of 44,750 grieving spectators. Today, there is a bronze statue of Busby in front of the main entrance to Old Trafford, and Warwick Road, which passes along the same main entrance, has been renamed Sir Matt Busby Way. In addition to these material manifestations of Busby's influence, it is perhaps more important that Manchester United in Alex Ferguson has a manager, who in the course of the last two and a half decades, has managed to find a balance between the commercial requirements and rules of the modern game and the ideological and philosophical heritage that Matt Busby made Manchester United world famous for in the 1950s and 1960s – and here I am first and foremost thinking about the investment in youth and the obligation to win by playing entertaining football.

* * *

There is one episode that the 1994/95 season is especially remembered for: the demonic black-suited Eric Cantona's kung-fu kick on a spectator during the match against Crystal Palace at Selhurst Park on 25 January 1995. Many see Cantona's subsequent suspension of nine months as the main reason why Manchester United failed to win the Championship for the third year in a row and the double for a second consecutive year. But Cantona's suspension – and an injured Schmeichel – destabilised the otherwise inexorable United machine's grinding enough so that Blackburn got in, arguably through the back door, and as the whistle sounded to get the last game of the season under way, Manchester United had to win at Upton Park against West Ham and at the same time hope Liverpool could beat Blackburn at Anfield. Liverpool did in fact win 2–1, thus giving their arch-enemies a lifeline. But in spite of opportunities galore Manchester United only managed to play out a 1–1 draw in London and had to settle for second place. Six days later, in the FA Cup final at Wembley on Saturday 20 May 1995, Everton rubbed salt into Manchester United's wounds by winning the match 1–0. In the Champions League, United were still suffering from the rules that allowed only five non-English players on each team. Meeting both Barcelona and IFK Gothenburg with Jesper Blomqvist meant an early exit from this year's tournament.

In addition to Cantona's kung-fu kick and the season's dramatic end, there were a number of other events that make the season worth remembering. In twenty-one home matches Manchester United conceded only four goals and kept eighteen clean sheets. Peter Schmeichel played seventeen of the twenty-one matches, and in the first sixteen matches he kept a clean sheet until Southampton broke the spell in the final home game of the season. But United still won 2–1. Three days before Cantona's kung-fu kick in the home victory against Blackburn on 22 January 1995, Ferguson gave his new star striker Andy Cole a debut. Ferguson had bought Cole from Newcastle for the record high amount of £6 million, plus Keith Gillespie. The purchase of Cole was an attempt to reinforce the team with English quality and counter the weaknesses in Europe. At Camp Nou in Barcelona, Ferguson had, for example, been obliged to let both Schmeichel and Cantona sit in the stands and the result was a noticeable 4–0 drubbing.

With his goal instinct and his 'penalty area feel', Cole seemed the perfect partner for Cantona, the goal poacher who could finalise the Frenchman's foreplay. However, they only got to have one and a half matches together before a devilish Cantona left Selhurst Park and served a subsequent nine months' suspension. Andy Cole, however, was not the only new name arriving at Old Trafford. Ferguson also signed David May from Championship rivals Blackburn. From the club's youth academy four future prominent names emerged: Gary Neville, Nicky Butt, Paul Scholes and David Beckham all had their share of games.

The 1–0 defeat at Wembley against Everton felt like the end of an era, and in the summer of 1995 this feeling was converted to action as Alex Ferguson took the controversial decision to sell a number of his established stars. Ferguson seemed to have had enough of Paul Ince's open mouth and self-proclaimed title as Old Trafford's 'guv'nor' and sold him to Inter Milan. Andrei Kanchelskis, whose relationship with Ferguson had also soured, was sold to Everton. Finally Ferguson sold Mark Hughes to Chelsea.

Ferguson's operation seemed so reckless and dramatic that many United fans were on the brink of revolt. The three players that were sold had, after all, been essential in the previous seasons' success where the club had won two championships and only missed out on a third in the season's dying minutes. Kanchelskis had just become the club's top scorer with fifteen goals, Hughes had led the attacks, and Ince had been the chief engineer of the team's engine room. When you review clips from Manchester United's matches during these years, when Ince controlled the midfield, it is strikingly revealed what a power and inspirer he was. He was always leading the way as the team's defensive garbageman where his relentless tackles destroyed his opponents' constructive play, but he also played an important role in United's offensive as motivator, scoring many important goals too. Alex Ferguson, however, felt several of the players from the talented class of 1992 were ready to replace Hughes, Ince and Kanchelskis.

If the away game against Huddersfield on 31 October 1953 signalled Matt Busby's youth revolution, then it was a similar case on 19 August 1995 at Villa Park in Birmingham when Alex Ferguson sent a clear signal about the direction Manchester United would go in the coming years. On the team sheet next to established names such as Schmeichel, Parker, Irwin, Pallister and McClair, the following names were listed: Lee Sharpe (twenty-four), Roy Keane, (twenty-four), Gary Neville (twenty), Nicky Butt (twenty), Paul Scholes (twenty) and Phil Neville (eighteen). The substitutes were, by the way, called John O'Kane (twenty), Simon Davies (twenty-one) and David Beckham (twenty), and the latter scored United's goal with a fantastic long shot. Unfortunately for Manchester United, Aston Villa scored three times, and after the match, the Liverpool legend Alan Hansen spoke his famous words on SkySport: 'You'll never win anything with kids.'

8½ is a famous film by Federico Fellini. A film about Manchester United's 1995/96 season could begin with Alan Hansen's statement and be named 8½, like Fellini's masterpiece. Eight and a half months after Hansen's badly misjudged analysis, Manchester United secured their third championship in four years, and it was done with a whole kindergarten of kids in the team. 'Fergie's Fledglings' they were soon baptised, these young comets and the symbol of England's future: Gary Neville, Phil Neville, Nicky Butt, David Beckham and Paul Scholes.

Six times in the spring of 1996 Cantona became the match winner in 1–0 victories and he also on several other occasions secured the team points in draws or one-goal victories. The match that really tilted the table in Manchester United's favour in the running for the title was the away match on St James Park on 4 March 1996 against Newcastle. Newcastle dominated events and were all over Manchester United, but in the second half Cantona scored one of his many match-winning goals in a classic counter-attack and secured Manchester United a priceless 1–0 victory.

In the FA Cup the club chased a historic repetition of the double. Never before had a club won the Championship and the FA Cup in the same season twice, but on 11 May 1996, 79,007 spectators saw Eric Cantona, back on the team after the Selhurst incident, crown an enchanting personal comeback to the football scene with a goal securing Manchester United a victory of 1–0 over Liverpool and the first 'double double' in English football. Two days before the crucial goal at Wembley football journalists had named Cantona Footballer of the Year, a title that had not gone to a Manchester United player since George Best received it in 1968. In view of the fact it was the very same journalists who, one and a half years earlier, had demanded Cantona be excluded from football for life and even expelled from UK, this shows Cantona's unique transformation and his impact on Manchester United's team. The previous year he had been prevented from playing in the final against Everton, and Manchester United had lost 1–0. In May 1996 he added that momentary magic to an otherwise boring match, which just four minutes before the final whistle sounded was enough to ensure Manchester United's victory and a place in the history books.

Thirty-six-year-old Steve Bruce played his last match for Manchester United at Old Trafford against Leeds on 17 April 1996. In nine years, Bruce played 414 matches for Manchester United and scored fifty-one goals. One cannot mention Steve Bruce without also mentioning Gary Pallister, who played 437 matches and scored fifteen goals for United in the period 1989–1998. In seven seasons, Bruce and Pallister made up the cornerstone of Manchester United's defence and they phenomenally complemented each other. Bruce lived to a great extent on his enthusiasm and played with his heart on the outside of his sleeve. He was a wonderful stimulus for his teammates and was also the club's captain for a few years. He was a regular goal-scorer, both from penalty kicks and headers. Pallister was the more intelligent central defender, whose defensive interventions were perfectly timed, and his touch of the ball made him the defence's natural play-maker.

* * *

In the 1996/97 season the Norwegian invasion of Manchester United began. At Besiktas in Istanbul Alex Ferguson signed an intelligent and stylish defensive player, the Norwegian Ronny Johnsen, who was joined by his fellow countryman, the striker Ole Gunnar Solskjær. Solskjær was a relatively blank slate, signed from Molde after Ferguson once again had failed to get Alan Shearer to come to Old Trafford. As a forewarning of the rest of his long career at Manchester United Solskjær marked his debut in the 2–2 match against Blackburn on 25 August 1996 by scoring his first goal for the club just six minutes after being substituted. Ferguson also purchased the Czech Karel Poborsky and Dutchmen Raimond van der Gouw and Jordi Cruyff.

In the UEFA competitions as well as in the English league the Bosman ruling from 1995 meant players from the European Union countries were no longer considered as foreigners. The decision had a tremendous effect on all European clubs, big and small, as it triggered an accelerating globalisation of the club's squads. The five purchases mentioned above are a clear example of this. The purchase of Andy Cole in January of 1995 had intended to boost the national element on Manchester United's team with English 'premium quality' since United couldn't field their strongest team in Europe as a result of UEFA's policy on foreigners. The Dane Peter Schmeichel, Ukrainian Kanchelskis and the Frenchman Cantona all were of course included in the foreign quota. But in contrast to the rules of the English league, the non-English players from Great Britain and Ireland also counted as foreigners when playing in European competitions. In United's case this meant the Scottish McClair, Giggs and Hughes from Wales, and the Irish Irwin and Keane were also counted as foreign players. Manchester United were only allowed to use five of these star players in the team at the same time.

Manchester United started 1996/97 by humiliating the title rivals Newcastle 4–0 in the Charity Shield. In the season's first league match, Wimbledon were defeated 3–0 at Selhurst Park and David Beckham delivered the match's gem by scoring from the centre line. After three draws Cantona & co. went to Elland Road and defeated Leeds 4–0, and when Liverpool were beaten 1–0 at Old Trafford on 12 October 1996 everything seemed the way it should be. But Newcastle apparently were of a different opinion, revenging themselves for the humiliation at Wembley when they beat the Red Devils 5–0 at St James's Park on 20 October. The match against Newcastle inaugurated an extraordinary streak of defeats as the following week they lost 6–3 at the Dell to Southampton, and then completed the hat trick in the league, when Chelsea defeated them 2–1 at an otherwise unconquerable Old Trafford. In the meantime the Turkish side Fenerbahçe had even destroyed Manchester United's European record of being undefeated on home ground when, after a goal by Elvir Bolic, they won 1–0 at the 'Theatre of Dreams'.

It was not entirely without reason many believed Ferguson had lost his grip. Three defeats in a row in the league were unusual for Manchester United, but it was not without precedent. However, the size of the defeats was unheard of. On top of that came the defeat by Fenerbahçe, and when that was followed by yet another 1–0 defeat on home ground against Juventus, Ferguson was under pressure. The European ambitions were balancing on the edge of failure, and the dream of defending the championship was crumbling. But Manchester United's response was typical: the team went undefeated in the next sixteen league matches, and in addition went to Vienna and beat Rapid 2–0, and thus secured for the first time ever advancement from Champions League's group stages after three victories of 2–0 and three defeats of 1–0.

On 11 May Manchester United could together with 55,249 spectators celebrate the club's fourth championship in five years, when, in the season's last match, they defeated West Ham 2–0 at Old Trafford. Solskjær made a cannonball arrival at the club as he became top scorer with eighteen league goals and one in the Champions League in his first season with the club.

In the Champions League's quarter-final, Manchester United were paired with Porto, from Portugal. On 5 March United won the first match 4–0 at Old Trafford, and two weeks later the team qualified for the semi-finals by playing out a 0–0 draw in Porto. The massacre of Porto at Old Trafford made Manchester United favourites along with Juventus, but in the semi-finals Dortmund showed typical German professionalism by defeating the Red Devils 1–0 in both matches. After forty years without defeats at home in Europe, United had suddenly suffered three of its kind in the same season, but more than the annihilation of the record, the defeat by Dortmund and the impossibility of revenge over Juventus in the final pained the team.

On Sunday, 18 May 1997, exactly a week after the season's last match, Martin Edwards announced at a press conference that Eric Cantona had chosen to end his career as a professional footballer. The decision came as a shock to Manchester United's fans, and probably also to Ferguson and his teammates, as the Frenchman was only thirty years old. But the decision was typical of Cantona, whose career had been one long series of controversial and unconventional decisions. Cantona stopped while he was at the top, and because of this people will always remember him as the exceptional footballer he was. In his five seasons at Manchester United he played 185 matches and scored eighty-two goals. Neither the number of matches nor the goals are enough to give him a place in the statistical record books, but his alchemical influence can hardly be overestimated. In five years he won four British championships, two FA Cup titles and three Charity Shields. In 1994 Cantona won the PFA Player of the Year, and in 1996, his comeback season after the Selhurst Park incident, he was announced FWA Player of the Year by the football journalists.

* * *

Before 1997/98 began Alex Ferguson replaced Eric Cantona with Teddy Sheringham, whom he signed from Tottenham. Ferguson also added another player to the Norwegian delegation when he purchased the defender Henning Berg from Blackburn.

In the league Arsène Wenger's Arsenal emerged as a new threat to Manchester United's championship chances. In his first season at Highbury in 1996/97 Wenger had transformed Arsenal into potential champions when the team finished in third place. On 9 November 1997 Arsenal showed they meant it, when they won 3–2 in an entertaining match at Highbury against Manchester United. To Manchester United the defeat fell midway between five victories, which otherwise indicated another championship for Ferguson's Fledglings: 7–0 at home against Barnsley, 6–1 at home against Sheffield Wednesday, 5–2 away against Wimbledon, 4–0 at home against Blackburn and 3–1 away against Liverpool. After the season's first eighteen matches, Manchester United also seemed to be directed toward the title, but in January the team allowed Arsenal to join the championship race. When Wenger's team defeated Ferguson's men 1–0 at Old Trafford, the road was paved for Arsenal to ensure the club won its first Championship since 1991.

In the Champions League, victories came both home and away against Kosice and Feyenoord, but the most encouraging performance in the group took place at Old Trafford on 1 October 1997 when Manchester United won 3–2 against powerful Juventus. At the Stadium Delle Alpi in Turin, United lost 1–0, but the tickets to the quarter-finals were secured with unfailing certainty. Here Jean

Tigana's Monaco awaited, and in the principality Manchester United secured an excellent starting point with a 0–0 draw, but in Manchester the young David Trezeguet scored for Monaco. Solskjær's equaliser was not enough for United, who were knocked out by the rule of away goals.

To Alex Ferguson the future still looked bright. In the last seven years Manchester United had won four championships and three times the club had finished in second spot after a close run in. The transition from Ferguson's 'first generation' to his 'second generation' had worked smoothly, and players like the Neville brothers, Beckham, Scholes, Butt and Giggs had shown that they were ready to take responsibility and strive for higher goals. In Europe the last two years' performances had also been uplifting, but both the Dortmund and Monaco matches had also shown that Ferguson and his Fledglings still had a long way to go before the European DNA-code was broken down.

To help crack the code Ferguson purchased the defender Jaap Stam from PSV Eindhoven, the attacker Dwight Yorke from Aston Villa and the winger Jesper Blomqvist from Parma. Stam was purchased as a direct replacement for Gary Pallister, and Blomqvist was intended as Ryan Giggs's back up. Yorke was brought to Old Trafford after Teddy Sheringham's first season at Manchester United had not convinced Ferguson he was the perfect partner for Andy Cole. In addition, Ferguson was aware of the fact that the season's many matches and the challenges in the Champions League demanded a large squad with at least four top-class attackers. In spite of second place in the league in 1997/98, Manchester United still qualified for the Champions League, which no longer only allowed participation of the national champions and defending title holders.

9 April 1995
Commercial cup

Outside Old Trafford in the early 1970s there was only one souvenir kiosk. It was registered in Matt Busby's name, and the shop was part of Busby's retirement package. For several years the kiosk was managed by Sandy Busby, Matt's son. Hence, this was the time when Manchester United were apparently still a cosy family club. Many of the fans from Busby's time thought it a clear signal of the club's distancing from the family atmosphere and club spirit the 'boss' had created when Manchester United's board refused to renew the kiosk agreement with Busby. The club had realised what a goldmine merchandise would turn into in the future and wanted to get their hands on the profits.

Today some believe Old Trafford is more of an amusement park and a shopping mall than a football stadium. Busby's souvenir kiosk is replaced by the Manchester United Mega Store, physically located under Old Trafford's large entrance, right under the statue of Matt Busby. Affiliate stores are also located in some of the world's major cities, as well as on the Internet as online shops. In addition to the Mega Store, small stalls spread themselves around Old Trafford on match days. Many local Manchester shops offer official and unofficial Manchester United merchandise. On match days evil tongues claim to see more so-called fans with a shopping bag from Manchester United's Mega Store in their hand than genuine fans with a United scarf around their neck on Sir Matt Busby Way.

On Saturday 11 August 2007, the day before Manchester United begin their title defence against Steve Coppell's Reading at Old Trafford, I take a bus from Mosley Street in Manchester's centre to Old Trafford Cricket Ground. From there I follow Sir Matt Busby Way towards the Theatre of Dreams. On the way I join up with Anne from France, who has lived in Manchester for a few years, and is also on the way to Manchester's mecca. I naturally assume she is a fan of Manchester United, but it turns out not to be the case. She actually cares very little about football. Anne is with her sister and her husband, who is visiting from the south-west of France. It's perhaps because of them she spends a Saturday at Old Trafford? No, they are actually not major football enthusiasts, Anne tells me. It's their nine-year-old son who is a big fan of Manchester United. He has asked his mother and father to visit Old Trafford to take some pictures home for him.

The meeting with Anne and her family leaves me puzzled, but the story gives some clues to Manchester United's global magnetism. After I've picked up my ticket for tomorrow's match, and after having been on a stadium tour, I spend a couple of hours at Old Trafford's impressive museum before I go back to the bus stop by the cricket ground. Here I start talking to Maggie and Claire, two older ladies from Edinburgh. They have taken the journey from Scotland to Manchester with the primary purpose of visiting Old Trafford. So there it is again: the global magnetism this club appears to possess, also confirmed by the stadium tour that included Americans, Dutch, Japanese, Koreans and Finns. I myself can be included as yet another component in the diverse group of middle-aged French, older Scottish ladies, young Koreans and American adults and children.

So are the evil tongues right? What do we learn from the stories of people like Anne, Maggie, Claire and me? Well, first of all they tell a story of globalisation and of the interdependence between the cultural and commercial. This development, without a doubt, has contributed to a shift in the balance between global and local fans. But who determines who is a genuine fan? Maybe as Scots Maggie and Claire have family, religious or cultural ties to Old Trafford. United's Scottish connection has always been strong, not least under Busby's and Ferguson's long regimes. And is Anne's nine-year-old nephew less an authentic fan than the local Mancunian who makes a short trip in the car to be here?

The new tribalism, which we see within the world of football today, is marked by the fact that the local links are loosened and there is a capacity to 'plug into' or 'connect with' a team no matter where you are. Loyalty and attachment are no longer exclusively based on the locally rooted, almost mythical, working-class communities with which club support was usually associated. Mega-clubs like Manchester United represent rather a fusion point for a neotribalism, which is not only transnational, but also media-based via the global satellite-distribution network.

In 2008 it was estimated Manchester United's global fan base amounted to 333 million people (of which 83 million are in Asia), or about 5 per cent of the world's population. According to United's own statements, the number in 2012 has doubled. The reason behind these monstrous numbers can't, however, only be found in aggressive marketing that focuses on the stars' here-and-now celebrity status. It is also a commercial exploitation of the historic and symbolic values linked to the club. Myth and tradition, as well as fractures and tragedy, have become good business. So do you really need to be born in Manchester and have seen the Busby Babes *live* to be a genuine fan? This kind of authenticity no longer seems to be suitable for the age of post-modernism and globalisation. This is not to say development does not have its problematic side. Personally, I am critical of the lack of historical knowledge – undoubtly one of the by-products of global capitalism – and this book bears witness to this by taking Manchester United's long and turbulent history seriously.

If we shift focus from the supporters to ownership, then Malcolm Glazer's purchase of Manchester United is also an example of this globalised reality. The American ownership of England's most mythologised and famous football club, with its strong territorial and historical roots in the north-west of England, inevitably provokes the question of whether the roots and myth will gradually dissolve in a transnational, capitalistic company culture. And Glazer's buy is far from unique in England, where Liverpool and Aston Villa are also US-owned, Chelsea is Russian-owned, and Manchester City is owned by a sheikh from the United Arab Emirates.

In the United States, one is not alien to the idea of moving a sports team from one city to another similar to a franchise (underlining the team's fundamental foundation as a business). In such cases, the tie to a new place is completely superseded by the media's ability to distribute the brand both nationally and globally. Could you imagine Manchester United transplanted to a different English city, or even to one in America? Hardly. The club's leadership and its new owners seem to be aware of the history and the team's local specificity. The purchases of, for example, Michael Carrick and Phil Jones under Glazer testified to the fact that Manchester United actively seek a balance between the English and the international by maintaining an English/British core of the team. In addition, the club is financially involved in a wide variety of local projects, communities and associations, as well as in local charity activities, which aim to strengthen and develop the local setting.

*   *   *

On 9 April 1995 the British broadcaster Channel 4 aired the controversial programme 'J'accuse: Manchester United.' The TV host and author Hunter Davies accused Manchester United of being greedy and selling the club's soul through the shameless exploitation of the fans. Davies criticised, for example, the club's high frequency of shirt changes. At this time Manchester United introduced six new shirts in four years, and once they even introduced two new shirts within just six months.

The phenomenon even became a discussion topic in the political arena. In an article in the *Guardian* on 16 January 1995, the Labour party leader and England's future prime minister Tony Blair criticised football's increasing commercial-isation and the clubs' seemingly endless greed. Blair also criticised players and managers for the escalation of violent incidents and bad behaviour. His comments fell nine days *before* Cantona's kung-fu kick. Blair insisted he did not want an unrealistic return to 'the good old days' with maximum wages, but he expressed his concern over the fact that increasingly money was the decisive incentive in the sport. Blair acknowledged there was a market, but he stressed the market's counterweight should be the club's roots in local and loyal communities. Manchester United received a special mention from Blair when he explicitly criticised the club's introduction of a new blue/white-away outfit in the match against Southampton on 31 December 1994: 'There is a fine line between fashion and exploitation. Fashion cannot justify the change of strips which parents then are pressurised to buy. How many children had been bought a Manchester United away strip at Christmas only to see them turn out in blue and white?'

In the 1992/93 season, the hundredth year of the club's entry into the Football League, we saw one of Manchester United's attempts to maintain a connection to its own humble origin when the club chose to introduce an away shirt modelled on Newton Heath's yellow and green-shirts with cord in the neck and black pants. Many laughed but it has since achieved a cult status. Indeed during the Glazer ownership the yellow and green colours have come to symbolise the humble and local origins and fans use them as protest against Glazer and the club's financial situation with large debts.

An event that also contributed to criticism of the club's shirt policy happened at the Dell on 13 April 1996 during Manchester United's match against Southampton. United were playing in their brand-new grey away shirt, but when the team was 3–0 down at the break, Ferguson chose to switch to the more traditional blue and white shirt. Ferguson claimed the grey outfit had brought the team bad luck, and he also claimed they had difficulty finding each other on the pitch, as the grey colour made it difficult for the players to distinguish themselves from the spectators. Manchester United never played in the grey shirt again, and Umbro ended up apologising for the colour's inappropriateness. The shirt was on the market long enough for thousands of fans to buy it, though.

The frequent change of shirts made the Independent Manchester United Supporters' Association accuse the club of cynical exploitation. This, among other things, is opposed to the idea of a harmonious relationship between club and fans and the idea of an acceptable balance between tradition and innovation, an idea I put forward earlier in the book. After all, there has been a great deal of unrest in the club's fan base where gaps between older and younger fans and between the 'authentic' fans from Manchester and the 'inauthentic' fans from the rest of England and the world have sometimes become clear. However, I maintain that Manchester United's success on and off the field can be attributed to a kind of balance between tradition and expansion. First, the rapid commercial development that the club has gone through in the last twenty years is a general development in the game of football globally, and perhaps particularly in England. Arguably, Manchester United (as well as Real Madrid and FC Barcelona) are leaders in marketing, but that does not mean other clubs do not try to copy their success, and that is why Manchester United is not a unique phenomenon, but perhaps one of the most extreme. Second, while unrest exists in certain fan factions and many older fans feel great antipathy towards the way that the club is run today, undoubtedly Manchester United will continue to attract new fans.

Hunter Davies also criticised the fact that in the club's annual report, the previous year's sporting success was completely overshadowed by long explanations of the club's commercial successes. He concluded the money had become the primary and the sport the secondary motive. Today, players are first of all seen as assets, not just players – and even less as humans. However, the question is whether players have ever been purely viewed as humans, independent of their financial value as assets. Admittedly, it was Busby's ideology to view players as people, but it was also Busby who, during a board meeting in the 1950s when youth policy was on the agenda, legitimised the policy by claiming the club had £200,000 of talent walking around in the reserve team. This story only emphasises the fact that football has never been a completely pure sport, free of economic thinking and moneymen.

Hunter Davies also meant that Manchester United was in the regrettable process of severing the ties to the club's cultural and geographical roots. In relation to my argument that the club's success is based on the balance between tradition and innovation, 'J'accuse: Manchester United' postulates that the club neglects its traditions and its historical legacy. Tommy Docherty, the former manager of Manchester United, said in the programme that Busby would be turning in his grave if he saw how things were run today. Docherty also claimed that, although Manchester United would end up not winning the Premier League in 1995, they would surely end up winning the 'Commercial Cup'.

It cannot be denied Manchester United in many ways embodies the phenomenon that the cultural historian Fredric Jameson describes as the collapse between the cultural and economic spheres. In other words, in the post-modern or late-capitalist age we see the blurring of boundaries between the cultural and commercial worlds. Football is in Manchester United's case inextricably linked to the values and guidelines in a global capitalist company-culture that is becoming more and more dominant in the world.

For Manchester United it means they are in a relational and dynamic field with other special interests (see also Andrews). On the one hand, they are placed in relation to external spheres and these are in many cases dominated and defined by commercial requirements. This for example applies to football's organisations and representative bodies (FA, UEFA, PFA, G14, FIFA), the club's primary sponsors (AoN, General Motors, Nike) and the media (ITV, Sky Sports). On the other hand, we find on the inside of the organisation shareholders, owners, directors, management and supporters. Before Malcolm Glazer took over the club, the shareholders had economic interests in the club's operation, but with Glazer as owner, only one person (or family) determines in which direction the club will travel.

Hence, Manchester United is located in a complex network consisting of tightly integrated, but also often divergent interests and claims pulling in different directions. We see conflicting interests between external and internal operators when Manchester United, together with other clubs in the G14, try to influence UEFA into creating better conditions for the big clubs. But the biggest problem is the conflict of interests between the internal operators, like, for example, between Glazer and the supporters, the latter believing that the American's takeover, huge debts and vision goes against their wishes and ambitions for the club.

*　*　*

The fourth pillar on which the club stands, aggressive marketing, is one of the main reasons for the club's global magnetism. At the same time it represents a development, which in many people's eyes threatens to destroy the club's cohesiveness, that is, among other things, its connection to the local fan: to the worker or older supporter, who saw the Babes in the 1950s or Old Trafford's 'Holy trinity', Best, Law and Charlton, in the 1960s.

When Roy Keane in the beginning of this century criticised the home crowd at Old Trafford for caring more about their prawn sandwiches than supporting the team, his remark was precisely bearing witness to the transformation that happened among the spectators up through the 1990s. Keane's attack was primarily directed towards the VIP and corporate boxes occupied by the so-called 'prawn sandwich brigade'. In January 2008 Alex Ferguson backed up his former captain's criticism when, after a home match against Birmingham which Manchester United struggled to win 1-0, he compared the atmosphere at Old Trafford with one at a funeral. This made a spokesman from IMUSA claim Old Trafford was to be compared with a police state, where every aberration from the strict rules led to an immediate and rough dismissal. Furthermore, IMUSA criticised Old Trafford's colony of 'corporate fans' whom they believed were responsible for the flat atmosphere. Manchester United's reply to this criticism was that only 10 per cent of Old Trafford's capacity was occupied by the so-called 'executives', which still left room for around 68,000 'normal' spectators. Furthermore, the 8,000 executives placed around the stands in special exclusive areas such as VIP boxes, were the reason why ticket prices were so low for the rest of the spectators.

My own experience from Old Trafford on 12 August 2008 does not stray much from Keane's and Ferguson's feelings. I do not sit at the Stretford End where the hardcore sits and where the sound is loudest. In fact, from my position up high under the roof between the North and East Stands I can hardly see the Stretford End (West Stand). But even though I am fully aware of not being among the hardcore fans I still wonder about the poor sound and atmosphere there is surrounding the match. Around me are solely 'nice men', most of them in jeans and T-shirt and only a few in a red club shirt. Before the match I am impressed with how many have turned up in official club shirts, most of them even in the newest version. Sir Matt Busby Way is simply a red/white sea of people. However, there are none with face paint or banners, and you don't hear any groups singing football chants. Everything is nice and calm; 'sanitised' both inside and out.

Keane's and Ferguson's statements testify to an internal problem, where the team suffers from the club's and the supporter's divergent interests. The growing commercialisation has thus led to groups of fans who hate the club, but still choose to stand behind the team. The transformation in the spectator segment and the resulting 'change of atmosphere' at certain stadiums has more reasons. The local club politics combined with increasingly expensive tickets leads to the dismissal of the traditional and loud working-class fans. Also the politically required sanitisation of the football stadium (only seating, a ban against banners, Roman candles, fog horns, wearing masks, etc) has a measurable effect on the atmospheric barometer of many stadiums.

The overall picture looks more or less like this: instead of the older fan who has faithfully supported the team for decades, there is a growing percentage of spectators at Old Trafford today, who do not possess the older fan's historical knowledge. Instead of the worker, who chooses to spend a large part of his weekly wage on a ticket, and indirectly demonstrates his feeling for the club, an increasing part of the spectators come travelling from afar, and for many a match at Old Trafford is a once-in-a-lifetime experience. And instead of the local boy from Salford who each week begs his mother for pocket money to buy a ticket, there's a growing number of spectators belonging to the upper middle class for whom a ticket does not represent a significant portion of their budget, and for whom the match is just one among many weekly diversions in the late-capitalist consumer society.

But this development is also characterised by the decline in hooliganism, both as a result of general social changes but also because of the abovementioned sanitisation. So yes, the transformations take place, but not all are necessarily for the worse. And again I ask the question: is the supporter who comes travelling from afar a lesser fan than the local Mancunian?

* * *

The marketing doesn't only represent a transformation threatening to disengage Manchester United from its roots. In its marketing the club also use these roots, more specifically its traditions and myths, whereby they are continually consolidated but also revised and made up to date. The club, its history, its stadium and its players are mobilised as buyable items in a multiplicity of branded experiences and products designed to stimulate people's interest and also create economic growth. The diversity is represented by magazines, computer games, DVD documentaries, DVD season collections and books (here one of the latest additions is the exclusive *Manchester United Opus* published in 2006, which consists of more than 800 pages, contains over 2,000 images and costs between £3,000 and £4,500). But there are also stadium tours, restaurants, mega-stores, the club's own television channel MUTV and the large-scale museum with three floors at Old Trafford. And we mustn't forget merchandise in the broadest sense, particularly the sale of clothes, both brand-new shirts, but also retro shirts from all decades.

An interesting example of how the club consolidates its tradition can be found on the front page of the book *The Official Illustrated History of Manchester United 1878–2006*, which was published on 19 October 2006. The front page is an excellent illustration of the inclusions and exclusions that are continually made in the official mythology of Manchester United – a mythology that has been continually updated and revised from a contemporary perspective. On the front page is a picture showing some of the legends in Manchester United's history. The picture makes me think of the French writer Bernard le Bovier de Fontenelle's *Nouveaux dialogues des morts* from 1683, in which Fontenelle came up with a series of dialogues between famous dead people. One of the dialogues is a conversation between Herostratus and Demetrius of Phalerum, who both lived in the fourth century BC. Herostratus desired at any cost to be famous (hence the term 'herostratic fame') and therefore set fire to the Artemis temple in Ephesus. Demetrius, a student of Aristotle, is known for having raised 360 statues in Athens when he served as Macedonian regent in the city. In Fontenelle's book the two celebrities are discussing the contradiction between tearing down and building up, and Herostratus at one point says to Demetrius: 'The earth is similar to those large tablets, on which every human being wants to engrave his name. When these tablets are full, it is necessary to delete the already typed names to have room to write new ones. What would happen if all of the ancient monuments lasted? The moderns would not know where to place their own.' Herostratus here gives his justification of why a Parnassus necessarily must be under constant revision: for new legends to be placed on the Parnassus, old ones must necessarily be sacrificed.

If we return to the front page of *The Official Illustrated History of Manchester United 1878–2006* it's clear to see Herostratus has been at work. The picture shows a group of players and two managers, who celebrate after having secured a trophy. The persons who appear in the picture represent Manchester United's Parnassus circa 2006; they are legends, we see. The actual trophy is the Champions League trophy, and the main picture is made up of the team who in 1999 triumphed 2–1 over Bayern Munich. We see Schmeichel, who, together with Ferguson, raises the trophy, and in front of them in the lower right corner of the picture, there is Giggs and Keane. Gary Neville, Beckham and Solskjær from the 1999 team are also found worthy for the Parnassus. When it comes to exclusions, it is interesting that Scholes (who couldn't play in the final, but in more than a decade has been the brain in United's well-oiled machine), Sheringham (one of the goal-scorers) and the 'twins' Cole and Yorke were not found worthy to be included in Manchester United's 'greatest hits'. But Herostratus is, of course, right: there is not room for all.

Compared with 1999 the past is represented by Busby; located in the front row right in front Ferguson, and far right we find Edwards. In the centre of the picture at an angle behind Ferguson we find Best, just as two other pre-1999 legendary number 7s have found their way into the picture, namely Robson and Cantona, who stand next to Beckham in front to the left. On top of all of them, as if he is standing on the other giants' shoulders, there we find Charlton, a giant himself. And finally, the future is represented by Rooney.

As I said, I am wondering about the exclusion of Scholes, but some other exclusions are interesting and tell us something about Manchester United's self-image and self-understanding in 2006. It is very telling that Busby and his Babes mark a temporal border, since no pre-Babes are included. Pre-1955 players like Stafford, Roberts, Meredith, Rowley and Carey are notable by their absence. As to the Babes, prominent names such as Byrne, Pegg, Foulkes, Colman, Whelan and Gregg are missing. From the decade after Munich, there is no room for Law, Crerand and Stiles. If we go from the 1968 team and move forward to today, then Herostratus also hasn't found room for players such as Macari, McIlroy, Wilkins, Whiteside, Hughes, McClair, Bruce, Pallister, Stam, van Nistelrooy or Ferdinand.

Seen with today's glasses the absence of one player in particular catches the eye: Cristiano Ronaldo, in 2007 Player of the Year in England and Manchester United's top scorer, in 2008 Player of the Year in England, winner of the Ballon d'Or and top scorer in both Premier League and Champions League. In 2006, Cristiano Ronaldo must have felt the same way about Manchester United as the Danish author Martin Andersen Nexø felt in Italy a hundred years earlier, where you couldn't 'spit for sheer predecessors and breathe freely for legends'. With his performances in 2006/07 and 2007/08 Ronaldo, however, undertook the role as a modern Herostratus and won a place among the legends – perhaps even the most noble as the club's best player ever.

Ronaldo is a great example of how the mythology surrounding the club is subject to a permanent revision, which fits today's Manchester United and today's Manchester United fans. For there is no doubt Ronaldo would be found on the front cover if this history book had been published today. The exclusion of the club legends before the 1950s Busby Babes must be seen in the context of one of mythology's purposes, which in this case is to sell books, annex new fan territory and maintain the already conquered. In such efforts, identification and recognition play an essential role. The Champions League final of 1999 is something many of today's young football enthusiasts can relate to and Robson and Cantona are still fresh in people's minds. Busby, Edwards, Best and Charlton are also known to most. Players such as Meredith, Roberts and Rowley would be totally unknown to most, so they work poorly as promotional objects of identification.

* * *

It is also interesting to see how conscious choices of the sponsor mark the club's desire to be an exclusive, transnational brand. The national and provincial Umbro logo is put aside in favour of the international and urban Nike™, just like exclusive companies such as Audi, Pepsi™ and Anheuser-Busch, contribute as essential sponsors to brand Manchester United. The cooperation with UNICEF also reinforces the club brand and results in profits on the ethical bottom line. For a while the telecommunication company Vodafone was the club's shirt sponsor, which helped the club's global appeal. Vodafone was replaced by the American insurance company AIG, which were considered by many to be Malcolm Glazer's attempt to create a closer transatlantic connection between Manchester United and the United States. In this context, the club also entered an agreement with the baseball club New York Yankees over how the two clubs could help to promote each other's brand in Europe and in the USA. Finally, Sir Bobby Charlton's 'Theatre of Dreams' concept should also be seen as the club's attempt to create a glamorous and exclusive image. With the concept of 'Theatre of Dreams' the club doesn't hide its desire to be linked with popular culture and the entertainment industry, and at the same time the concept speaks directly to some of man's deepest needs (fairy tales, stories and entertainment) and instincts (dreams and fantasies).

There has in recent years has been an explosion in sales of merchandise and club shirts in Asia. It is not a coincidence that Manchester United's official website is available in English, Chinese, Japanese and Korean. Players such as Ji-sung Park from South Korea and Shinji Kagawa from Japan are interesting in this context, not least because many consider particularly the former to be purchased by Manchester United for the sole purpose of selling shirts in South Korea, and thus disseminate the brand Manchester United in Asia. In the case of Park and in context with the preparation of the prestigious *Manchester United Opus*, there has been printed a special Asian version signed by him, which is more expensive than the standard version. The example shows how the global market utilises national specificity in the distribution of merchandise.

* * *

There will always be differing views on the development within the world of football. After the recruitment in 2008 of Italian Fabio Capello as England manager, Sepp Blatter, FIFA's president, accused England of having violated the unwritten rule about not hiring foreigners to be in the vanguard of the national team. And because it was England, football's motherland, it gave Blatter an even worse taste in the mouth. Michel Platini, UEFA's president, expressed in 2007 his concern about the many foreign owners of English football clubs as he thought it weakened the links to local people, who are the very lifeline of a football club according to Platini.

For many of us, Blatter and Platini's opinions, in a way, call for sympathy; but they can in fact also be seen as reactionary because they are completely lacking an understanding of the transformation of the relationship between the global and the local that has been caused by globalisation. Whether one prefers sympathy or shaking one's head, the two remarks capture the tensions in the relationship between the national and international, between the local and global and between the commercial and the sporting aspects that characterise the world of football in the decades before and after the millennium.

The transformations that are now taking place within the world of football are complex. For my own part I find a lack of historical consciousness, exploitation and lack of identity problematic. However, I do welcome the internationalisation and phenomena such as the Champions League, which for many years has served up sublime football and entertainment for football enthusiasts. The problems arise when the progressive elements (internationalisation) reach extremes and, perhaps in conjunction with money, destroy identities that have been laboriously built and slowly evolving during decades. I find it wrong when Inter Milan line up eight Argentinians, two Brazilians and a Dutchman, or when Arsenal and Chelsea line up without English players. I appreciate Arsène Wenger's prodigious work of developing talents, and I enjoy Arsenal's beautiful football, but I am annoyed about the lack of English players in the team. In Chelsea's case there is neither local talent nor beautiful play to appease the circumstances. Here the lack of history, the lack of historical identity and the presence of oil money are united in an ungraceful and unsympathetic mixture. John Terry is, of course, the exception.

I salute once again the balance I think characterises Manchester United more than any other club, and which in my opinion is the main reason for the club's success on a global as well as a local level. There is a balance between the British and the international, between history and development, between sport and business, between myth and metamorphosis, and between the local and the global. A club such as Chelsea is light years away from being able to match Manchester United on immaterial resources such as image, reputation and brand. The statement in 2006 by the then executive director of Chelsea Peter Kenyon that predicted Chelsea would be the world's largest club in 2014 is, and was, wishful thinking in my opinion, as it takes many decades to build the kind of strong image that Manchester United enjoys. When Kenyon claimed the main difference between Manchester United and Chelsea was that the Londoners are not in possession of a 'Munich', it is only a small part of the truth. Chelsea not only lack a plane crash, they also lack stability and continuity regarding both managers and players, they lack an attractive football style, they lack titles, they lack glamour, they lack a new stadium and they lack identity. Admittedly, Chelsea have a story, but it has no connection to today's Chelsea.

Sport and business do not necessarily have to be polar opposites. On the contrary, much evidence suggests they are directly interdependent in both Chelsea's and Manchester United's cases. A successful business side is important to be able to attract the best players and create the best team, but success on the field is also the best prerequisite for economic progress. Chelsea are unable to manage to capitalise on symbolic values such as continuity in the same degree as Manchester United. It is precisely continuity and its strong presence that prevents constant rupture and disorder (as in the case of Chelsea). Instead Manchester United's continuity produces a constellation of 'marketable' dramatic events and myths.

As a brand, Manchester United have in fact benefitted from their reputation as a commercially well-managed company. Of course, there are also those who believe the commercial ethos undermines the sport of football. But as long as an appropriate percentage of the club's profits are channelled into the team in the form of wages, talent development and transfer funds it is difficult to argue the strategy is poor. However, this does not mean that some elements of the profit-making are not problematic and on the borderline of exploitation.

26 May 1999
The Treble

Today most look back at Manchester United's historic Treble triumph of 1999 as a natural culmination of a fantastic season. Only Bayern Munich were close to spoiling the festivities, but then Manchester United replied with a double salvo in the dying seconds of the final on 26 May 1999 at the Nou Camp in Barcelona. What most people may have forgotten is that the road to the Championship, the FA Cup and the European triumph was littered with many obstacles, setbacks and last-minute rescues.

On the one hand, Manchester United's season seems, at many times, to balance on the edge of failure and elimination, and therefore the prospect of the Treble seems undeniably an emerging fantasy as a result of time's power to alter detail. On the other hand, the miracle in Barcelona actually seems an almost *natural* consequence, as, on several occasions that season, overcoming any obstacle, the team had managed to score earthquake-triggering goals in injury time. If considered an isolated event, the final is perhaps the ultimate example of contingency being an essential feature of football – anything is possible. 'Oh, I can't believe it! I can't believe it! Football! Bloody hell', as Alex Ferguson, not particularly articulate, but to the point, expressed straight after the final. But seen as an integral part, the last one, in a chain of previous events, the final is transformed into the very embodiment of the unification of contingency and continuity.

On 9 August 1998 67,342 spectators at Wembley saw the champions and cup winners from Arsenal trounce Manchester United with a 3–0 victory in Charity Shield. I do not recall the concept of the Treble in any way crossing my mind after the match. But I do recall watching the match in a shady bar in south-west Turkey, and that it was close to having ruined the remaining part of my holiday because of this miserable effort by the Red Devils.

The season's first league match at home against written-off Leicester City gives a very good picture of what Manchester United's fans could expect in the subsequent ten months. Falling 2–0 behind, it was an uphill struggle for Manchester United, but after Sheringham in the second half redirected a long shot from David Beckham and reduced the score to 2–1, there followed an onslaught against Leicester's goal. When the stadium clock crossed the ninety-three-minute mark the score remained unchanged, though, but Manchester United were then given a free kick just outside the penalty area. Beckham ran to the ball in his distinctive perpendicular way, and Becks succeeded in directing the ball into the goal via the base of one post. The redeeming goal couldn't, however, hide the fact a single point at home against Leicester wasn't good enough.

On 16 September Manchester United played their first match in Champions League's Group D, which included Barcelona, Bayern Munich and Brøndby. The opponent this Wednesday night at Old Trafford was Barcelona, with players like Luis Figo, Rivaldo and Sonny Anderson. In the first half Beckham sent one of his many millimetre-precise crosses from the right into Giggs, and with a powerful header the Welshmen put the home team in front 1–0. A little later Beckham once more sent a diagonal cross into the penalty area, this time from deep in the opposition's half, uncharacteristically, with the left foot, and Dwight Yorke responded to the inward spinning pass with a spectacular overhead kick. Barcelona's goalkeeper pushed the ball back out, only for it to hit a Barcelona player and roll to the feet of an alert Paul Scholes, who mercilessly knocked the ball in the net to make it 2–0. In the second half, Sonny Anderson managed to reduce the deficit, and then Geovanni equalised from a questionable penalty kick. A few minutes later, Beckham brought himself into the spotlight again, when he scored to make it 3–2 from a free kick. But Barcelona were awarded another penalty, as Butt stopped a Barcelona-shot with his hand on the goal line. Butt was sent off, and Luis Enrique equalised with twenty minutes left of the match. Manchester United succeeded in keeping out Barcelona with ten men, and the 'Group of Death' kicked off in a proper way.

*   *   *

David Beckham's name is already mentioned several times in this chapter. There are primarily two reasons for this: his cross assists and his free kicks. After the 1998/99 season, which may be described as his career's best, Beckham was runner-up to Rivaldo in FIFA's crowning of 'World Player of the Year'. In fifty-five matches for Manchester United this season he scored nine goals and made an impressive twenty-three assists with his precise crossing from the right wing and his dangerous corners. From his debut in 1992 until 2003 Beckham played 394 matches and scored eighty-five goals for Manchester United, winning six

Championships, two FA Cups, a Champions League trophy and an Intercontinental Cup.

Beckham has, in my opinion, not always received the credit he deserves. The obvious reason is that his public image and iconic status tends to block the appreciation of his football qualities. His escalating media exposure during his career at Old Trafford makes even George Best resemble a media-shy hermit. One of the main reasons why the club chose to sell him was that he, as an individual, competed with Manchester United as a brand. However, another, and even better (football-related), explanation of the lack of credit is that Beckham, the football player, has often been judged on completely wrong premises. At Manchester United it was, first and foremost, an inevitable, but essentially unfair, and deeply problematic comparison with Ryan Giggs that contributed to veil Beckham's unique qualities; however, the comparisons with his predecessor Andrei Kanchelskis and his successor Cristiano Ronaldo have also played a part in this. In Real Madrid it was primarily the analogies to Luis Figo that contributed to the discrediting of Beckham.

The main problem is that from the outset, Beckham is categorised as a winger and not a midfielder. The comparisons with Giggs, Kanchelskis or Ronaldo prevent a true appreciation of Beckham's distinctive contribution to *the story of football's great innovators*, and, what is more, the comparisons never tilt in his favour as they constantly point to his shortcomings in relation to these players. Giggs is elevated to the platonic ideal of a winger, and in relation to this idea of the 'winger' Beckham is merely a simulacrum, a false pretender: he lacks speed and penetration; he is unable to dribble and 'lose' an opponent; and he rarely crosses the ball from the goal line as real wingers are supposed to do. Compared with Giggs with his sliding run and Ronaldo and his potent penetrations, Beckham is just a sedentary supporting actor.

All this is not entirely wrong, but we owe it to Beckham to define him in a positive manner – that is to say, to use David Beckham as the starting point for passing judgements on David Beckham, and from here to delineate the contours of his exceptional footballing profile. Let us begin by stating that Beckham the footballer starts from the central midfield (a position he has characterised as his favourite position). In Manchester United's youth team – the team that won the FA Youth Cup in 1992 by defeating Crystal Palace and whose backbone was the famous Class of 92 – Beckham usually (and naturally) played alongside Butt in the centre of the midfield. So, during the next couple of years, on his journey from the centre to the right, Beckham brings with him a series of distinctive characteristics of a typical engine room operator, not least ball control, stamina and hard work, but he is also an excellent tackler and supreme passer of the ball. These attributes – combined with his leadership qualities and long shot abilities – would no doubt have made Beckham into one of the world's best central midfielders if his career had unfolded in the centre of the midfield.

But on the right – a position he more or less accidentally ends up in as a result of Kanchelskis's sudden 1995 transfer – Beckham invents a completely new type of winger never before seen by the world of football, and this invention ought to secure not only his immortality, but also a permanent seat on the Parnassus of great football players. What basically characterises Beckham's new type of winger is the fusion of Euclid's geometrical and Einstein's relativistic worldview. Beckham's special shooting technique endows his crosses with a geometrical ultra-precision, but at the same time this technique means that Beckham is capable of 'bending space', that is, space is wringed out of its geometrical and three-dimensional coordinate system and into a whole new fourth dimension. This happens through the extreme curl that Beckham is able to give the ball, and which in itself makes it difficult for the opponent team to find secure anchoring points for their defensive actions, for example during a corner kick, but also when Beckham executes one of his dangerous set pieces. However, when the ball is in play, and the curled crosses are combined with Beckham's timing and his 'sense of space' – that is, when the crosses are executed halfway between the centreline and the goal line, early on and without any ambition to reach the goal line before making the cross – they are epiphanies of a new spatial dimension in which the drawing of hitherto unseen and unimaginable attacking patterns becomes possible. This long cross from deep inside the opposition's half, a condition of timing and sense of space, is the key element in Beckham's successful re-invention of the winger. When the crosses are executed from this position on the pitch and with the right timing, there exists a vulnerable space between the opposition's goalkeeper and defensive line – a space that would be minimised or downright eliminated if the crosses were executed from the goal line. However, midway between the halfway line and goal line is not enough, because if the crosses from this chosen position were only executed with Euclid's foot, the defenders could easily deal with them. However, when they are executed with a combination of geometrical precision and relativistic curl they become a paralysing blow in the opponent's solar plexus: the defenders cannot meet these crosses straight on, instead they have to move backwards into the vulnerable space; the attackers, in contrast, have the advantage of being able to meet the crosses more directly and with their front towards goal. In that sense, Beckham is granted what only very few players are granted, namely the privilege to add new pages to football's ABC. Those pages are all about timing, curled crosses and this precision of positioning.

* * *

During the season's many goal flurries Peter Schmeichel announced the current season was his last for Manchester United. Peter Schmeichel is a legend at Manchester United. He is, together with Edwin van der Sar, the best goalkeeper the club has ever had. Cantona was perhaps the alchemist who transformed the club into pure gold after his arrival in November 1992, but Schmeichel had at this time already inoculated the team with a rigorous winning mentality and competitiveness. From day one his performances between the posts meant that a crucial self-confidence had spread to the rest of the team. With his arrogant and antagonistic nature the great Dane simply seemed to be born with a Manchester United shirt on.

Schmeichel's strength was first and foremost his ability to intimidate the attackers in advance. This ability was inextricably linked to the arrogant and antagonistic nature, but it was exacerbated by his sheer size, which made the goal smaller for the attacker. His reflexes were another strength, one that came from his past as a handball goalie, and which made him a phenomenon on the goal line. Furthermore, he also dominated the penalty area like no other keeper before or after him, and despite his size he was also incredibly agile. And we must not forget Schmeichel's throws, which were both long and precise, and which often served as foundations for counter-attacks and subsequent goals. Schmeichel was therefore not just a defensive bulwark, but a major component in Manchester United's feared counter-attack machine. The title harvest says it all: in eight years he played 398 games, scored a single goal and had a record 'clean sheet' ratio of 42 per cent for Manchester United. Peter Schmeichel won the English championship five times, the FA Cup three times, the League Cup once, Charity Shield four times, the Super Cup once and Champions League once. In addition, in 1992 and 1993 he was named the world's best goalkeeper and won the European Championship with Denmark in 1992.

*　*　*

But we shouldn't forget Camp Nou on 25 November 1998, when Barcelona, after two defeats to Bayern Munich, have the knife at their throat against goal-seeking Manchester United. The Catalans, who are favourites to win, apparently have no problem playing under extreme pressure, because in the first minute Sonny Anderson hammers the ball past Schmeichel to make it 1–0. Shortly after Barcelona's jump-start Yorke equalises with a shot that runs along the turf. Before half time Schmeichel saves an impudent attempt by Figo, and in the same action the Dane just manages to get the ball away from the feet of an oncoming Rivaldo, millimetres from intercepting the riposte.

Eight minutes into the second half Cole puts Manchester United 2–1 up, after he and his 'twin', Yorke, have magically combined themselves to cut through

Peter Schmeichel makes a flying save.

Barcelona's defence. The lead-up and the goal stand as the prototype of their interaction and as an example of how pure telepathy transcends football's geometry. As Keane from his position at the centre and a little to the right plays the ball diagonally forward to Yorke, he chooses to step over the ball, which continues onwards to Cole. He in turn, with a first-touch pass, sends the ball on to Yorke, who, having stepped over the ball, has turned around and is heading toward Barcelona's goal. As Yorke receives Cole's pass he sends the ball directly back to Cole, who now has set course towards the goalkeeper. The one–two combinations across the field have totally torn the Spanish defenders away from each other, and Cole can easily score against Ruud Hesp.

The telepathic communication between Manchester United's 'Glimmer Twins' is the main reason why two footballers, who individually perhaps weren't as good as the Brazilian Ronaldo, Alan Shearer or Gabriel Batistuta, were in unison transformed into the most feared attacking duo this season. Cole and Yorke could well be out of sight of each other, but they were never out of each other's minds. They were constantly on the same wavelength and had an instinctive feel for where the other was on the field. Not just in the immediate now, but also in the next second and the next again. It was perhaps the pace in their combinations that tore up defences, but the pace was very much dependent on their telepathic ability to be able to anticipate the other's movements, which left their opponents one or more steps behind. In the Cole–Yorke partnership, the dash symbolised the unbreakable connection. They were football's answer to Aristophanes' myth of origin, as it is depicted by Plato in his *Symposium*. In this famous dialogue on the nature of love, Aristophanes develops the idea that Zeus once chopped all people into two, but that we are able to retrieve out lost half and thus become whole and harmonious creatures again. It was only with Yorke's arrival at Old Trafford that Cole became a complete striker, and it was only in combination with Cole that Yorke developed his full potential.

After the exhibition of the effects of synergy, Rivaldo luckily manages to score from a free kick, when the ball's direction is corrected by the wall and thus tricks a chanceless Schmeichel. Yorke then spurns an enormous opportunity to put United in front 3–2 when, close to the goal, he heads a cross from Beckham just past one of the posts. But why not try a second time? An outward swinging cross from Beckham on the right-hand side and Yorke, throwing himself forwards, results in a third goal for the Reds. After Rivaldo has equalised to make it 3–3 with an overhead kick, the Brazilian is close to scoring again, but his long shot hits the upper post, and Schmeichel needs to produce a world-class save as Geovanni breaks through the defence alone. But here it ends, 3–3, as at Old Trafford two months previously.

The match between United and Bayern at Old Trafford on 9 December 1998 was a question of who should proceed from the group's first and second place.

The second-placed club wasn't automatically guaranteed advancement, but Manchester United were sure to advance if they managed to draw or win against Bayern. The team had rightly felt the victory had been stolen from them in Munich (2–2), first of all because of the double offside when Bayern scored their first goal, secondly because the equaliser was an unfortunate mix of Schmeichel's fumble and Sheringham's own goal, and thirdly, because the goal came so late in the match. At Old Trafford Keane put Manchester United on a winning course with a low shot from long range. But in the second half, Bayern's Hasan Salihamidzic managed to equalise making it 1–1. Two wins over Brøndby and four draws against Bayern Munich and Barcelona respectively proved sufficient to secure Manchester United access to the quarter-finals.

The two drawn second-leg matches against Barcelona and Bayern Munich coincided with a period in the league in which the team had difficulty winning, but after a home defeat against Middlesbrough shortly before Christmas, Manchester United went undefeated through the season's remaining thirty-three matches.

* * *

Manchester United started 1999 with a 3–1 victory at home against Middlesbrough in the season's first FA Cup match. Three weeks later, and after two league rounds against West Ham (4–1 at home) and Leicester (6–2 away) Manchester United face Liverpool in the FA Cup's fourth round. 54,591 spectators are at Old Trafford to witness a remarkable comeback for the Red Devils. After Michael Owen has put Liverpool in front 1–0 in the first half, Manchester United dominate the rest of the match, but Liverpool's goal seems bewitched. In the middle of the first half, Keane sends a header towards the goal, which hits the inside of the post, but Liverpool are rescued by the Stretford End's old superhero, Paul Ince, who blocks the ball on the goal line. In the second half a long shot from Keane is redirected, so instead of going into the goal it sneaks millimetres around the outside, and shortly after Keane hits the inside of the post with a bang.

Time is running out for the home team. But two minutes before the end of ninety minutes Beckham lifts a free kick into the head of Cole, and he controls the ball across the goal area to a completely free Yorke, who sends a well-deserved equaliser into the net. It is not over yet, because long into stoppage time Manchester United score once again – and guess who the goal-scorer is? That's right: Ole Gunnar Solskjær! 'An incredible comeback by Manchester United! A complete turnaround in the closing minutes of the match and Liverpool are left absolutely stunned!' the TV commentators yell. Behind 1–0, Manchester United turned the match completely upside down in the dying minutes with a double salvo and the victory goal in stoppage time is assigned to the 'Baby-Faced Assassin.' Sounds familiar? The same scenario happens again four months and two days later, and this match is remembered by most of us while the Liverpool match has slipped out of most people's minds.

But let us not be hasty. Before Solskjær at the Nou Camp concretised Friedrich Nietzsche's idea of the eternal return, there are a few eventful dramas and remarkable achievements to recount. For example, Solskjær's introduction against Nottingham Forest two weeks after the 'omen' against Liverpool. In the meantime Yorke had also ensured Manchester United received six points and first place in the league by scoring the only goal in matches against Charlton Athletic (another late winner) and Derby County. Yorke continued to build a phenomenal first season at Old Trafford as he scored two goals in the following match against Nottingham Forest, and the happy marriage to Cole was only underlined by the fact Cole copied his act. But at 4–1 to Manchester United, the time was ripe for Solskjær's entrance at City Ground. With ten minutes left of the match the Norwegian scored to make it 5–1, then 6–1, and then 7–1 and finally 8–1. Four goals in ten minutes by 'Super Sub'.

In the fifth round of the FA Cup awaited another team from the Premier League. At Old Trafford the home team won 1–0 against Fulham with a goal by Cole. The match programme now became very condensed for the Red Devils, and just three days after the victory over Fulham, Arsenal awaited at Old Trafford in a match that could decide the championship of 1999. A penalty kick was missed by Yorke in the first half. But the home team maintained the momentum, and Cole later spurned another enormous chance, when he was one-on-one with David Seaman. In the second half Nicolas Anelka put Arsenal in front 1–0 against the play. But Cole equalised to gain a well-earned point. In the dying minutes an unfortunate Yorke missed a great chance when, four yards from goal, he placed the ball past one of the posts. 1–1 and the title race was still completely open.

On 3 March 1999, Manchester United played the first quarter-final in the Champions League against Inter Milan at Old Trafford. After six minutes Beckham put a cross in to Yorke's head, and it was 1–0 to the home team. A little later Beckham repeated the move, but Cole headed past one of the posts. Beckham tried a third time and Yorke converted his cross in the same way as before, as he put United in front 2–0. In the second half, Schmeichel, vertically hanging in the air and with both arms and legs spread out, managed to block a header from a flying Ivan Zamorano with one lap. At the end of the game Schmeichel once again rescued United when Nicola Ventola cut through the defence. Francesco Colonnese slammed the riposte towards the goal, but, unfortunately for Inter, hit exactly the place in the goal where substitute Henning Berg was placed.

In Milan two weeks later, Ferguson chose a cautious approach and paired Keane and Johnsen in central midfield. Inter immediately put pressure on Schmeichel's goal and was on several occasions unlucky not to score. Zamorano felt cheated out of a penalty kick and Berg once again cleared on the line. Javier Zanetti also hit the post. In the second half Ventola finally succeeded in scoring for Inter, and United had their backs against the wall. Zé Elias was alone with Schmeichel, but missed inexplicably by sending the ball way past the goal. Instead substitute Scholes equalised to make it 1–1 after Cole's intelligent cross and thereby sent Manchester United into the semi-finals.

* * *

On 7 April 1999 Manchester United met Juventus at Old Trafford in the first semi-final of the Champions League. Juventus are slight favourites due to their busy match schedule that has brought them into the final for the last four years. This seems to be justified when the captain Conte puts Juventus in front 1–0 early in the match. Shortly afterwards the home team are lucky when Pessotto shoots slightly past a post. Manchester United are transformed in the second half, and Giggs appeals with justification, but in vain, for a penalty when a Juventus player uses his hand in the penalty area. In the scramble for possession, Scholes gets to the ball and sends it right past one of the posts, but United aren't going to give in. A little later, Keane drills a long shot in the box, but Sheringham, who grazes the shot with his head, is dubiously called offside, and the goal is ruled out. Long into stoppage time United finally equalise as Giggs knocks a drop-down ball into the roof of the net.

Fourteen days later, Filippo Inzaghi seemingly extinguishes any red hope, when in just eleven minutes he put Juventus in front 2–0. Manchester United now have to score twice at Stadio delle Alpi and at the same time keep the experienced Italian team from scoring. At first glance a utopian idea, but if there is a season in Manchester United's (and football's) history in which utopia plays a leading role, it is in 1998/99. The first building block of utopia is laid down by captain Keane, when he irresistibly rises at the near post and heads a corner from Beckham into the opposite corner of the net. The lifeline Giggs had thrown to Manchester United two weeks previously in injury time is taken up by Keane.

2–0 is a dangerous lead. With United's goal, the nervousness rises in the Juventus players because now Manchester United with one single goal can play themselves into the semi-finals on away goals. The confidence beams out of Ferguson's Red Devils, as they resolutely seek the equaliser. It falls shortly before the break as Cole, latching onto a cross from Beckham, finds his 'soul mate' Yorke in the free space between a defender and the goalkeeper. Yorke throws himself forward and heads the ball down in the corner, leaving Peruzzi without a chance. Juventus are shaken, and just a few minutes after their equaliser Yorke knocks a long shot onto the post, which contributes further to the Italians' wavering. In the second half, it is Irwin's turn to hit the post before Cole hammers the last nail in the Juventus coffin and scores to make it 3–2. Yorke is alone with Peruzzi but is tripped by the Italian keeper, and instead of giving a penalty and a red card to Peruzzi the referee plays the advantage rule. Cole rounds both Yorke and Peruzzi to send the ball into the empty goal. The match is without question one of the most impressive performances in the club's history, and Keane more than any other player embodies United's regeneration. With his opportunistic goal, he is the one to keep hope alive. Although in the course of the match Keane receives a yellow card that triggers a suspension from the final, it is he who, with a titanic effort, constantly and consistently drives his teammates forward. Keane is, however, not the only one who gets an untimely booking. Scholes also gets a yellow card and will miss the final.

In between the two semi-finals against Juventus, the team also plays two semi-finals in the FA Cup against Arsenal. The ruled-out goal in the home match against Juventus had no consequences for further advancement in the Champions League. But four days after the home match against Juventus, United once again get a goal annulled, and this time it's even more incomprehensible. The goddess of fortune doesn't seem to be a fan of Manchester United. The match ends without goals, and just three days later the two teams face each other again. As already mentioned in this book's introduction, it is 14 April 1999, and the place is Villa Park in Birmingham.

David Beckham puts Manchester United in front 1–0 in the first half with an excellent long drive and in the second half Ole Gunnar Solskjær is close to increasing the lead, but David Seaman makes a world-class save. Instead, Dennis Bergkamp equalises for Arsenal, as his long-range effort is redirected and tricks an unlucky Peter Schmeichel in the United goal. Then Schmeichel mishandles a shot from Bergkamp, which lands at the feet of Anelka, who must surely score. But fortunately for Schmeichel and United, the Frenchman has just moved into an offside position as Bergkamp fires the cannon. Then Keane makes it hard for his teammates when he receives his second yellow card, and Manchester United have to play the rest of the match one man short. In stoppage time Phil Neville fouls Ray Parlour and Dennis Bergkamp gets the chance to finally end the Treble dream from the penalty spot. He shoots hard and places the ball wide by the right-hand post. But Schmeichel saves the shot. Hope is still alive. In the second half of the re-match's extra time Ryan Giggs makes the temperature rise from absolute zero to 100°C, when he becomes match winner for Manchester United with a phenomenal solo goal. The goal inaugurates a seismic tremor that the football world rarely has seen before, and a series of aftershocks spreads all the way from Birmingham to Barcelona, where they can be felt six weeks later.

With Arsenal and Juventus defeated, Manchester United can now look forward to an FA Cup final and a European Champions final, just as they are still pursuing the Championship. In the league, Liverpool are waiting at Anfield with four games to play. This is going to be yet another dramatic evening in a dramatic season. Yorke puts Manchester United in front 1–0 when he heads in a cross from Beckham. In the second half, United are given a penalty kick when Jamie Carragher kicks Blomqvist in the stomach, and Denis Irwin cold-bloodedly puts United in front 2–0. Referee David Elleray, who controversially had disallowed a United goal in the first FA Cup semi-final against Arsenal, is now giving Liverpool a penalty kick. Øivind Leonhardsen falls in the penalty area after close combat with Blomqvist. Jamie Redknapp converts the penalty with twenty minutes left of the match. Irwin a little later receives his second booking for kicking the ball away, and the suspension doesn't only cost the full back the FA Cup final, but Manchester United will also lose 2 points. Liverpool, with less than two minutes remaining, make it 2–2. The goal-scorer is none other than Paul Ince.

Ince's goal means Arsenal overtake United in the league. When the Red Devils defeat Middlesbrough 1–0 away and Arsenal lose 1–0 to Leeds at Elland Road, the two teams find themselves level. But the Gunners have played thirty-seven matches and United only thirty-six. United's goal difference is plus 42 and Arsenal's plus 41. With a victory away against relegation-threatened Blackburn, Alex Ferguson's men can more or less secure the Championship, while Brian Kidd's team needs a victory to stay in Premier League. The match ends 0–0, thus leaving everything open for United until the last league game on 19 May 1999.

On this day Tottenham visit United and a victory will, no matter the result of the match between Arsenal and Aston Villa, bring the championship back from Highbury to Old Trafford. Les Ferdinand gives the majority of the 55,189 supporters at Old Trafford an early scare when he scores for Spurs. The away team are in front 1–0, but scares, setbacks and hard conditions are an everyday occurrence for the United fans. In the minutes after the goal Scholes is close to equalising twice, but Ian Walker saves superbly. Beckham spurns a huge opportunity when he heads the ball over the top from close range but gets revenge shortly after when, from a sharp angle, he curls the ball into the net to put United back on track. In the second half, and just three minutes after entering the match from the bench, Andy Cole lobs the ball over Ian Walker and secures Manchester United's fifth Championship in seven years.

At Wembley on 22 May 1999 Manchester United face Newcastle in the FA Cup final. Ferguson's initial master plan is, however, in pieces after just two minutes when Keane is injured. But instead of replacing Keane with a midfielder, Ferguson introduces Sheringham and rearranges the team. The gamble pays off within a few minutes as Sheringham scores an excellent goal, after he links up well with Scholes. In the second half, the roles are reversed when Sheringham serves the ball up for Scholes, who knocks it into the net with his left leg. End result: 2–0, and the club's third double is in the bag.

∗ ∗ ∗

Camp Nou, Barcelona, on 26 May 1999. The year's Champions League final is played out between Manchester United and Bayern Munich. Manchester United have to do without two of their central midfielders, the captain Roy Keane and the conductor Paul Scholes, through suspension. Alex Ferguson is therefore forced to rearrange his midfield pieces. Nicky Butt is the obvious choice as one of the replacements as Butt has played as often as Scholes.

Possible partners to Butt are Ronny Johnsen and David Beckham. Ferguson chooses the latter and teams up Johnsen with Jaap Stam in central defence. It's good logic to choose Beckham over Johnsen as Butt's partner as both Butt and Johnsen have strong defensive qualities, and centrally Manchester United might be short on creativity. Moving Beckham to central midfield from the right wing must not have been an easy decision for Ferguson, though. On numerous occasions, crosses from Beckham on the right wing have led to United goals, and by moving Beckham Ferguson actually removes United's best attacking weapon. The obvious replacement for Beckham on the right of midfield is either Solskjær or Phil Neville, but Ferguson instead chooses to place Ryan Giggs on the right side and lets Jesper Blomquist play on the left. The attack consists of Andy Cole and Dwight Yorke, while the backs consist of Gary Neville and Denis Irwin. In the goal we find Peter Schmeichel who, because of Keane's suspension, is captain.

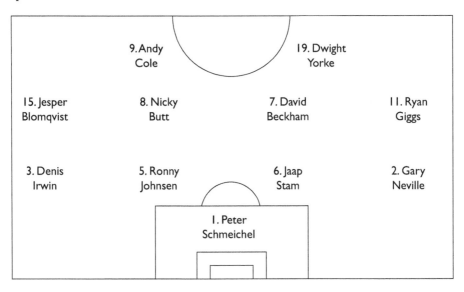

Disaster strikes after just six minutes when Manchester United go behind. A free kick from Mario Basler is redirected and Peter Schmeichel is caught on the wrong leg. The Red Devils have been behind many times this season and managed to turn things around, but as the final progresses, it's obvious the new midfield is having trouble creating chances. The fluid attacking play and the fascinating patterns, which have been the team's trademark all season, aren't materialising this evening in Barcelona, and the telepathic communication between Cole and Yorke seems to be blocked. In other words, Manchester United are not capable of lifting their play out of the predictability of geometry.

When Manchester United in the second half start to invest more in attack it unavoidably leaves holes at the back. Mehmet Scholl hits the post after having lobbed the ball over Schmeichel, and in the eighty-fourth minute, Carsten Jancker scissor-kicks the ball onto the crossbar. But from the eighty-seventh to the eighty-ninth minute United produce four good chances. First Solskjær creates a chance for Sheringham by passing on the ball with his heel, but Sheringham doesn't place his shot out far enough to pass Kahn. Then Yorke heads across, but Sheringham misses the ball by millimetres. Yorke then completely misses a cross from Neville and finally Giggs sends a cross into the head of Solskjær, but it isn't a problem for the keeper. The clock says 88:10, and one of the English commentators says: 'I think they'll win this. They are going to win it.' His partner exclaims: 'They are creating chances for fun now.'

When the match passes the ninety-minute mark there are just three minutes of stoppage time to play. The Red Devils are still behind 1–0, but they win a corner kick in their left side. Beckham places the ball and gets ready to execute the corner kick, but waits for Schmeichel to reach the penalty area and then he kicks the ball towards the great Dane who, right in front of the goal, jumps but misses the ball. But his presence creates panic in the Bayern defence and when they try to clear it, it ends up at the feet of Giggs who is placed right outside the penalty area. With his right foot he aims an instinctive shot towards Oliver Kahn's goal, and Sheringham reacts just as instinctively when, close to goal, he redirects the ball into the net by one of the posts. The time is on 90:35 and Manchester United have equalised Bayern Munich's lead in stoppage time.

When a minute later Beckham once again sends a corner kick into the penalty area, Schmeichel stays back. However, Sheringham meets Beckham's perfect cross by the near post and from here sends it across the goal area, where another substitute, Ole Gunnar Solskjær, is perfectly placed. Solskjær reacts impulsively and gets his foot on the ball and directs it into the roof of the net. The time is 92:18 and Manchester United are suddenly 2–1 in front.

After ninety-three minutes and thirty-three seconds Pierluigi Collina blows the final whistle and Manchester United have miraculously turned the match around. On the field, German players, grown-up men, are scattered around and

Champions League triumph at the Camp Nou, 26 May 1999, after the most dramatic of comebacks ever.

tears flow from many of them in sheer disbelief. In the stands 45,000 are distraught and the other 45,000 are joyous. Unashamedly, I admit that I myself cried tears of joy watching this historic final, and the tears still sometimes come when I re-watch the goals.

Both Manchester United goals are examples of what Karl Heinz Bohrer has called 'the transformation of geometry to energy, that explosion in the penalty area, which makes one crazy with happiness'. If Manchester United throughout the match had trouble transcending the pure and simple geometric – among others because (1) the Cole–Yorke telepathy didn't work, but also because (2) Giggs wasn't able to make his normal defence-splitting runs from left to right, and because (3) Beckham in the middle is more a Euclid than an Einstein – then both Sheringham's and Solskjærs's goals are like explosions of pure energy, leaving Bayern Munich's organisation defenceless. The discharges of pure energy are the culmination of both accumulated defiance and sheer determination, and they are Manchester United's last way out on an evening, when their usual geometry-transcending strategies don't work. Alex Ferguson expresses it this way after the match: 'A manager can talk about tactics, but if the players can't bring that inner beast out of them, then he's wasting his time. Well, they've got that beast inside them and found it when it mattered.' Tactics and geometry are football as craftmanship and intellectual practice. It's the inner beast, telepathy, the bending of space, timing, the actualisation of the virtual space, the destabilising dribbling and so on, that make football into an existentialist gesture – that is, into art.

6 August 2003
The Portuguese connection

The big question in the summer of 1999 for Manchester United was whether the team was still hungry for success, or whether the Treble in May was enough for the players. Another pressing question was who should/wanted to/would be capable of taking over after Peter Schmeichel. The answer to this complicated second question are as follows: Australian Mark Bosnich should and wanted to, but wasn't capable of replacing Schmeichel; the Dutchman Raimond van der Gouw should therefore replace Schmeichel, and he also wanted to, but, like Bosnich, he wasn't capable of taking over from the great Dane. Bosnich was simply not in possession of a sufficiently tough psyche needed for life at Old Trafford. Van der Gouw was a fine goalkeeper, but on an impossible mission – that is, taking over from a legend that is still today considered as the best goalkeeper in United's history. With regard to the first question, the answer given by an almost unchanged Manchester United team sounded like this: the English Championship was won again with 91 points and a record lead of 18 points over Arsenal, and the team also won the Inter-Continental Cup in Tokyo with a 1–0 win over Palmeiras from Brazil, thanks to a goal from Roy Keane.

Roy Keane had been head chef behind the unforgettable three-course menu in 1999, but the 1999/2000 season was perhaps his best of all. He was named Player of the Year in 2000 both by the PFA and FWA. From 1992 to 2005, Keane played 480 matches and scored fifty-one goals for Manchester United, and from 1997 he was the club's captain. Alex Ferguson has repeatedly characterised the Irish captain as the best, most important and most influential player that he has worked with during his long reign at Old Trafford. Keane could do it all. He could shoot, he could tackle, he could head, he could pass – and he was always playable. His most important characteristic, however, was his winner instinct, which made him an extremely inspiring captain, and Ferguson's alter ego. His perfectionism, passion and uncompromising attitude helped lift his teammates, and his warlike posture often scared away opponents with delicate souls. No one more than Roy Keane incarnated the balance between *agon* and *arête* that characterises Manchester United.

When Keane left the club in November 2005 under high drama, one of the main reasons for his shock exit was an interview he had recently given to MUTV. The interview has been censored as Keane, in unambiguous terms, is supposed to have criticised the conditions at the club, in particular the squad's declining quality and Carlos Queiroz's increasing responsibility and tactical influence. The interview is a clear example of Keane's uncompromising temper and perfectionism. It was precisely these qualities that, in more than twelve years, made him Alex Ferguson's extended arm on the field, but which now also forced the Scot to sell his Irish captain. Keane in all likelihood did something unforgivable in the interview, namely breaking Ferguson's code of conduct to never to criticise the club, the players or the coaches in public, but most of the people with some kind of relationship to Manchester United were at that time inclined to agree with Keane in his criticism.

* * *

In the Champions League, mighty Real Madrid awaited in the quarter-finals. With a 0–0 at Santiago Bernabéu, Manchester United secured a reasonable starting point for the return match at Old Trafford. But in Manchester, Roy Keane gave the Spanish team the lead with an own goal midway through the first half, and when Rául scored twice early in the second half – who doesn't remember Fernando Redondo's solo run, pirouette and cross for one of Rául's goals? – the match seemed settled. Manchester United managed to send a clear signal that perseverance was still one of the team's main qualities, as first Beckham and then Scholes pulled back goals for the home team, but in spite of a tremendous pressure on the Madrid goal they couldn't turn the match around.

In the summer of 2000, Alex Ferguson bought Fabien Barthez from Monaco, the French national team's goalkeeper. He quickly became a fan's favourite due to his charismatic personality, his eccentric play and his amazing reflexes. Barthez played an awesome first season for Manchester United when the club won its third championship in a row (and its seventh in nine years).

This season was Teddy Sheringham's last for Manchester United, but what a season, and what a goodbye to the club in whose history he will always be inscribed because of his goal and flick-on in the dying seconds of the Champions League final of 1999. Sheringham ended his stay at Old Trafford as the club's top scorer with twenty-one goals and, like Keane the year before, he was named Player of the Year by both the FWA and PFA. Although Sheringham turned thirty-five in the spring of 2001, his age didn't show. The Englishman was equipped with one of the best football brains in the Premier League. But why did Ferguson choose to part with a player just named Player of the Year? Besides Sheringham's advanced age, the main reason was the arrival of a Dutch goal machine in the summer of 2001, as well as Ferguson's considerations about changing his game concept.

* * *

The goal machine's name was Ruud van Nistelrooy, whom Alex Ferguson had been head-hunting for years, and who had actually already signed a contract with Manchester United in April of 2000. But back then van Nistelrooy's transfer was cancelled as a result of a cruciate ligament injury. Ruud van Nistelrooy cost Manchester United £19 million, but the Dutchman wasn't this summer's most expensive purchase. Ferguson also bought the Argentine midfielder Juan Sebastián Verón for £28 million from Lazio. Both players were purchased to enhance Manchester United's chances in Europe.

The last two years of quarter-final defeats to Real Madrid and Bayern Munich had convinced Ferguson that Manchester United had to develop a more flexible and continental playing style. 'When we won the European Cup, we won it because we had a great front two of Andy Cole and Dwight Yorke who scored nineteen goals between them in Europe. Next season we lost games because we tried to play the same way as the year before and our opponents punished us. That's when I changed it around, by adding a third midfielder', Ferguson says to Gianluca Vialli in *The Italian Job*. In reality Ferguson shifted his 4–4–2 to a 4–4–1–1. The Scottish manager had according to himself never played a 'traditional' British 4–4–2 with two attackers in line: 'I don't know why English clubs have been so fixated for years on playing the 4–4–2. I seldom play it . . . What English teams did was always predictable. It's stupid to say "you have to always have two up the top of the park." If you do that, you only have one point of attack, whereas, if you have one guy dropping off, you have two points of attack', he says to Vialli. When the attack was McClair–Hughes, McClair fell back in the field, Cantona did the same when he formed an attacking duo with Hughes or Cole, and it was the same for Cole and Yorke, where Cole was the frontman, while Yorke's task was to 'roam' around in the free space between the opponent team's defence and midfield.

The change may therefore not so much have been in the formation as in the choice of player types and in having more opportunities and thus more flexibility. With the purchases of van Nistelrooy and Verón, Ferguson's master plan was to let Scholes function as a deep-lying attacker behind van Nistelrooy. Scholes, who began his career at Old Trafford as a striker, had developed into one of England's

– and the world's – best midfielders. He had usually been playing next to Keane in central midfield, but now Ferguson planned to push him up in the room between midfield and attack, partly in an attempt to continentalise the team, partly to make room for Verón next to Keane in the engine room.

This didn't mean that Ferguson permanently abandoned the more traditional 4-4-2 set up with two strikers. But the purchases of van Nistelrooy and Verón marked the Scot's attempt to develop a new and alternative concept in order to regain the Champions League title. The elaborations and fine-tunings of this concept have since continued with the purchases of players like Louis Saha, Kléberson, Cristiano Ronaldo, Wayne Rooney, Ji-sung Park, Michael Carrick, Carlos Tévez, Owen Hargreaves, Dimitar Berbatov and Shinji Kagawa. With the arrival of these players Manchester United have, since 2001, developed a tremendous flexibility regarding formations as well as styles under Ferguson and his Portuguese assistant Carlos Queiroz (and Queiroz's work is continued today by Dutch Rene Meulensteen), and after two semi-finals and one quarter-final in six years the efforts finally bore fruit in 2008.

The arrival of Verón and van Nistelrooy was part of a rebuilding project, where the existing British style was to be grafted with continental virtues. The kind of 'all-out attack' mentality, which had characterised the team in 1999, was not only goals galore, injury time miracles and the Treble. In fact, several times during the season the team had been close to collapse in important matches. In 2000 and 2001 it had meant quarter-final defeats in the Champions League against tactically more flexible opponents. They had found a way to paralyse Manchester United's almost mythological 1999 offensive with Beckham–Keane–Scholes–Giggs in midfield and Cole–Yorke in attack.

In many ways the 2001/02 pre-season therefore was to compare with 1995/96, when Alex Ferguson replaced his first generation with his second. Then, in 1995/96, it paid off instantly when a bunch of fledglings ripened with the speed of light and secured Manchester United the championship. Ferguson's second generational change, which he began in 2001 with the purchase of van Nistelrooy and Verón, did not pay off immediately. There were several reasons for this. The first was that Ferguson's severely criticised system changed from the traditional British style of 4-4-2 to a more continental 4-4-1-1 didn't work optimally. The other reason was Verón had problems adapting to life in Manchester and the Premier League. He was never a great success at Old Trafford and only displayed his undeniable qualities (changes of pace in between soft transversal passes and explosive killer passes in depth) in glimpses.

The third reason for Manchester United's difficulties this season was the surprising sale of the defensive colossus Jaap Stam. One day Stam was in the process of slowly but surely securing a place among the legends of the club, the next day he was at the baggage carousel at Rome airport. He was astonished by football's commercial cynicism and his former manager's uncompromising attitude. The official explanation of Stam's departure was that the Lazio bid of £16 million had been too good to pass up, especially when you consider the player's dive in form and injury problems. But there was speculation about whether Stam's autobiography *Head to Head* could have played a role, because of remarks about Ferguson's alleged illegal attempts to contact Stam for the purpose of a transfer while he was still under contract to PSV. Ferguson later admitted the sale of Stam was a mistake. Stam's replacement, the Frenchman Laurent Blanc, was not the great success Ferguson had hoped him to be. The Scot had previously attempted to bring the French World and European Champion to Old Trafford. But in 2001 Blanc was thirty-six years old and if his experience and vision still were worthy qualities, then his speed wasn't impressive.

Adding to the club's difficulties was Alex Ferguson's announcement, early into the season, that 2001/02 would be his last season as manager of Manchester United. The announcement sowed unrest among the players and made it difficult for Ferguson to maintain his usual standards of discipline. In February of 2002, he changed his mind and quickly agreed an extension of his contract with Manchester United.

2001/02 ended without titles for Manchester United. In the league, the club ended in a disappointing third place, the worst since 1991. However, there are also a few encouraging things to say in the middle of the misery. The first is a series of notable victories in the league, which bore witness to the team's continued offensive power: 4–1 at home against Everton, 4–0 at home against Ipswich, 5–3 away against Tottenham, 5–0 at home against Derby, 6–1 at home against Southampton, 4–0 away against Bolton, 4–1 at home against Sunderland, 4–0 at home against Tottenham, 5–3 away against West Ham, 4–3 away against Leeds and finally 3–0 away against Chelsea. The second encouragement was Ruud van Nistelrooy, who shot himself directly into the hearts of United's fans when, in his debut against Liverpool in the Charity Shield, he scored Manchester United's only goal. The Dutchman continued to bomb goals in his first season at Old Trafford, thirty-six in total, and van Nistelrooy crowned a superb first season with the PFA's Player of the Year award.

The season's third encouragement came in the Champions League, where Manchester United reached the semi-finals. An achievement indicating Ferguson's 'continental turn' was beginning to work. In the semi-final Manchester United were favourites against the German team Bayer Leverkusen. It is possible Ferguson's new continental concept had not been completely successful in the Premier League and that Verón had trouble convincing in the league. But both game concept and Verón seemed to work in Europe. On the way to the semi-finals, the Argentinian had contributed four goals. On 24 April 2002, 66,534 spectators watched Manchester United play out a 2–2 draw against

Bayer Leverkusen at Old Trafford. A disappointing result that still left the Red Devils with a good chance of further advancement, though. But the two away goals to Leverkusen proved to be decisive, as the match in Germany ended 1–1, after Roy Keane had put Manchester United in front 1–0.

*   *   *

In the summer of 2002 Alex Ferguson hired Carlos Queiroz as his assistant, a position that had been vacant since Steve McClaren's departure in 2001. With Queiroz, Manchester United got a cosmopolitan face to complement Ferguson's Scottish dock-worker one. His arrival was also a clear indication of Ferguson's efforts to make Manchester United more competitive in Europe.

Carlos Queiroz is Portuguese, but was born and brought up in the Portuguese colony of Mozambique in Africa. Besides England, his coaching career has also led him to South Africa, Japan, the United States, Portugal, the United Arab Emirates and Spain. Queiroz is perhaps primarily known for being the discoverer of 'the golden generation' in Portugal in the early 1990s; a generation of players such as Luis Figo, Rui Costa and Fernando Couto. Queiroz is also a coach with experience in the 4–4–1–1, 4–2–3–1, 4–3–2–1, 4–1–4–1 and 4–3–3 formations. This tactical flexibility, and his merits in the development of young Portuguese players, were the main reasons for Ferguson to bring Queiroz to Old Trafford. The Portuguese coach has since played a major role in the development of Manchester United's hybrid flamboyant football style.

The second new face in the club this summer was the defender Rio Ferdinand. Manchester United once again set a British transfer record when they bought Ferdinand from Leeds United for £30 million. Since the partnership between Bruce and Pallister, Ferguson had struggled to get his defensive set-up hermetically sealed. In Rio Ferdinand, Alex Ferguson saw the team's long-term defensive centre of gravity, and he saw correctly. Ferdinand is technically brilliant and endowed with an impressive physical stature. He is tall but has excellent balance. He heads well and is an excellent distributor of the ball. He is a leader on the field, strong in close combat and fast. The only weakness Ferdinand previously had fought with were his momentary lapses of concentration. But during the course of his first year at Old Trafford he overcame these and developed into one of the world's absolute best central defenders. In his first four years at the club Ferdinand, however, suffered under changing partnerships. But with the arrival of Nemanja Vidic in January 2006 Ferdinand finally got his ideal partner and Ferguson his ideal fit.

In 2002, Manchester United won their eighth championship in eleven years after a fluctuating autumn and an irresistible spring. Ruud van Nistelrooy improved his harvest of goals from the previous season, as he scored a total of forty-four goals – only two away from emulating Denis Law's club record of 1963/64. In the League Cup Manchester United lost disappointingly 2–0 to Liverpool in a match that the Merseysiders dominated from start to finish. In the FA Cup's fifth round on 15 February 2003 the team faced their rivals from Arsenal at Old Trafford. Manchester United lost the match 2–0 and in the dressing room after the match Ferguson was so furious over this toothless effort that he kicked a football boot in a fit of temper. Unfortunately for Beckham the boot struck him over one eye and United's icon needed several stitches. Later Ferguson characterised the episode as 'a freak accident', but consciously or not it symbolises the collapse of the relationship between Alex Ferguson and David Beckham.

In the quarter-finals of the Champions League, Manchester United met the Spanish champions Real Madrid for the second time in three years. This year, the Champions League final was to be played at Old Trafford and many saw the clash between Manchester United and Real Madrid as being the moral final. Both teams had played great football this season and Manchester United's performance in both Champions League and Premier League demonstrated this. Ferguson's work with a more flexible and continental style had started to bear fruit. Van Nistelrooy's forty-four goals and Scholes's twenty goals indicated the partnership worked, and Ferguson and Queiroz's 4–4–1–1 formation didn't only work in Europe, but also in the domestic tournaments.

The first quarter-final was played at the Santiago Bernabéu in Madrid, where the home team dominated largely and got ahead 3–0. First Figo scored with a gem of a strike from the left-hand side, and then Scholes lost the ball just outside of United's penalty area and Raúl immediately punished Manchester United by scoring to make it 2–0. In the second half Raul scored his second goal, as from 20 metres he dumped the ball down into the corner to make it 3–0 for Real Madrid. Ruud van Nistelrooy handed Manchester United a lifeline when he pulled a goal back at the end of the match.

At Old Trafford on 23 April 2003, 66,708 spectators witness a historic match against Real Madrid that ranks as one of the tournament's best ever. Manchester United line up in the formation shown overleaf:

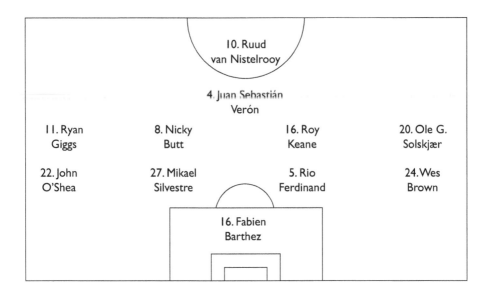

The advantage Manchester United's away goal may have given them is quickly punctured by the Brazilian Ronaldo, who fires a clinical cannonball to put real Madrid in front 1–0. The scoring's abruptness has a paralysing effect. The goal is like one large black hole, sucking sound and noise at Old Trafford into it. Barthez, by the way, doesn't look too good in the goal, and many people afterwards think the French keeper has signed his own redundancy notice with his performance in this match. A little later in the first half, the majority of spectators explode as Solskjær serves the ball to van Nistelrooy who, close to the goal, equalises. The excitement is back, and with United's goal machine in top form, you never know what may happen. But in the second half, the Galácticos play games with United's defence. First Figo hits the crossbar, and then Ronaldo scores his second goal after a Real Madrid power play demonstration in front of United's penalty area. Manchester United soon answers back as a cross ball from Verón hits Ivan Helguera and ends up in the net to make it 2–2.

Just as United's fans think the Red Devils' comeback has forced the White Angels to their knees, Ronaldo fires another thunderbolt and puts Real in front 2–3. Manchester United now have to score four times to advance – apparently a hopeless task. As Beckham, who was controversially benched but now comes on as a substitute, equalises to make it 3–3, then I actually believe it is possible. This is quite simply the kind of miracle that Manchester United is capable of. And if not in a game between Manchester United and Real Madrid when the score is 2–3 with a quarter of an hour left of the game, when would one have a gut feeling that the drama might actually end 6–3 to United? The feeling intensifies as Beckham scores his second goal to put Manchester United in front 4–3. Another foul just outside the penalty area, but Beckham has no more miracles up his sleeves this evening, and the United machine runs out of steam. The historic evening was one of Beckham's last at Old Trafford in a Manchester United jersey. In the summer of 2003 Manchester United sold him to Real Madrid for £25 million, though for a long time Barcelona had been favourites to get his signature. Beckham left the Old Trafford family and the father figure Ferguson reluctantly, but the relationship between Becks and the manager had deteriorated badly. As already indicated, Alex Ferguson also parted with Barthez. The third victim of the cleansing was Verón, who ended up at Roman Abramovich's and Claudio Ranieri's Russian-revolutionised Chelsea.

To many Manchester United fans the parting of Barthez, Verón and Beckham came as a bit of a shock. At least it did for me. The team had, despite everything, just ensured the club their eighth championship in eleven years. Their performance in the Champions League, in particular the two victories over Juventus and the home match against Real Madrid, had shown the team was close to regaining the trophy. Beckham had, in the last eight years, made the position at the right of midfield his own. In the last six years he had even carried the legendary number 7 jersey. Who could possibly fill the space after him, and who was worthy enough to wear number 7?

Speculation buzzed in the summer of 2003, and after the departure of three high-profile stars there was a massive demand from the fans about bringing new world stars to Old Trafford. Manchester United and Alex Ferguson had set their eyes on Paris Saint Germain's Ronaldinho as the club's new attacking trump card. In Barcelona, the newly elected president Joan Laporta had promised to bring Beckham to the Nou Camp, so when Beckham instead signed an agreement with the rivals from Real Madrid, Barcelona and Laporta were obliged to look around for alternative options. The Catalan telescope pointed towards Ronaldinho, and United suddenly had competition in a transfer most had seen as completed.

In the end Ronaldinho went to Barcelona and Manchester United were left with a long face, and without a new number 7. I still remember the disappointment, when in a newspaper in Rome I read about Ronaldinho's switch to Barcelona. Ronaldinho was perhaps the only person, who could have replaced David Beckham at Old Trafford, or so I thought. The allegation of hesitation and stinginess from Paris Saint Germain's management against Manchester United only rubbed salt in the wound. You could say Beckham was indirectly responsible for the fact Ronaldinho ended up at the Nou Camp instead of Old Trafford. Was this the irony of fate?

The summer offered a number of purchases for Manchester United, but none of them could soothe the fans' impatience for some stardust. Ferguson bought the unknown goalkeeper Tim Howard from New York Metro Stars. He signed the midfielder and World Cup winner José Kléberson from Brazilian

Atlético Paranaense, and in Nantes the club picked up defensive midfielder Eric Djemba-Djemba, a Cameroon international. Finally Ferguson bought the French attacker David Bellion from Sunderland. None of the purchases were a success except Howard, who impressed in his first season, where he was named Premier League's best goalie. But much like Barthez, a 'mistake' in a Champions League match, this time against José Mourinho's Porto in 2004, cost Howard his Old Trafford career.

* * *

On 6 August 2003 the club played a friendly match against Sporting Lisbon at the opening of their new home, Estádio José Alvalade. United lost the match 3–1, but on their team Sporting had a unique talent and a future golden star, the eighteen-year-old Cristiano Ronaldo, and he played so flamboyantly and technically brilliantly that on the plane home, several of United's established stars urgently asked Ferguson to buy the wonderboy. Ferguson was indeed impressed with Ronaldo and acted quickly. He bought the Portuguese for £12.6 million and immediately assigned him the magical number 7.

My first reaction when I heard about the transfer was something along the lines of 'He can't bloody well be named Ronaldo'! The boy could be as talented as he liked, but there was only one Ronaldo. He was Brazilian, and only three and a half months previously he had slammed three goals in behind Barthez at Old Trafford thus putting an end to the English team's European dreams. Today, ten years later, there is in a way still only one Ronaldo, but he is Portuguese and his first name is Cristiano, and he alone brought the Theatre of Dreams to life again.

The purchase of a raw and edgy talent wasn't really what Manchester United's fans wanted. The summer of 2003 was clearly a watershed year as Ferguson didn't only part with a goalie, who had won the French and the English championship, the European Championship and the World Cup, he also parted with two world-class midfielders. But in themselves these kind of ruthless actions were not unusual for Ferguson. What made the whole thing sad and seminal was that he had neither talent from the academy ready to jump in at this time, nor had he managed to buy replacements to match the three stars going out. The summer of 2003 began a period of three years, where Manchester United went through their worst crisis since 1991. The difference was that the crisis back then wasn't a surprise. But from 2003 to 2006 the crisis followed in the wake of eleven years of total dominance in the Premier League and seven years with a guarantee of at least a quarter-final spot in Europe.

Much could perhaps have been different in 2003/04 if Rio Ferdinand had carried out the doping test he so notoriously forgot to do on 23 September 2003.

The omission ended up costing Ferdinand eight months' suspension effective from 1 January 2004. For some, this was a much too severe punishment, for others too merciful. With Ferdinand on the team Manchester United had won the Charity Shield against Arsenal, and they had won five of the six group matches in the Champions League. In the league, the team's form also made the fans forget all about Barthez, Beckham and Verón. However, with Ferdinand suspended the Manchester United engine stuttered all the way through the spring.

Ferguson reinforced the team in January when he bought the attacker Louis Saha from Fulham, and the Frenchman was an instant hit. He made his debut with a goal in the 3–2 home victory against Southampton and then scored two goals in the 4–3 away win against Everton. Saha's season was, however, ruined by injuries, and injuries have been the attacker's Achilles' heel ever since. Arsenal played for their part a historic season, where they went undefeated, finishing 15 points ahead of Manchester United in third place. In the Champions League Manchester United, as already mentioned, lost to the subsequent winners from Porto as Tim Howard didn't manage to hold on to a Portuguese free kick in the dying minutes of the second leg.

The season's positive history was written in the FA Cup. On April 3rd 2004, just six days after drawing 1–1 at Highbury in the league, Manchester United and Arsenal faced each other once again. At Villa Park and with a brilliantly collective performance marked more by *agon* than *arête*, Manchester United won the match, which many viewed as the true final, 1–0. In the final at the Millennium Stadium in Cardiff, 71,350 spectators witnessed a one-sided performance when the favourites from Manchester United brushed aside Millwall from the Championship 3–0.

* * *

The purchase of Cristiano Ronaldo in 2003 didn't only mark the beginning of a new Manchester United generation, it also signalled the beginning of the club's Portuguese–Brazilian connection. This connection was already under way with the appointment of Carlos Queiroz in 2002, and the formalisation of a cooperation with Queiroz's former club Sporting Lisbon. But with the arrival of Cristiano Ronaldo the rebuilding of Ferguson's third generation was kicked off.

Compared to the first generation, with warriors like Hughes, Ince and Bruce, and with the defiant second generation, with players like Schmeichel, Keane and Beckham, Ferguson's third generation was less British and more Portuguese–Brazilian in its playing style. The English–Portuguese and British–Brazilian hybrid was in 2007 reinforced with the arrival of the Portuguese Nani and the Brazilian Anderson. Portuguese and cosmopolitan Queiroz, who after just one

Wayne Rooney scores the fifth goal of the match and completes his debut hat-trick at Old Trafford, 2004.

season as head coach at Real Madrid came back to Old Trafford in 2004, was a crucial factor in both deals, and Ronaldo's presence also helped to persuade Nani and Anderson to replace the Portuguese sun and heat with rainy Manchester.

Manchester United has also maintained a strong British–English component in the team. What first and foremost characterises the English players in Manchester United's team today is that they are technically better than their English predecessors. This was and is the case for players like Ferdinand, Carrick, Hargreaves, Rooney and Cleverley, all of whom have a distinct Britishness about them. But they are also more elegant and technically sound players than, for example, Pallister, Keane, Ince, Stapleton and Robson were in their time.

* * *

The most controversial and talked about transfer in the summer of 2004 was Manchester United's purchase of the eighteen-year-old attacker Wayne Rooney from Everton for £25 million. Rooney was England's new wonderboy, who during the recent European Championship had managed to score four goals in three matches before an injury stopped the comet. That summer Newcastle were very close to winning Rooney's signature, but just a few hours before the transfer deadline expired, Rooney signed a contract with Manchester United. Wayne Rooney made his debut on 28 September 2004 in a Champions League match at Old Trafford against Fenerbahçe. There, 67,128 spectators watched Rooney celebrate his debut with a fairy tale hat-trick. United won the match 6–2.

Wayne Rooney embodies today's Manchester United. Although he is a Scouser, he is from a working-class background in the industrial north-west of England. This makes him a natural successor to players like Duncan Edwards and Bobby Charlton. On the field he also embodies a number of typical Manchester United virtues: an admirable work ethic which means that he always sacrifices himself for the team; he is aggressive defensively, opportunistic and direct in his offensive actions; finally, he is technically excellent. In many ways he reminds me of Mark Hughes, and like Hughes one of his trademarks is his spectacular goals. He is a more mobile forward than Hughes, and one of his signature moves is the long raids he makes from midfield, where his drive with the ball is irresistibly assisted by something which almost reminds us of an inner anger. To me Rooney only has three weaknesses: he is not selfish enough; his waste percentage in obvious scoring opportunities is too large; and his lifestyle seems to spoil his focus on football and the seriousness that it requires.

At his arrival in 2004 Rooney symbolised the future of Manchester United – for a number of years together with Ronaldo, before the Portuguese was sold to Real Madrid. They both arrived at the club as eighteen-year-olds and have each

THE PORTUGUESE CONNECTION

contributed to the fascinating balance which I characterised in the introduction as the main reason for the club's unmatched attraction. Rooney is English, aggressive and hard-working; Ronaldo is Portuguese, elegant and glamorous. They represent the national and the international, the local and the global, the collective and the individual.

If the big topic of conversation at Old Trafford in the summer of 2004 was the arrival of the 'assassin-faced baby' Wayne Rooney, then it was the arrival of 'The Special One' José Mourinho at Stamford Bridge, who pulled the big headlines in London. With Mourinho at the helm, Chelsea's team set a new standard for what was demanded in order to win the Premier League. Manchester United compensated for their poor shape in the league with three fine cup runs, but ended the season without any silverware.

In Manchester, the spring and summer of 2005 were not so much influenced by the usual transfer talk as the rumours of a takeover of United. American Malcolm Glazer from Florida, owner of, among others, the NFL club Tampa Bay Buccaneers, had already started buying shares in Manchester United in 2003. On 12 May 2005, the American succeeded in obtaining the share majority, and four days later Glazer reached 75 per cent, which allowed him to sign off Manchester United on the stock exchange and transform the club from a public limited company to a privately owned company. This happened formally on 22 June, eight days after Glazer had increased his shareholding majority to 97.3 per cent. On 28 June he reached 98 per cent, which then allowed him to buy up the remaining 2 per cent. At this time Manchester United was valued at almost £800 million.

Malcolm Glazer's buy led to a number of controversies between the club and its fans, not only because the club was now owned privately and in American hands, but especially because Glazer had to run up a giant debt in order to achieve control of the club, and the fans were afraid that it would affect the transfer budget. Even Sir Alex Ferguson commented critically during the course of the potential take over. At first the fans' concern about the transfer budget seemed to be confirmed, but since then Manchester United has invested heavily in the team. They have also invested in the expansion of Old Trafford's capacity, which now holds 76,212 spectators. In addition, the new owners seem to have an understanding of the club's long history. From the beginning they said both Alex Ferguson and David Gill were part of their future plans.

In the summer of 2005 Manchester United only bought the Dutch goalkeeper Edwin van der Sar and the South Korean winger Ji-sung Park. Edwin van der Sar was exactly the goalkeeper Alex Ferguson had been looking for since Peter Schmeichel left the club in 1999. In January 2006, Alex Ferguson secured an additional two players when he bought the Serbian centre back Nemanja Vidic from Spartak Moscow and the French left back Patrice Evra from Monaco. After a difficult start, they established themselves as key players in the team.

The 2004/05 season had been disappointing, and Manchester United were left without a single trophy. 2005/06 was in many ways worse than the previous season, although this campaign brought a single title, namely the League Cup trophy. In the league Chelsea continued to dominate and set the pace, and even though United did well they ended in second place, eight points below Chelsea. Given the circumstances, it was quite surprising the Red Devils were able to infuse a little excitement into the tournament in the spring with a series of nine consecutive victories, but when it finally counted, they lost 3–0 at Stamford Bridge in the season's third from last match. And when I say 'under the circumstances', then I'm referring to Roy Keane's departure in January 2006 after his famous diatribe against named players and coaches in an MUTV interview in autumn 2005, but also to Alan Smith's horrendous injury in an FA Cup match at Anfield against Liverpool when he broke his leg in two places. Then there was Paul Scholes's mysterious eye disease, which kept him out of the team for more than four months. And adding to Manchester United's woes, Ole Gunnar Solskjær's knee injury spoiled another season for the Norwegian super sub just as Gabriel Heinze's knee injury kept him out throughout the season.

The many injuries meant Ferguson tried an alternative solution in central midfield, where Giggs and O'Shea established an excellent partnership. This was essentially the foundation of United's impressive run in the league in February, March and April. The club's major problems, which the league form partially hid, stood out clearly in the Champions League, where Manchester United for the first time in nine years didn't proceed from the group stage. The FA Cup adventure also ended in the fifth round away against Liverpool. In the League Cup, however, Manchester United went all the way, as they defeated Wigan 4–0 at the Millennium Stadium. The match is perhaps best remembered for Ferguson's decision to bench van Nistelrooy.

Before the final in Cardiff there had been rumours about a collision between Ronaldo and van Nistelrooy. During a training session, the Dutchman supposedly accused Ronaldo of concentrating more on pointless tricks than on purposeful crossing. The discussion allegedly ended with van Nistelrooy saying to Ronaldo: 'run to Daddy.' 'Daddy', in this case, was not an allusion to Ronaldo's real father, who had died just a few months before, but to Carlos Queiroz who, according to the Dutchman, gave Ronaldo too much protection. Both players have since denied the incident, but whether the incident is real or not, it tells us something about the radical change that Manchester United was facing. On one hand there was the old guard, with players like Roy Keane and Ruud van Nistelrooy, who were critical of Queiroz and the 'Portuguese turn' in the club, and on the other hand there were Queiroz and Ronaldo, whose influence grew. In the spring of 2006 Keane was already gone, and in that summer van Nistelrooy was shipped out after five hugely successful years at the club.

In five seasons van Nistelrooy had played 219 games for Manchester United and scored an impressive 150 goals. With thirty-eight goals in forty-seven European matches, he holds the club record of most scored goals in Europe. The Dutchman was simply the king of the penalty area, as, with a single exception he scored all of his goals within this region. His unparalleled instinct for goal-scoring was supported by a dazzling technique and his robust physique. He had the same ability to suck the ball to him that also characterised Mark Hughes, but he could do more on his own than the Welshman could. Ruud van Nistelrooy will, because of his outstanding finishing skills and his goal ratio, always be remembered in Manchester United's history as one of the club's best strikers.

10 April 2007
A new history of the decline and fall of the Roman Empire

The historical connection between Rome and Manchester goes all the way back to the heyday of the Roman Empire. Manchester's residents even owe the Romans their name. In the year 79 AD the conquering Romans settled down in that area, which is known today as Castlefield in Manchester. In this alluring part of town, a fifteen-minute walk west of Manchester's centre, you can still see traces of the Roman fortresses. Here you can also find the excellent Museum of Science and Industry. The museum's fascination is only strengthened by its location in the buildings of the old Liverpool Road Station, the world's first railway station for passenger traffic. After their arrival the Romans built the fortress Mamucium ('breast-shaped hill'), whose name was transformed into Mancuniun. This is why today's inhabitants of Manchester are called 'Mancunians', and the town's name is likewise derived from the Roman fortress's name. But just as happened in 2007, the Roman world conquerors ended up being defeated on English soil back then.

Among historians there are disagreements as to when the Roman Empire collapsed. One possibility is the year 395 AD, when the Roman Empire was divided into a western and eastern sector. A second possibility is the West Roman Empire's break-up on 4 September 476. Finally, there are those who believe it wasn't until 29 May 1453, when the Byzantine Empire was conquered by the Ottomans, that the Roman Empire was over. Regardless of whether you support the first, second or third option, the dating uncertainty indicates the Roman descent was quite a slow and complex affair. Many centuries later, I sit in my apartment in Copenhagen and witness history repeating itself – although in a smaller scale of course – in one of football's most famous amphitheatres, Old Trafford in Manchester. On this occasion the time and date cannot be questioned, though, and the Romans' fall is in no way dragged out. It's 10 April 2007 and in barely two hours AS Roma are massacred by Manchester United.

Since the middle of the 1980s, Roma has stood in the shadow of Milan, Inter, Juventus and Lazio. But in 2006/07 they look like a team on the verge of re-creating themselves as a football super power, and experts are even talking about Roma as outsiders for the Champions League title. But on this evening, Roma's dream of a new European reign is shattered when the match ends with a scorching 7–1 defeat. The monstrous result makes Alex Ferguson characterise the match as Manchester United's biggest European performance in his time as manager of the club. The match is not only remembered for the result, but also for a number of outstanding individual performances, one of which results in Cristiano Ronaldo's international breakthrough at club level. Most of all the match is remembered because Manchester United's attacking machine on this evening in April simply embodies the claim by the German man of letters, Karl Heinz Bohrer, that 'the creative invention' cannot be reduced to 'aesthetic grammar'. By this, Bohrer suggests there are elements of the creative expression, for example, a football match, which cannot be reduced to formulas, schemas or automatisms.

* * *

Just six days prior to the match between Manchester United and Roma at Old Trafford, I, along with millions of European football enthusiasts, experience the zenith of this new 'Roman Empire'. AS Roma simply eradicate the otherwise strong Red Devils at the Stadio Olympico and are unfortunate to win only by 2–1. In addition to surprising us with a readiness to attack in numbers – an uncharacteristic quality for an Italian team – the Roman greatness also stems from the fact that Luciano Spaletti's troops practise an entirely new kind of football, which the football world has never seen before. During the match I get the feeling that I'm looking straight into football's future. What is new in Spaletti's deeply fascinating, but also demanding tactical concept is that Roma is playing a kind of 4–6–0 formation; that is, without a traditional striker. Admittedly, the graphics shows that Francesco Totti is situated on the top, but in reality his defence-spoiling 'falling deep' and his constant involvement in the play means he often ends up playing with his front to United's goal (as opposed to a more sedentary target man, who often receives the ball while he has his back to goal).

If Roma lacks the traditional front man, then their six midfielders – one defensive and five offensive – show an incredible will to run. This results in a previously unseen movement and flexibility that is impossible for Manchester United to cope with. With concepts from physics, it can be argued that a defence's primary task is entropic, that is, to ensure that a system keeps a high degree of disorder and randomness. The attack's task, on the other hand, is negentropic, that is, to create order and patterns that challenge, destabilise and override the defence's chaotic state of equilibrium. Roma's offensive is this evening a constant negentropic threat to Manchester United's entropic intentions.

In addition to the overall tactical breakthrough of 4–6–0, there's also a more visible Roman strategy that makes the match memorable. I refer to the speed with which the home team execute throw-ins, free kicks and corners. In fact, it is a quickly taken corner that leads to Roma's first goal. It then requires a world-class counter-attacking move, consisting of a defence-tearing raid by Ronaldo, a visionary Solskjær pass and a technically brilliant shot executed by Rooney, to ensure that Manchester United (with one man short for almost an hour) can travel from 'the eternal city' with an important away goal.

After the match in Rome, as a United fan, I look forward with mixed feelings to the return match just six days later. On one hand, the Giallorossis' demonstration of what the future of football is probably going to look like makes me doubt Manchester United's abilities and makes me fear that the team (or, rather, the manager) belong to the past. But on the other, the second leg is played at Old Trafford, the arena where great European nights have more or less established themselves as laws of nature. And while a thought may slip in that Alex Ferguson is 'over the hill', it helps to hear his confident words about Manchester United's impressive statistics at Old Trafford in a European context and the club's (not to say Ferguson's own) repeated ability to rise in adversity. And the team has, in fact, been playing impressively throughout the season. In the spring of 2007 there is a new optimism for the future. After three title-bare years there is much to indicate the club is finally able to defeat Roman Abramovich, José Mourinho and Chelsea.

Alex Ferguson, who has to do without Scholes, Neville and Vidic, has a surprise up his sleeve on this historic evening. In his 4-2-3-1 team line-up (see previous page), Ferguson's surprise is Alan Smith, who has been out following a double fracture of the leg in the FA Cup defeat to Liverpool on 18 April 2006.

After only ten seconds of play we get a premonition of the result, when Ronaldo, with one of his characteristic changes of pace, ghosts past three Roman midfielders. His pass in depth is not accurate enough but, by throwing himself down into a tackle and winning the ball from Christian Panucci, Smith shows why he was selected. Pace and technical ability from Ronaldo combine with drive and brawn from Smith. United have immediately shown to themselves and to the home audience that they are prepared to invest everything in the match.

After ten minutes and fifty-seven seconds Michael Carrick repays some of the £18 million that United paid for him last summer. From the right Ronaldo passes to an oncoming Carrick in the centre. Carrick, who is still running, gets control of the ball with the outside of his right foot, and without stopping his movement he punches deeply to the ball with the right inside of the foot in his next step. The ball is lifted in an arc above Doni in Roma's goal and bends out of his range, landing in the net. The goal comes quite unexpectedly and Old Trafford is ecstatic.

With a superb shooting technique supported by a balanced elegance in the moment of the shot, Carrick creates a goal out of nothing. Thought and technique come together in a dimension that transcends Bohrer's concept of grammar. If grammar is a structure in which C naturally follows B, and B naturally follows A, then Carrick's action represents a creative leap out of grammar's traditional causality. We will not find Carrick's manoeuvre described in one of Ferguson's or Queiroz's manuscripts from the training field. Carrick doesn't follow a script, but acts in relation to a suddenly emerged opportunity, which only he sees, and that intuitively. At first glance, it may seem as if Doni is misplaced, but this would be a wrong analysis. Doni is actually positioned correctly, as by moving a few metres forward he will have a better coverage of his goal. Carrick's spinned lob is a perfectly executed technical action exploiting the only weakness hiding in Doni's position: the implicit invitation to lob. Should anyone be blamed, then the Roman defence will stand guilty because of its passivity.

Sixteen minutes and forty-five seconds have been played when Smith finishes a perfect orchestrated attack composed of four first touch passes, which means that Manchester United attacks with extreme speed. It all starts with Brown in the back four, who plays the ball up to Rooney, located on the centre line on United's left side. Rooney, closely marked, lifts the ball towards the centre where Carrick gets a foot on the ball, and with a precise cross he plays it out to the left side again where a running Heinze sends it toward Giggs in the middle. Giggs here produces his first masterstroke on an evening that must be included among

Michael Carrick scores the sixth goal in the second leg of the UEFA Champions League Quarter Final against AS Roma.

his greatest. As Giggs – halfway turned towards the Roman goal, halfway towards the left side – receives the ball from Heinze he hits the ball with the inside of his left foot and thus bends it in between two Roma defenders, who are completely caught off guard by the suddenness of the pass. The defenders are standing with their backs to their own goal and suddenly have to move backwards. Smith, on the contrary, can run forward in the ball's direction, and with precision and some force he kicks the ball with his instep into the corner to the left of Doni and puts Manchester United in front 2–0. But my description doesn't do justice in temporal terms to the whole scenario: it only takes five seconds from Brown's pass until the ball streaks in behind Doni.

It is possible the build-up involving Brown, Rooney, Carrick and Heinze has to do with automatisms practised again and again at the training facilities at Carrington, but Giggs's deep pass, or rather his sense of the timing of the pass, cannot be trained. Giggs's action is geometry transformed into pure intuition, an intuition that leaves the gates of the Roman fortress wide open and actualises a space on the field, which only existed as a virtual space in the seconds before. With Giggs's timing a spatial hypersensitivity (his sense for the virtual space) is merged with the launch of a qualitatively transforming movement, in this case Smith's destabilising run in behind the Roman defence. The result is a goal whose cause is not to found in any defensive error, but in the abovementioned causality-neglecting intuition and timing.

The clock shows 18:09 as Giggs once again prepares the ground for a goal. This time the assist's addressee is Rooney. 3–0 to United, and in just seven minutes Roma have lapsed into a coma. It gets even worse for Spaletti's troops. Before the match there has been much talk about Ronaldo's excellent season and his many goals in the Premier League, but strangely enough he has not yet scored for United in the Champions League. This changes after forty-three minutes and twelve seconds. With a long pass, Giggs sends Ronaldo going on the right wing. The Portuguese takes the ball with him and cuts into the field, but instead of continuing his drift to the left and attempting a long shot with his left leg, he makes a feint move with his body that leaves Christian Chivu caught on the wrong leg and instead Ronaldo draws the ball to the right. The way is now clear for a shot with the right leg, and Ronaldo doesn't fail. He sends the ball down into the nearest goal corner with a hard, flat kick with his instep.

Cristiano Ronaldo's first goal in the Champions League is a reality. Incomprehensibly three and a half years have passed from his European debut on 1 October 2003 against Stuttgart to 10 April 2007 against Roma. Ronaldo has been phenomenal in the entire first half, like Giggs, who for the third time has been the architect behind the crucial pass. After the match Ronaldo is crowned 'Man of the Match', but Giggs isn't far behind him in terms of performance. The Welshman (with his fourth assist) and the Portuguese (with his second goal) are also behind Manchester United's fifth goal shortly after the break. After fifty-nine minutes and twenty-seven seconds Carrick scores to make it 6–0 with his second pearl of a long shot. This time Carrick torpedos the ball up into the goal corner as if drawn by a ruler. Compared to his first goal, thought has been downgraded and power has taken over; accuracy and balance are still major components.

After further goals from Daniele de Rossi for Roma and Patrice Evra for United the match ends 7–1 to the home side. Both Roma and Manchester United are unrecognisable compared with the match that had been played in Rome just six days earlier. The roles are reversed, and the dynamism and flexibility shown by Roma's offensive at the Stadio Olimpico is now adopted by Manchester United. Wayne Rooney, Ryan Giggs and Cristiano Ronaldo have shown their football intelligence by making full use of the positional freedom given to them by the manager. Their interaction and positional shifts all come together this evening. Ferguson is often criticised for his European line-ups featuring only one striker, especially by those conservative Englishmen for whom a traditional 4–4–2 with three 'flat' units is a God-given gift that cannot be questioned. In particular, Ferguson's use of Rooney on the left wing often arouses amazement. But the match against Roma shows Rooney can be deadly when his starting point is on the left-hand side, just as Giggs uses his experience and overview to swing the baton from his position in the middle. Without question, Giggs is Manchester United's maestro on this historic evening. However, the precondition for the elegant trio's triumphant actions is the presence of three workmen. Smith constantly stresses the Romans central defence with his willingness to run, his aggressive style and physical volume. In the engine room behind them Fletcher is winning balls, while Carrick distributes them. Both players' performances this evening are memorable, Carrick's primarily because of his two goals, Fletcher primarily because of his herculean effort in preventing Roma from playing their own fluid game.

* * *

While the match between Manchester United and Roma is being played out, and the scoreboard glows, memories of another match played forty-one years earlier begins to emerge in my mind. Perhaps these memories emerge to help me? The fact is that I find it difficult to come to terms with what is happening this April evening in 2007 at Old Trafford. I slowly realise, perhaps only after the game or during the days that follow, that I am witnessing a so-called historic event. Historic precisely because it is a watershed, unique and outstanding. Such singular events our intelligence finds hard to understand – that is, to conceptualise (and the concept is, of course, the mind's defence against chaos and the march of time) – since the singular events all represent something never seen before. Our traditional concepts are not sufficient in such cases, but previously experienced events that in certain ways are similar can help our intelligence in its attempt to understand what we have just experienced.

In 1966 Manchester United triumphed 3–2 over Benfica at Old Trafford in the first quarter-final of the European Cup. In the second leg in Lisbon, Busby planned to start carefully. 'We always played a 4–4–2 away from home. Especially in Europe. At home we always played the 4–2–4. But we used to pull the two wingers back', Nobby Stiles says on the DVD *Manchester United: The Official History 1878–2002*. He recounts Busby's instructions: 'The first twenty minutes, play it nice and tight, don't get over-adventurous, keep the ball, pass the ball, keep it. Quiet the crowd. And that was the plan in Benfica. But somebody had forgot to tell George. You know, George just destroyed them, absolutely destroyed them, I mean, that night was when George came of age.' Stiles refers to the performance that many consider to be George Best's best match ever.

More specifically, Stiles refers to the match's opening minutes, where Busby strongly stressed to his players they had to go easy and reduce any willingness to take risks. But as Stiles laconically remarks, that message didn't seem to have been received by Best. When the match was just six minutes in, Best, with a mixture of elegance and fearlessness, attempted to reach a cross from the left. He hit the ball perfectly with his head and directed it in an arc over the keeper and into the opposite corner of the goal. So much for the cautious start. But Busby had not seen the last masterstroke from his jewel, because after thirteen minutes Gregg sent a goal kick into Benfica's half, which Herd headed down at the feet of Best. Best was already in full speed forward when 45 metres from the Portuguese goal he elegantly tamed the drop ball. Because of his pace and his directional taming of the ball, he lost the first opponent, after which he twisted around the next and then with great force and accuracy kicked the ball diagonally past a chanceless keeper and into the opposite corner of the goal. The goal was spectacular, a result of physical strength, technique, and (the forbidden) spirit of adventure.

Benfica had barely kicked off when John Connelly scored to make it 3–0 for United. Benfica, with Eusébio in the team, had dominated Europe at the beginning of the 1960s and had never lost a European home match. However, things were to be even more miserable for 'The Eagles' on this April evening in 1966. After fifty-two minutes the home team did reduce the deficit through a Shay Brennan own goal, but with a quarter left of the match Law tore up the Portuguese central defence with a brilliant deep pass, and the oncoming Crerand could make it 4–1. In many ways Laws's assist to Crerand is similar to Giggs's assist to Smith forty-one years later. In the last minute, Charlton completed a perfect attack he started himself in his own half. After several good combinations the ball was played up to Herd at the edge of Benfica's penalty area. With his back to the goal Herd flicked on the ball with the outside of his right foot to Charlton, who dribbled it into the penalty area. With his favourite left leg he made a feint, which in turn made Benfica's goalkeeper balance to the right. Charlton pulled opposite and finished with his right leg to send the ball into an empty goal and make it 5–1.

Manchester United sent shock waves through most of Europe with their dazzling performance. Just like Ferguson said in connection with the Roma match in 2007, Matt Busby revelled in the 1966 performance, saying the Benfica match was, in his opinion, the club's best performance to date. Foulkes expresses this without any fuss. 'The team was the best team in Europe then. No question. I've never seen a team or played in a team that played as well as United did that night in Lisbon.'

Three days after Manchester United's super match in Lisbon the Italian referee Concetto lo Bello is quoted in the *Daily Mirror* as saying Manchester United, in his opinion, is a better team than the English national team. In the same newspaper the respected sports journalist Peter Wilson wrote in a tribute to Busby: 'Today Busby's Manchester lives up to its name by uniting the best from England, Scotland and Ireland.' Wilson's dream was that a team modelled, guided and inspired by Busby could represent Great Britain in this summer's upcoming World Cup. It might not win, Wilson writes, but it would play the kind of football that the spectators would love to watch. (As most people will know, Alf Ramsey actually led England to its first and only World Cup triumph a few months later, thanks to great performances from Stiles and Charlton. But Ramsey's playing style was severely criticised for being cynical, pragmatic and without flair and elegance.)

The showdown between Benfica and Manchester United was transmitted to an international audience. And this, combined with George Best's magical performance and his Beatles haircut, meant Best, who travelled to Lisbon as a star in the making, returned home a superstar. He was football's first pin-up boy. From the female spectators during the entire match one could hear the cheers 'El Beatle! El Beatle!' The front pages of the English and European newspapers the next day were adorned with a picture of George Best wearing a sombrero hat. The photo supported Best's status as the fifth Beatle, a pop star rather than a football player; the long, tousled hair; the sideburns; the full lips and the white string of teeth with the charming little gap between his front teeth; the bedroom eyes with their irresistible power of attraction. Best, the rogue, resembled a hybrid between Elvis, Jim Morrison and a Beatle: seductive, provocative and slightly decadent, but also still a little innocent.

The Benfica match marked George Best's international breakthrough in the same way that forty-one years later the Roma match marked Cristiano Ronaldo's. They also both wore the magical and iconic number 7. George Best was the first in the club's history to turn number 7 into a special number. After him the number has been worn by players such as Bryan Robson, Eric Cantona and David Beckham. Cristiano Ronaldo was the latest superstar to bear the legendary number.

In addition to this parallel between Best and Ronaldo, the Benfica and Roma matches also resemble each other because they were European Cup matches. Both matches ended with great victories against a tough opponent, and the results made Manchester United's manager describe the respective games as the club's greatest performance during the time that he had been in charge. This parallel emphasises what a so-called historical consciousness and memories of past events can contribute: The awareness of past events and episodes in Manchester United's history can intensify the experience of a contemporary event by (using Gumbrecht's words) making it more complex and polyphonic, while the contemporary event on the other hand can help to recharge our memory and ensure that the contours of the historical events don't fade away.

* * *

2006/07 marked Manchester United's reconquest of the English throne. It may seem a little surprising that United managed to surpass Chelsea, since Mourinho had supplemented his already powerful squad with Michael Ballack, Andrei Shevchenko and John Obi Mikel, while Ferguson had only purchased Carrick, and even said goodbye to both Keane and van Nistelrooy. However, there were two reasons why the championship ended up at Old Trafford and not at Stamford Bridge. The first was that the purchase of Ballack and Shevchenko broke the harmony of Chelsea's system, as Mourinho was forced to change his successful 4-3-3, and Chelsea's new 4-4-2 without players out wide simply didn't work. The second reason was the fact Ferguson's confidence both in his team and in his young players proved to be justified. In particular Rooney and Ronaldo in attack, Carrick in the middle, Ferdinand and Vidic in the defence and the versatile O'Shea, who had a great season. A total of eight Manchester United players were chosen for this year's team in the Premier League, and Cristiano Ronaldo crowned a formidable year by winning the PFA's Player of the Year, PFA's Young Player of the Year and FWA's Player of the Year.

In addition, the season offered one of Ferguson's most inspired and surprising transfer actions, when he secured the thirty-five-year-old Henrik Larsson on a loan deal, which ran from 1 January to 15 March. Larsson was an excellent addition to the team as he was familiar with British football from his many years at Celtic. His football intelligence meant he effortlessly slipped into the team. Larsson's stay was even perfectly timed, as he arrived just after a packed Christmas programme began to bear its marks on forwards such as Rooney, Saha and Solskjær. In thirteen matches Larsson contributed to Manchester United's championship hunt by scoring three goals.

21 May 2008
The red circles come together

On 5 August 2007 the English season was kicked off with a match between Manchester United and Chelsea. The match was the traditional Community Shield and was played at Wembley. The showdown ended 1–1 and was settled after a penalty shoot-out. When the season ended on 21 May 2008 the combatants were once again Manchester United and Chelsea. The match was the final of the Champions League and was played at the Luzhniki Stadium in Moscow. The showdown ended 1–1 and was settled after a penalty shoot-out. The English Championship race, which took place between Wembley and Luzhniki, developed into a duel between Manchester United and Chelsea. In all three cases – the preliminary match, the championship duel and the final match – the Red Devils got the best of it. From start to finish there was thus a clear red circle drawn around 2007/08.

The red colour was intensified by the fact 2008 was the hundredth anniversary of the club's first Championship and the fiftieth anniversary of the Munich disaster. In the stands at Luzhniki Stadium in Moscow on 21 May 2008, fifty years after Busby's young pioneering team was wiped out in Munich in the club's first hunt for a European triumph and forty years after Manchester United first conquered Europe, five of the survivors from Munich were there as living monuments to both Manchester United's tragic history and the club's inextricable ties to the European Cup: Harry Gregg, Bill Foulkes, Kenny Morgan, Albert Scanlon and Bobby Charlton. A victory in Moscow would be a timely tribute to the Busby Babes and an appropriate culmination of a season devoted to the Munich accident.

That the Munich tragedy motivated the Manchester United players during the dramatic final against Chelsea in Moscow can hardly be doubted. After the victory, Alex Ferguson said: 'I said the day before the match we would not let the memory of the Busby Babes down. And fate played its hand even in John Terry slipping. We had a cause and people with causes become difficult people to play against. I think fate was playing its hand today.'

Fate? Others think the victory was pure luck. But whether you swear to fate or luck, the reality is the events and their triumphant outcome once again converged in a beautiful pattern, which not only brought together Manchester United's past and present, but also helped to strengthen the club's mythological dimension. Just like back in 1999, when the club's second European Cup triumph was secured on a night, when Matt Busby would have turned ninety years old.

* * *

Copenhagen. An early Saturday morning in August 2007. I am ready for the long anticipated pilgrimage. Not to Mecca, but to Manchester. To Old Trafford and the 2007/08 season's first Premier League match. The weather in Copenhagen this Saturday morning oozes an almost tropical moisture, and when I arrive in Manchester I immediately feel a similar heat and humidity. It doesn't rain. Which they say it always does in Manchester.

To me, the name 'Old Trafford' is a container of multiple meanings, magical myths and rich reminiscences. If I may suggest that you try for yourself to stay inside the cathedral on a day when it's completely empty, as I did on this Saturday, you will find there is nothing less empty than an empty Old Trafford. Nothing less mute than its empty stands. Right beneath the surface of silence, a wealth of past voices and sounds are struggling to push through, and occasionally they succeed in breaching the armour of the present. Eduardo Galeano's vision of the empty football stadium is that it is a storage room for the memory.

Along one of Old Trafford's sidelines I still sense the contours of Billy Meredith and the grass seems to show imprints of his equilibristic raids. As an echo from Joe Spence's time, you can still hear a weak shout from the stands: 'Give it to Joe!' By one of the penalty spots I can hear Charlie Mitten asking the opponents' goalie where he should place his shot. And there, in the middle of the field, in the very epic space of football, Duncan Edwards's intense presence can be sensed for all eternity, and a little further up the pitch I seem to catch a glimpse of Eric Cantona with his collar turned up and jutting his chest proudly. Down at the other end the net is still fluttering after one of Bobby Charlton's powerful shots from long range, and for a short while the pitch bears traces of George Best's energetic arabesques. And there, right in front of the old player's tunnel in the middle of the stand that faces the railway, was where Bryan Robson, in the company of Ron Atkinson and Martin Edwards on a Saturday in October 1981, was seated when signing his contract. I even feel the aftershocks from the time when Robson's two goals helped beat Barcelona 3-0. Peter Schmeichel's voice also echoes everywhere, and in the midst of all his motivational and inciting roar I suddenly hear a thumping sound when David Beckham hits the ball with the inside of his foot and bends it over the wall and into the net. Down at the Stretford End I can hear Denis Law and Ruud van Nistelrooy still being honoured; but sometimes I also hear a sigh of disappointment, reminding us of Law's relegation-sealing back heel goal against the Red Devils in 1974. However, this sigh is swallowed by an ecstatic roar of exultation, partly due to a Cristiano Ronaldo goal from a free kick and partly due to Wayne Rooney's goal from an overhead scissor-kick goal against Manchester City in February 2011.

A few hours later when I find myself at the newly restored Piccadilly Station in Central Manchester, I immediately notice two well-known faces on the newspaper's front page. One is Carlos Tévez's impertinent Apache mug. It is the day after the Argentinian attacker officially became a Manchester United player after a legally complex and summer-long transfer saga. The other face is Anthony Howard Wilson's. He died on Friday evening at a hospital in Manchester, as cancer got the best of him. Tony Wilson is a legend in Manchester and often credited as the man who, more or less single-handedly, turned an industrial town of decline into a vital cultural metropolis of global significance. Wilson was the host of the 1970s culture and music show *So It Goes*, where he introduced the British public to the Sex Pistols. He is also one of the five founders of Factory Records, co-owner of the legendary nightclub La Haçienda and the man behind bands like Joy Division and Happy Mondays.

Seeing the two faces side by side, it strikes me they in many ways symbolise a condensation of what I want to do with this book on Manchester United. Wilson and Tévez represent the balance between tradition and innovation, between past and present and between Manchester's local roots and the town's global impulses, all of which have a leitmotif throughout this book. And Wilson's death doesn't mean a farewell to traditions and local roots, on the contrary, because in Manchester they recall the city's past in the middle of the present's turmoil and all the expectations of the future.

Twenty-three-year-old Carlos Tévez, who was bought from West Ham, was one of the four new players at Manchester United by the beginning of season 2007/08. The twenty-six-year-old Canadian–English midfielder Owen Hargreaves was signed from Bayern Munich. Twenty-year-old Portuguese winger Nani was captured from Sporting Lisbon. And finally, the nineteen-year-old Brazilian midfielder Anderson was prised away from Porto. The four were bought for a dizzying combined total of £60 million pounds.

First of all, this sent a clear signal that Malcolm Glazer's regime would not lead to a lack of activity on the transfer market, which certain fan fractions had feared. Second, the purchases testified to Alex Ferguson's European ambitions. At the end of the 2006/07 season, Manchester United's squad proved to be too small to be able to compete on three fronts, which the 3–0 defeat at San Siro in Milan and the defeat to Chelsea in the FA Cup final after extra time quite clearly had shown. The bench had been too weak, as they say. With Hargreaves, Anderson, Nani and Tévez in the team, Manchester United possessed double quality in all positions and a considerable variation in terms of player types. Both Hargreaves and Tévez already had great experience on the international scene, while Nani and Anderson were both challenging types, who would be able to make a difference.

Thirdly, the transfer strategy points to Ferguson's preoccupation with making the squad and the club geared for the day that he may choose to step down as manager. All four players were young and could serve Manchester United for many years to come. So, therefore we can conclude that Ferguson, Queiroz and David Gill paid constant attention to the squad's age, and ever since the famous 'cleansing' in 1995, where Ince, Hughes and Kanchelskis had to give way to the Fledglings, Ferguson had been focused on keeping a 'healthy' average age in the squad: an age that on the one hand means future, development and hunger while on the other it guarantees past, experience and routine.

Upon my arrival in Manchester and at Old Trafford in particular I feel immediately the high expectations surrounding this new season. The four new players are a major cause of this, precisely because they represent a mixture of proven quality and unquestionable, if unknown, potential. Another major cause is that Manchester United begins the new season as defending champions. The Championship in 2007 was secured after three ugly and empty years during which the fans had begun to adjust to the fact Chelsea and not Manchester United was the dominant force in England. But the 2007 title – and the beautiful play on the field – had not only raised the atmosphere in and around the club, but had also created a promise of more to come.

* * *

On 12 August 2007, Manchester United open the new Premier League season at home against Reading. A week earlier at Wembley the club had secured the Community Shield against Chelsea after extra time and a penalty shoot-out. The season is therefore kick-started with silverware. On a sunny Sunday 75,655 spectators have turned up at Old Trafford. Prior to the match some of the most well-known songs Tony Wilson co-produced are broadcast over the PA. You can also see a perfect pitch in the most beautiful shade of green. Unfortunately, the Red Devils are not inspired by Wilson's music, the sunshine, the many thousands of fans or the greenness of the grass. The match ends 0–0, and the most significant event occurs shortly before the break, as Wayne Rooney is accidentally injured in a tackle. The verdict is a fracture of a metatarsal bone in his foot and a six-week break.

It was already clear a few months into the season that Manchester United's team was better than the season before. Both media and people inside the club even speculated on whether the Treble was within the team's reach. Rooney and Ronaldo had matured, and Ronaldo in particular showed a terrifying power and a goal-scoring prowess of another world. In addition, the four new players slipped seamlessly into the team and reinforced it in a way no one had expected. Hargreaves, who was intended for a role as anchorman in the midfield, distinguished himself both as right back and in the right of midfield, but he also filled out the role on the centre neatly. Tévez, whom people knew was good, but who many doubted would function with Rooney in attack, took on an almost Cantona-like role, when he scored vital point-winning goals not less than seven times, goals which often fell in the match's final phase. Furthermore, not only did Rooney and Tévez seem to be able to play together, they actually seemed to be made for each other.

As for Nani and Anderson, people knew they had plenty of talent, but for them to actually step into the team and make a difference in their first season was a long call. However, that was precisely what they did. Nani gained more matches than expected, both as a substitute and a starter; and the occasional fall-outs and small faults that were only to be expected of so young a player whose game was founded on taking risks were overshadowed by many excellent performances and decisive actions. Anderson also played a much greater role in the team in his first season, than both the fans, Ferguson, and he himself had expected. And those who believed Manchester United had purchased the new Ronaldinho were in for a surprise, as Anderson wasn't a forward, but rather a herculean, totally unimpressed and technically well founded midfielder, somewhat similar to Dutchman Edgar Davids.

* * *

In the FA Cup's fifth round Manchester United and Arsenal met at the Theatre of Dreams in one of the season's most memorable matches. Scholes, Hargreaves, Giggs, Ronaldo and Tévez were left out of the starting line-up, but Nani, Anderson and Fletcher were impressive. The Red Devils annihilated Arsène Wenger's team 4–0 with two goals by Fletcher, one from Nani and one from Rooney. The defeat – and not least the obvious difference in strength as the match made clear – left Arsenal with deep wounds and in effect inaugurated the decline that led to the London team's derailment in the championship race. Admittedly, Arsenal managed to get back up for a short time to get involved in what otherwise turned into a duel between Manchester United and Chelsea. But once again, it was United that struck the nails into Arsenal's coffin as they defeated Wenger's troops 2–1 at Old Trafford on 13 April 2008 – courtesy of goals from the penalty spot by Ronaldo and a free kick by Hargreaves.

After the vital 2–1 victory over Arsenal and after a point-saving equaliser in stoppage time by Tévez in an away match against Blackburn, three important matches in six days awaited Manchester United. In between two Champions League semi-finals against FC Barcelona, United would meet Chelsea at Stamford Bridge in a match that would crown the Red Devils as champions if they won, but it would also send Chelsea level with United if the reverse happened.

The Nou Camp, 23 April 2008. Less than one minute had been played of the match between Barcelona and Manchester United when the away team were given a penalty kick. Cristiano Ronaldo, the world's most talked about and best footballer, was to take it. But the Portuguese misplaced his shot, and Manchester United missed a golden opportunity to score an important away goal. Barcelona played nicely, but ineffectively, and Ferdinand and Brown in Manchester United's central defence effectively closed down any imminent Catalonian chances. The showdown ended as it started: 0–0.

In an unequivocal declaration of the club's top priority and in acknowledgement that the home match against Barcelona was completely open, Alex Ferguson made a highly controversial decision. He chose to rest some of his key players in the away match against Chelsea. Not that this kind of reshuffle meant a weakening of the team – just think back to the 4–0 massacre of Arsenal in the FA Cup. But the exclusion of many stalwart players, in particular Ronaldo, pointed towards Ferguson's preoccupation of improving Manchester United's European title collection. Chelsea also dominated the first half without seriously threatening United, but just before the break Ballack put the home team in front 1–0.

In the second half United showed more will, but it took a mistake from Ricardo Carvalho before Rooney could equalise for United. Rooney had been injured shortly before and had to be substituted by Ronaldo midway through the second half. A few seconds after his substitution Ronaldo was felled in Chelsea's penalty area by Ballack, but the referee didn't respond to the misconduct. However, his assistant referee, four minutes before time, with the match otherwise destined to end in a tie, made the controversial decision to award Chelsea a penalty when the ball hit Carrick's hand. Once again Ballack scored, and his goal secured Chelsea the victory of 2–1, and brought the thrill back into the Premier League. With two matches left, both teams had 81 points, but Manchester United led with a much better goal difference.

Just six days after the Camp Nou and three days after Stamford Bridge, Manchester United and Barcelona played the return match in the Champions League semi-final. United had to do without both Vidic and Rooney, who were out with injuries, and a little surprisingly this meant a place in the line-up for Park and Nani, who occupied the wide midfield positions. Hargreaves continued to stand in for the now centrally located Brown at right back. Up front Ferguson placed Tévez together with Ronaldo, who in several matches in the season's final phase were used as a striker. In a match that did not offer great goal-scoring opportunities, the absolute peak occurred after fifteen minutes of play when Paul Scholes intercepted a transversal pass from Gianluca Zambrotta just outside of Barcelona's penalty area. Scholes then made two short moves before he cannoned the ball into the opposite corner of the net. The early lead made Manchester United leave most of the initiative to Barcelona in the conviction their defence was solid enough to keep the Catalans from creating chances. The conviction proved correct, for the Red Devils bought a ticket to Moscow with a 1–0 victory.

Two decisive matches in the duel against Chelsea now were in the offing, and their outcome would sort out both the English championship and the Champions League title. In the matches against Barcelona, Manchester United's play had not been as fluid as it had been earlier in the season. The same was the case for the three away matches against Middlesbrough, Blackburn and Chelsea, which had only brought the team two points. With Chelsea's recent victory of 2–1 over United there was speculation about whether the London team had the psychological advantage over United. However, if the play hadn't been dazzling, United's players had at least demonstrated an indisputable winning instinct and determination, both in the Barcelona match and in the three away matches in the league where Rooney and Tévez had secured points with late goals against Middlesbrough and Blackburn, and where the team had only lost one point at Stamford Bridge on the grounds of a dubious penalty award.

All speculation about Manchester United and 'rubber souls' were brushed aside on Saturday 3 May 2008, when they demolished West Ham and won 4–1. As Chelsea defeated Newcastle 2–0 away, the ground for the most dramatic final day of a Premier League season in many years was prepared. In their final match Chelsea played at home against Bolton, while Manchester United met Wigan away. Neither Bolton nor Wigan had anything to play for, but as the match progressed, it became clear they both wanted to put a spanner in the works.

In London a relatively uneventful first half ended without goals. In Wigan, however, all sorts of things happened as three significant refereeing decisions in the first half played a big role in the match's outcome and maybe thus also in the ultimate Championship ranking. The first was the referee's decision not to give Wigan a penalty as the ball hit Ferdinand on the hand. The second was the referee's decision not to give Scholes a second yellow card for a foul on Wigan's Wilson Palacios. The third was the referee's decision to give Manchester United a penalty kick as Rooney, shortly before the half hour, fell in a tussle with Wigan's Emerson Boyce. Ronaldo, who had spurned a penalty at the Nou Camp in Barcelona a few weeks previously, was cold-blooded in sending Wigan's goalkeeper Chris Kirkland the wrong way and thus scored goal number forty-one of the season.

In the second half, Chelsea managed to get in front 1–0 with a goal by Andrei Shevchenko. This meant that the title would end up at Chelsea if Wigan equalised against Manchester United. As the second half proceeded, it was not at all unimaginable, because Wigan played impressively. Ferguson chose to bring on Giggs from the bench in order to bring calmness and experience to an under-pressure Manchester United team. Nine minutes before time the Welshman repaid Ferguson's faith by making it 2–0 for Manchester United in his 758th match – an emulation of Bobby Charlton's club record. Ferguson called it 'fate'. Others would call it 'luck'. The goal sealed the match, and when Bolton simultaneously equalised Chelsea's lead in the dying minutes, Manchester United could be hailed as champions for the second year in a row.

* * *

Luzhniki Stadium in Moscow, Wednesday, 21 May 2008. Oh, what a match! Oh, what a drama! And in the end this apotheosis of beauty culminates in an English version of Russian roulette.

Roman Abramovich, Chelsea owner, has, for a short while at least, returned home. The same can be said of Manchester United's Nemanja Vidic, who had his home here for a few seasons when he played for Spartak Moscow. This cannot be said about many of the other 67,000 people in the stadium. In the weeks leading up to the event UEFA's decision to play the Champions League final in Moscow has been criticised, because so many thousands of supporters had to travel so many thousands of kilometres, but all in all the arrangement went off in a splendid way. There is one thing that is not quite as it should be, though: the pitch. And this turns out to have a significant influence on the outcome.

Alex Ferguson has chosen to line up in an offensive 4–4–2 with a team consisting of six Englishmen, a Dutchman, a Frenchman, a Serb, a Portuguese and an Argentinian (opposite).

The match proves to be far better, more lively and more rich on goal-scoring chances than expected. Often when Manchester United and Chelsea meet the two teams neutralise each other's strengths. Manchester United's art cancels out Chelsea's force and Chelsea's Apollonian virtues tames Manchester United's Dionysian ones in what often develops into a deadly boring trench warfare, or, as they say in German, *Stellungskrieg*. This evening in Moscow something completely different happens. After a cautious first ten minutes it is as if Manchester United's flow, courage and creativity get the upper hand. After twenty-six minutes of play, Ronaldo, with his forty-second goal of the season, puts the Red Devils up 1–0. It is a well-deserved goal. On Manchester United's

right side Wes Brown and Paul Scholes combine nifty one–two combinations, and Brown suddenly gets enough space to deliver a curled pass over towards the back post with his left foot. Here Ronaldo rises above Michael Essien, and with his head he precisely and powerfully directs the ball into the nearest corner of the goal.

The goal falls after a longer period of United dominance, where Rooney and Ronaldo distinguish themselves. The goal only makes Manchester United intensify the pressure. In the thirty-fifth minute, Rooney sends Ronaldo on a run with a great sixty-yard pass. Ronaldo crosses from the left wing into the penalty area where an oncoming Tévez, in a completely free position and just few yards away from the goal, throws himself forward hitting the ball with his forehead. Petr Cech in Chelsea's goal parries the header from Tévez with a reflex safe, but the ball then rolls to the feet of Michael Carrick. In front of a virtually empty goal he sees his drive pushed around one of the posts by Cech. After forty-three minutes of play Tévez is once more millimetres from increasing Manchester United's lead, as he only manages to graze a cross with his boot in front of an otherwise open Chelsea goal.

The play is excellent, and it wouldn't have been undeserved if the Red Devils had led 3–0 or 4–0. The lead, however, is only 1–0, and in the dying seconds before the break Chelsea suddenly strike back with a messy goal. Essien, who until now has been run around by the nose of an effervescent Ronaldo, now does what he does best: drives the ball forward. Thirty-five metres from the goal he fires an opportunistic shot. On its way towards United's goal the ball hits two United defenders and thus changes direction twice, which means, first, that it lands at the feet of Frank Lampard and, second, makes Edwin van der Sar slip a little on the controversial surface. The goal is a bitter pill to swallow for the

Manchester United players, who have dominated the first half completely and even allowed themselves to pass up three obvious scoring chances. Instead of a possible 4–0 it's now level at 1–1.

In the second half the balance of power is turned upside down. Now it's Chelsea's force and will that takes over, strangling any signs of United artistry. In fact, it is as if Chelsea's physical dominance not only neutralises United's flow but at the same time also allows the emergence of Chelsea's own technical qualities; in the same way as when Manchester United's creative dominance before the break not only neutralised Chelsea's physical power, but also allowed the emergence of the Manchester team's own power. Chelsea now control the match and also threaten van der Sar's goal in the process. Twelve minutes before time the Red Devils are lucky when Drogba, with an excellent shot out of nothing, hits the post. The second half is in fact remarkable, because so many players are hit with cramp. After sixty-eight minutes we see Rio Ferdinand prostrate on the pitch, followed by many others, not just because the grass is wet, but also, and more importantly, because it hasn't properly attached itself to the foundation yet.

In the eighty-seventh minute Ryan Giggs writes history as he enters the fray and plays his 759th match for Manchester United, exceeding Bobby Charlton's record. In extra time the match once again changes as Manchester United slowly start to dominate again. This only happens, though, after Lampard, four minutes into time, slams the ball against the underside of the bar. In the eleventh minute it's Ryan Giggs's turn to spurn a big chance, as his shot, seemingly destined for the net, is blocked on the line by John Terry. The last significant event occurs four minutes before time, when Drogba, after a scuffle with Vidic, is shown the red card for punching Vidic in the face.

The final now has to be settled in a penalty shoot-out, and anything can happen. Manchester United win the draw and kick first. Tévez scores for United, then Ballack equalises for Chelsea. Then both Carrick and Belletti score. Next man up is Cristiano Ronaldo. Ronaldo, who had fluffed the important penalty at the Camp Nou, but conversely put away a vital penalty against Wigan. The Portuguese, upon whom everyone's eyes are turned, not just in this moment but all the time, walks up to the spot in deep concentration. The rain pours down, as it has done most of the match. He takes the ball between his hands and brings it up to his mouth to kiss it. The pictures show that he is fully focused. He places the ball on the spot, takes a few steps back and adjusts his run-up. Ronaldo has everything to lose and nothing to gain. For Cech, it's the other way round. Ronaldo now runs to the ball, but stops halfway to tempt a reaction out of Cech. The Portuguese has done this before, but this time his pause seems to last a little too long. It is as if he is stationary for several seconds and you sense his hesitation. Cech is cool, however, and just waits for Ronaldo's kick. As the Portuguese pulls the trigger, Cech throws himself to the right and parries the shot. Ronaldo has missed.

The score is 2–2 during the penalty shoot-out between Manchester United and Chelsea. Cristiano Ronaldo is next to kick.

The trophy is now just a hair's breadth away from the Chelsea players, and it comes even closer, as Lampard scores to make it 3–2. Hargreaves equalises, but Ashley Cole puts Chelsea in front again. Now it's Nani's turn, who had come on as a substitute. If he misses, he pushes the cup into Chelsea's hands. The young Portuguese withstands the great pressure and equalises to make it 4–4. But Chelsea can still ensure the title, if only John Terry manages to score on their last attempt.

I must admit that at this moment I am resigned to a Manchester United defeat. Until now, the match has given the spectators an emotional roller-coaster ride, because of its peculiar rhythm and many peripeteias. But it has also been a display of beautiful football, tactical intelligence and physical intensity. My resignation is not marked by irritation, instead it is what could be termed 'sad happiness': sad because of the impending defeat, happiness as a result of the game's unsurpassed beauty and unique rhythm. I have, in short, surrendered to the idea that Chelsea will win the Champions League, and that it somehow also has been deserved as they in the course of the match, especially in the second half, have played very (and for them unusually) attractive football. In addition there is a certain symbolic beauty in that it is John Terry who holds the key to Chelsea's success. Mr Chelsea, as he is called, is the epitome of the club, but – and in this there is a certain amount of irony – at the same time he is also Chelsea's antithesis.

John Terry is not only the epitome and antithesis of Chelsea, he is also the very embodiment of a winning mentality and a strong psyche. He has a good shot and is a defender who often scores goals. As Terry places the ball on the spot, the world holds its breath. We see him take a few steps back. As he begins his run-up, time suddenly goes faster – in contrast to Ronaldo's run-up where time stood still – because suddenly something unexpected and totally awkward happens that one barely has time to perceive. Terry slips just before he has to kick and, unfortunately for Terry and Chelsea, his shot hits the outside of the post. By the way, it shouldn't have been Terry to take fifth kick. The sent-off Drogba should have. Ferguson calls Terry's slip 'fate'. I call it poetic justice, because did van der Sar not slip at Lampard's equaliser just before the break?

Everything is now open again. Perhaps the momentum is even with Manchester United now. Anderson, at just twenty years old, shows 'that Brazilian mentality' (Ferguson's praise for the Brazilian players' apparent coolness in highly demanding situations) and scores to make it 5–4, and the road to red triumph is almost complete. Kalou equalises for Chelsea, but Ryan Giggs, legend and club record holder of most played matches, shows his experience when he outplaces Cech and scores to make it 6–5. The scene is now set for van der Sar's great moment. As Nicolas Anelka runs to the ball, the shrewd Dutchman reads his shot and parries the ball. The drama is over, and Manchester United have won their third European Cup.

The giants' manager: Alex Ferguson with the Champions League trophy 2008.

The 2007/08 circle has come together as it ends where it began: with a Manchester United triumph over Chelsea, with a 1–1 stalemate, extra time and a penalty shoot-out. But bigger and more mythological circles – 1908/2008, 1958/2008 and 1968/2008 – have also come together. One hundred years after Mangnall and Meredith ensured the club's first championship, fifty years after the Munich disaster and forty years after the club's first European triumph, Manchester United pay a tribute to its past heroes. Both the living heroes who watch from the stands in Moscow, and the ones who have passed away, who see it from the club's pantheon. What they see is perhaps Manchester United's best team ever. Alex Ferguson, for his part at least, declares after the final in Moscow that this third generation of players is his 'best team ever'.

22 August 2011
A new brood of Babes are born

The five years that have passed from the great culmination at the Luzhniki Stadium in May 2008 to the present day, 2013, don't seem for Manchester United's part to contain major changes or historic events compared with those of 1999 and 2008. The manager is, in contrast to clubs like FC Barcelona, Real Madrid, Chelsea and Liverpool, still the same. United have not had any Pep Guardiolas or José Mourinhos coming in and predicting a new era as those two did at Barcelona and Chelsea. The ownership is still the same, and the voices criticising the Glazer family haven't weakened; quite the contrary.

Under this surface of seeming uniformity there are, however, a number of incidents and events that, due to the lack of an obvious culmination or upending episode, fight for the position of the most defining moment. In this chapter I'll try to identify what I think defined Manchester United's history between 2008 and 2013, but since this is also the book's final chapter, I will also look forward and try to outline where Manchester United is going, and identify which challenges the club and the team are facing.

If we look back over the last five years, then we can ask the following questions. Is it the two losing finals to FC Barcelona in 2009 and 2011 that stand out as the defining events? Is it the sale of Ronaldo to Real Madrid for £80 million in the summer of 2009? Is it the humiliating 2–1 defeat to FC Basel in December 2011 (leading to a Champions League exit after the preliminary group stage)? Is it the championships in 2009 and 2011 (where Manchester United emulated and exceeded Liverpool's previous record of eighteen championships)? Is it Wayne Rooney's controversial revelation in the autumn of 2010 that he wished to leave Manchester United? Is it the purchase of Robin van Persie in the summer of 2012 from Arsenal? Or is it the breakthrough for new, young players like Chris Smalling, Tom Cleverley, Danny Welbeck and Phil Jones?

There is no doubt in my mind Rooney's statement was not only endowed with a potential cataclysmic effect inside the United camp (this destructive potential was, however, minimised by his subsequent regret at his words), but also, and especially, carried a symbolic significance of global dimensions. It sent shock waves through the football world (I know it is a cliché, but nonetheless, this is what happened) when a clearly emotionally affected but also collected and soberly summarising Alex Ferguson announced during a press conference on 19 October 2010 that Wayne Rooney did not want to extend his contract with Manchester United. But why react like this, you might ask? Players who do not wish to extend their contract are commonplace in the modern football world. But there are players and clubs . . . and then there is Wayne Rooney and Manchester United.

As to Rooney, he represented for many football fans – before this Tuesday in October 2010 – the last residual of innocence, loyalty and genuine sincerity in a modern football world marked by disloyalty and greed. No ulterior motives, but a pure and simple (childish) joy of the game. In addition, Rooney's roots are deeply entrenched in north-west England's industrial soil, and in a world where everything floats, Rooney had quite simply looked like someone who felt *at home* at Old Trafford during the last six years (and some will even say that in the years before his arrival at Old Trafford he always looked like someone who was destined for that stadium). This is why Rooney's announcement that he wanted a 'divorce' from Manchester United, in my eyes, symbolises football's final fall – not the first fall for those we have seen plenty of in the past, but the ultimate and last fall. From 19 October 2010 we are no longer able to endure any other sins, because on this day the very last remnant of football's innocence was flushed down the drain. Rooney was a last remnant, a relic from a bygone era, and in the future there will never be another Wayne Rooney again. He was standing, like the Busby Babes did it in the 1950s, with one leg in a world of yesterday – a world that is about to disappear (or maybe it's already gone) – and with the other leg in a world of today, a world that erases the past at a furious pace.

As I have already mentioned, one of Manchester United's characteristics is *continuity*. This makes the Red Devils a very special club in relation to other global mega clubs like Real Madrid, Inter Milan and Chelsea. Continuity relates to both the manager's post (Busby's almost twenty-five years, Ferguson's more than twenty-five years), the playing style (an offensive philosophy founded by Busby and continued by Ferguson) and to the squad (the belief in youth means players like Bobby Charlton, Bill Foulkes, Ryan Giggs and Paul Scholes make up long red micro-threads in the club's rich red tapestry). Of course, there are many examples of players whose Old Trafford career wasn't anything more than parenthetical. Think of Garry Birtles, Massimo Taibi and Eric Djemba-Djemba. The point is, however, that these players' careers as Red Devils were short-lived because Manchester United wanted it so. Manchester United is not a club one leaves voluntarily (unless you're named Cristiano Ronaldo), and certainly not if you are an Englishman. As a result of Wayne Rooney's incorruptible character, on one side, and Manchester United's traditions on the other, there had been a consensus in the football world up until October 2010 that Manchester United and Wayne Rooney formed the perfect couple.

Ferguson's announcement concerning Rooney's reluctance to extend his contract and Rooney's own version of the proceedings the day after have, as I see it, consequences on three levels. First, they challenged the idea of the United-continuity. Second, they destroyed the idea of Manchester United as an irresistible magnetic force to English players. Third, they questioned the image of Rooney as an untainted footballer. In the following days the media and fans speculated about what possible motives Rooney could have for wanting to break with Manchester United. Some intimated Rooney had simply tried to achieve the best possible contract by playing hardball. But I don't believe this. Rooney himself explained the club's lack of assurances over both its spending power and its ability to compete had been a worry to him. This explanation achieved a certain resonance among the Glazer-sceptical fans, for whom the American owner has burdened Manchester United with an overwhelming private debt. In this respect, Rooney's statement can be seen as a tactical manoeuvre, its purpose being to persuade the club to come out of the passivity it showed during the summer transfer window in 2010. In this lies potentially a genuine concern about the club's future from Rooney's perspective, something I consider likely, and at the same time it relativises his apparent transformation from uncomplicated working class kid to corrupt footballer.

A further twist in this version is that Ferguson possibly was Rooney's puppeteer. The Scot used Rooney to press the Glazer family into promising more transfer money. I think this completely unlikely though. Rooney's announcement, whether motivated by a genuine concern for the club's future or not, appears as an indirect criticism of Ferguson's long-standing principles to focus on the development of young players; principles that have not only been behind several successful generations of teams, but also behind controversial 'cleansings' in which stars such as Paul Ince, Andrei Kanchelskis, Mark Hughes, David Beckham and Ruud van Nistelrooy have been chucked out of Old Trafford to make room for 'kids'.

So the question is whether Rooney's U-turn just thirty-six hours after Ferguson's historic press conference blots out the intense one and a half day's public separation process and thus cancels out the aforementioned consequences in relation to the club's continuity, the club's magnetism and Rooney's own incorruptness. Not in my eyes. Something broke into pieces. A flirtation with the newly rich neighbour's wife (Manchester City), a love affair with a city-babe

(Chelsea) or with a southern beauty (Real Madrid) cannot be undone. The same can be said of a fling, and especially a *fait accompli* affair, with an escort. And here was perhaps (together with Rooney's agent Paul Stretford and his role as the bad guy working behind the scenes) the real *misère* in all of this.

If we can conclude Rooney's announcement has an enormous symbolic significance – the last remnant of club loyalty and innocence in modern football disappeared on 19 October 2010 (and this in spite of the fact Ferguson and United actually were left as the big winners) – then in the weeks that followed the question remained in what condition the prodigal son would return from his week-long exile in Nike town. Would Rooney end up as the new Norman Whiteside or Paul Gascoigne, whose promising careers were destroyed by problems in their private life? Or would he regain his form from 2009/10 (in which he scored thirty-four goals and almost single-handedly filled up the empty space left by Ronaldo's departure) and meet his immense potential? Posterity has shown that Rooney seems well on the way to meeting his potential, and one of the main reasons is quite simply that he *belongs at* Old Trafford (and thus the infamous thirty-six hours might still be forgotten by some fans for this reason alone). If Rooney's announcement undoubtedly contains a great deal of symbolism in relation to the football world's condition generally, then internally in Manchester United the wounds seem to be healed. Rooney – after a few public apologies and many big matches – is back in the role as the club's culture carrier and Ferguson's alter ego.

* * *

And now another event that in my eyes comes closer to being the truly defining event in the time after Ronaldo and the Champions League victory in 2008 (or rather, and now this chapter turns into a more speculative tone) will come to be considered as such. In ten years, when Manchester United fans in all likelihood will look back at a long period of success because of players like Phil Jones, Chris Smalling, Tom Cleverley and Danny Welbeck, many of them will, I will argue, look back at Monday 22 August 2011 as the day that it all began. This day will undoubtedly be inscribed into the club's history as a legendary date on equal footing with 31 October 1953 and 19 August 1995. But what do these days have in common? The answer is that on each of these three days a brood of Babes was born.

On 31 October 1953 the mythical Busby Babes were born in a match against Huddersfield, when Sir Matt Busby had no less than seven teenagers in his starting line-up. These included Roger Byrne, Duncan Edwards and Dennis Viollet. On 19 August 1995 the unforgettable Fergie's Fledglings were born in a match against Aston Villa, when Sir Alex Ferguson had included five teenagers in the starting line-up and introduced three from the bench – including Paul Scholes, Gary Neville and David Beckham. On 22 August 2011 a third and brand-new brood of Babes was born. It happened in a match against Tottenham, when Ferguson lined up with five teens and five young players, including David de Gea, Edwin van der Sar's young substitute, and the above-mentioned Jones, Smalling, Cleverley and Welbeck. On the bench was the young Mexican comet Javier 'Chicharito' Hernández, who in his first season at the club had managed to relegate Dimitar Berbatov, the £31 million record purchase, to the reserves.

If all three events have in common the fact that a new generation of young Manchester United players was born on these days then there is also a number of differences between them. The match against Huddersfield was played away and ended without any goals. The only thing memorable about the match was Busby's teenage revolution, which, in all fairness was also noted in the English newspapers in the following days – and actually had been noted already in 1951 when the journalist Tom Jackson from the Manchester *Evening News* for the first time introduced the concept of the 'Babes'. It happened in connection with a match against Liverpool, where Jackson, referring to Roger Byrne and Jackie Blanchflower, said that 'United's "Babes" were cool and confident'.

The match against Aston Villa that launched the 1995/96 season was also played away, and here Manchester United actually lost 3–1. Again, the result wasn't especially memorable. But, as I said, it was the introduction of a new generation of players that would come to dominate Manchester United's history to this day. As well as Ferguson's 'baby boom', the match is, however, also remembered for the former Liverpool player Alan Hansen's famous comment: 'You can't win anything with kids.' The comment fell immediately after the match, but the background was not only United's defeat to Villa. Hansen's remark was also a response to Ferguson's controversial decision in the summer of 1995 to get rid of Mark Hughes, Andrei Kanchelskis and Paul Ince. All three had been stars on United's team in the prior seasons. But, given Manchester United's history, not least the role of the Busby Babes, Hansen should have known better. His comment came back to haunt him when United not only won the Championship but also the FA Cup that season.

22 August 2011 differs from the two previous births as the labour pains weren't as long or hard this time. The new babes not only won the match against Tottenham at Old Trafford, they also won the match with style. The result, the play, the birth of new babes: three components that together create mythology. The young team, with an average age of just twenty-three years, demonstrated nice, fluent and creative attacking football. In the defence Smalling, Jones and Evans showed a maturity that was in stark contrast to their young age. Was it a one-off event, you might ask? No it wasn't, because in the following match Ferguson started with the same team, and they sent Arsenal back to London shell-shocked after having been thrashed 8–2, and they followed up with a 5–0 win at Bolton with only two changes to the line-up.

There are of course still a number of issues in relation to the present United team's potential, which only time can answer. To me there are at least five questions with no certain answers: (1) Will David de Gea prove a worthy successor to van der Sar? (2) How will the young team react to adversity? (3) How big a threat will Manchester City develop into in the coming years? (4) Can Manchester United meet the standard set by FC Barcelona in Europe? (5) Who will be and can be Ferguson's successor? The first question relates to the goalkeeping position. Manchester United, after a number of years with safe quality between the poles in form of Edwin van der Sar have now chosen to bet on the twenty-year-old great talent David de Gea. The Spaniard in his first season at Old Trafford made genuine mistakes, but De Gea grew with the task when he replaced an injured Anders Lindegaard in the spring of 2012. He has only gone on from there and both coaches and manager seem optimistic about the future.

The second question is how the team will react when they meet a period of adversity. It's one thing to triumph over Tottenham and Arsenal at Old Trafford in great style but something else to continue the point harvest at, for example, the Stadium of Light and the Britannia Stadium, where the youngsters come up against physically imposing teams who certainly know how to tackle, not to speak of places like Stamford Bridge, Anfield and the Etihad Stadium, where the home teams are both physically and technically strong. Here it is possible the team will get the so-called 'wake-up call'. But on the other hand, if anybody is able to make his team learn from mistakes and adversity, it is Ferguson.

And since we are talking about the Etihad Stadium, we can appropriately move on to the third question mark about this new United team. 2011/12 clearly showed that the top four monopoly of Arsenal, Chelsea, Liverpool and Manchester United that once had been taken for granted, seems to be broken for good. The break happened in 2010, when Tottenham displaced Liverpool from one of the Champions League spots, and it was repeated in the next season, when Manchester City sneaked in on third place. And it is precisely the 'Sky Blues' from Eastlands in Manchester who mark the third question. After Manchester City's thunderous opening of the 2011/12 season, including a 6–1 victory at Old Trafford, the entry phase to the top of English football, which the club began together with the rich Sheikh Mansour in the summer of 2008, was finally completed. This was fully confirmed, when City dramatically (and in true United fashion on top of that) secured the English championship in May 2012 on the final day of the season with two stoppage time goals against Queens Park Rangers.

To me, City will in the coming years be United's fiercest rivals in the battle for the English championship, a greater threat even than Chelsea. Where the latter are in a double transition with a new manager (who since writing this has already been replaced by yet another manager, despite winning the Champions League) and a forthcoming generational change, I think the patience with Roberto Mancini at City has borne fruit (although nobody knows what will happen to him after a possible trophy-less 2012/13 season). The many new players he and his predecessors have brought to the club – and continue to bring to the club – have begun to blend. In short, the team plays like a unit but it also contains the individual pearls that are so essential for great teams. If the first two questions regarding De Gea and the response to adversity don't really constitute obstacles in the short and long term, then Manchester City is definitely an obstacle – at least on a national level. City's lack of experience of being able to navigate simultaneously on a European level and an English once can perhaps offer hope to United. City's obligations and unambiguous ambitions to conquer Europe can interfere with their focus on the English league. A second advantage Manchester United seems to have is the club's mythical history and strong traditions. Manchester City have set a new standard of what is economically possible (in relation to transfer sums and wages, and this despite UEFA's and FIFA's economic fair play-action) with which United simply can't compete, but a player such as Robin van Persie shows that United on certain parameters, such as aura, flamboyant football and history, have a head start compared with City.

Fourth, on an international level FC Barcelona have set a new standard any ambitious football team on the planet must strive to emulate, or rather surpass. The standard was set at Wembley Stadium on 28 May 2011 when a bubbly Barcelona team wiped out Manchester United 3–1 in the Champions League final. The way it happened inevitably reminds us of the final two years earlier, in which the same match rhythm between the very same teams prevailed. United in initial domination, but after around fifteen minutes' play there was an irreversible inversion of the hierarchy. Ferguson himself acknowledged after the match: 'In my time as a manager it is the best team we have faced.' But then immediately a look to the future from the Scot: 'It's not easy but that's the challenge and you shouldn't be afraid of the challenge.' So this is the challenge that drives the seventy-year-old manager – and thus also his team – forward. But is youth the answer to the challenge? Is it realistic that players like Jones, Smalling, Rafael, Powell, Cleverley, Hernandez and Welbeck can challenge Barcelona? My guess is that Barcelona will continue to set the standard in the next couple of years, but give these new Babes a season or two to ripen, and *they* will set new standards and dominate for years to come.

As Ferguson has so correctly argued, football teams come and go in cycles. FC Barcelona's cycle has reached the top and may stay there another year or two but from then on, as you know, there is only one way to go. Manchester United's cycle, however, is only just beginning again.

* * *

This reminds me of the fifth and final unanswered question. It may be that the new United team's cycle has just begun, but Alex Ferguson's time as manager of United is probably soon over. Where to next? Does this collision between Ferguson's impending departure and the new brood's upward curve mean the young players simply won't manage to redeem their potential for the simple reason that no one can replace Ferguson?

As I see it Manchester United have, on the day Sir Alex Ferguson chooses to resign, four different options in the search for the Scot's successor. The first option is to recruit a manager who himself has played for Manchester United, and who has since achieved coaching experience in smaller clubs. It is someone like Steve Bruce, Mark Hughes, Roy Keane or Ole Gunnar Solskjær (who, in his first two seasons as head coach of Molde, won the club's first ever Norwegian championships). Ryan Giggs, who at the time of writing is without coaching experience, could also be an option.

Manchester United could also choose to go internal with one of Alex Ferguson's assistants. At the moment these posts are occupied by Mike Phelan and the Dutchman Rene Meulensteen. The latter could be a qualified guess on a future Manchester United manager. Meulensteen is schooled in a mixture of Dutch (passing game, wing play) and Fergusonian footballing traditions (youth, work ethic), and this cocktail could easily match United's requirements.

The third option is to select a British manager with relative success, and who is not too old. Everton's David Moyes is a good example of the kind of coach I mean. He has shown a solid level of expertise and continuity at Everton over many years and has often been praised by Ferguson. And he is also a Scotsman, and Manchester United, as we know, have had success with Scots earlier in their history. Steve McClaren, who was an assistant of Ferguson when the club won the Treble in 1999 and who since then has, among other things, led Twente to a Dutch championship, is another interesting British name. But from the younger generation of managers, where Tottenham's André Villas-Boas and Molde's Ole Gunnar Solskjær also belong, there is the Northern Irishman Brendan Rodgers. I had him down as a possible and very exciting candidate, but in the meantime he has been employed by Liverpool FC.

Finally there is the possibility the club selects a foreign top manager who has proved he can win titles. Here focus seems to be directed at one person, namely José Mourinho, who doesn't do too much to hide that he would like to see himself as Ferguson's successor. However, I am far from sure this scenario will materialise. The controversies that we saw in the four 'El Clásico' showdowns between Real Madrid and Barcelona in spring 2011 displayed on several levels that Mourinho probably has no future at Old Trafford. The charismatic Portuguese, who I at some point actually considered my top candidate, and also the best candidate, for the post as the next Manchester United manager, not least because of his strength of character, wrote himself off with his scandalous behaviour, which couldn't be further away from English sportsmanship.

As many commentators over the years have pointed out, Mourinho has been a gift to football and I have personally nothing against his so-called arrogance and general sharpness. When it's going well for Mourinho's team then his attributes help to make football more politically incorrect and fascinating. The limit, however, has often been exceeded when things don't go well for Mourinho's team. The Portuguese's trend hasn't only been to express all the possible (and, in particular, impossible) conspiracy theories against him. Even worse, he has often shown an utter disrespect towards colleagues, referees and football. Sir Alex Ferguson is certainly not a choirboy in that respect, especially not when it comes to referees, but he's still basically imbued with an Anglo-Saxon respect for the game and its virtues. He has generally shown much respect for colleagues (of course, he has had his fall outs and controversies with Arsène Wenger and Rafael Benítez through the years), but in contrast to Mourinho, Ferguson doesn't hesitate to praise colleagues of the same age as well as the younger ones.

However, the main reason why Mourinho and Old Trafford will probably never happen is not because of the Portuguese's behaviour and statements – Manchester United's 135-year history is after all pervaded by polemical statements and problematic behaviour – but it's his approach to the game on the field; his football philosophy in other words. I have been in doubt as to whether Mourinho's defensive starting point with risk minimising as the principal component would be an obstacle to his employment at Old Trafford. Previously, I came to the conclusion his title collection sufficiently outweighed his football philosophy's incongruence with Manchester United's traditions as they were founded by Matt Busby after the Second World War and have been continued by Alex Ferguson since 1986. In addition, Manchester United, as several people have noted, have become a little more continental in their approach to the game, a development that began around the turn of the millennium when Alex Ferguson realised the uncompromising (but relatively naive) kind of attacking football with which the club had won the Treble in 1999 no longer could be successfully practised, especially in Europe.

But in spite of the slightly more cynical approach to the game Manchester United have developed under Ferguson in the last decade – and his Portuguese assistant Carlos Queiroz undoubtedly contributed significantly to its foundations – it seems to me that Mourinho's philosophy (despite certain similarities such as the emphasis on collectivism and hard work) is far from the tradition that Manchester United rightly likes to associate themselves with: offensive and fluid attacking football, where a (Celtic-inspired) romantic urge for adventure and risk plays a key role. Under Mourinho, Real Madrid has sometimes played showy and attractive attacking football, both in La Liga and the Champions League, but in the matches against Barcelona in the spring of 2011 Madrid's focus was only about one thing: destruction of the Catalan carousels, and that in spite of the fact they themselves possessed intelligent and eminently good passing players like Xabi Alonso, Gonzalo Higuaín, Cristiano Ronaldo, Kaká and Mesut Özil.

I normally don't belong to the self-righteous faction who only see football's beauty unfolded in attack-oriented teams. To me, it is a great pleasure to see a defence turn away another team's offensive patterns or sudden individual explosions, whether it be through collective organisation (think of Mourinho's Chelsea and Inter Milan in the matches against Barcelona), semi-violent tackles (just think of Berti Vogts, who always went to the line or slightly above) or surgically precise actions (think of Rio Ferdinand, who played more than thirteen matches without committing a single foul).

Discussions about football style and beauty haven't only a tendency to unequivocally valorise the offensive above the defensive, they also have a tendency to overlook the fact that the two trends are not absolute values, but are relative, that is, dependent on one another. Inter's victory over Barcelona in 2010 was beautiful in its own way because everyone knew Barcelona's attacking machine at this time was the most well oiled and well functioning. The same is also applicable in relation to Di Matteo's Chelsea and their semi-final victory over Barcelona in 2012. Barcelona's Champions League triumph over Manchester United in 2009 was beautiful, so incredibly beautiful, because it was known the English at this time possessed the sport's best organisation as well as one of the most dangerous attacking sides (in addition, the victory only became more beautiful by the fact Manchester United, with just a bit of luck, could have led 2–0 after the first ten minutes: the match had thus a unique rhythm where one of the styles – United's more aggressive, physical and vertical style – totally dominated for ten minutes, after which the other – Barcelona's more indirect, patient and horizontal style – presided over the rest of the match). One last example. The beauty of Denmark's semi-final victory over Holland in 1992 did very much lie in the fact that Holland could show a frightening attack, which among others consisted of high-profile players such as Marco van Basten and Ruud Gullit, and also, of course, in the truly enchanting fact that the Danish players arrived in Sweden directly from holiday and the beach and hadn't, like all the other teams, spent weeks in a training camp working on optimisation and risk minimisation. The point is this: without defensive entropic greatness, there is no offensive negentropic greatness, and vice versa.

The four 'El Clásico' showdowns in spring 2011, and in particular the first semi-final in the Champions League at Santiago Bernabéu, however, showed such a destructive Real Madrid team that all talk about 'beautiful' defence, for example organisational discipline, physical semi-violence, surgical precision, would quite simply be inappropriate. It was not hard to see what Mourinho wanted. Nevertheless, he had been successful with his tactics against Barcelona in 2010 when he was head of Inter, just as he had been tactically successful, but not successful in terms of result, when he was head of Chelsea and faced the Catalans with a similar Catenaccio-like tactics). In addition, Real Madrid's 5–0 League defeat to Barcelona in autumn 2010 undoubtedly played a role in Mourinho's preparations for the four 'El Clásica'. But the impression one was left with after the first semi-final at the Bernabéu was of an unusually dirty anti-football approach: both before, during and after the match; both on and off the field; and both verbally and in a football-playing respect. Of course, Mourinho and Real Madrid were not alone in contributing to this scenario, but they were largely responsible.

And when Cristiano Ronaldo immediately after the match indirectly criticised Mourinho by expressing frustration over playing in such a defensive team, didn't he also then suggest a fundamental difference between Real Madrid and Manchester United, or perhaps rather between José Mourinho and Alex Ferguson? Yes, that was exactly what he did, and that difference, as I see it, is simply too large to let Mourinho's wish to be Ferguson's successor be fulfilled. His inheritor he certainly will never be.

My speculation as to who will replace Ferguson is, at the end, unresolved. Not only because it is hard to imagine *who* Manchester United can replace him with, but also because it is fundamentally difficult to imagine Manchester United without him. But we must remember that in Manchester United's turbulent and tragic history, no person has ever been bigger than the club. This applies as much to Ernest Mangnall and Matt Busby as it does to George Best and Alex Ferguson. Ferguson will undoubtedly leave a gap, and it will undoubtedly be impossible for his successor to live up to his legacy. It is inconceivable that one manager again will manage Manchester United for a quarter of a century, and the United fans will have to adjust to less continuity and a higher frequency of managerial changes, as they are accustomed to in other big clubs.

Sir Alex Ferguson has in the last years been busy future-proofing his team, so he can leave a competitive team with a potential to develop and a healthy mix of British and foreign qualities to his successor. He has done this by investing in and believing in his young players like Rooney, Nani, Hernández, Anderson and Fletcher, but also in the next generation of players such as Welbeck, the da Silva brothers, Smalling, De Gea, Cleverley and Jones. The major question is how this generation will react to any new manager.

Does Manchester United have the courage to believe in an untried name, whose football philosophy matches the club's culture, like they did in 1986, when Ferguson arrived from Aberdeen (admittedly, he'd already won major trophies in Scotland and Europe)? Ferguson himself has said football and the large clubs, including Manchester United, have changed so much since 1986 it today requires experience, and experience of large clubs, to run a massive club like Manchester United.

If you are to point out one name who has both experience and the right philosophy, then it must be Pep Guardiola. He was for a number of years an epitome of FC Barcelona and its culture (which not only reminds us of United in terms of footballing philosophy, but also in its commitment to youth and its regional revolt against the capital city). But Guardiola is on the other hand also a declared 'independent' – he never ties himself to a club for more than one year at a time. This would suggest there is a real possibility Guardiola one day might be found in the manager's seat at Old Trafford – his recent appointment by Bayern Munich is thus not an obstacle in the long run.

The inevitable managerial change should perhaps not create so many worry lines, even though the traces from Busby's retirement are still serving as a reminder of what can go wrong. As a United fan one must console oneself with the phoenix embedded in Manchester United's DNA, as this symbol precisely points out that the club will always rise again, be it after burning defeats, gap-leaving departures, or, worst-case scenario, dramatically destructive events.

Acknowledgements

A special thanks to Morten Langager for infectious enthusiasm and unwavering confidence in critical times; (there is only one) Tom Jensen for fulfilling the role as 'ideal reader' and for sharing his impressions from Luzhniki with me; Henrik Kragh (the midfielder that never has tackled) for critical input and 'brotherly' confidence; Mads Stougård Kristiansen for insightful discussions and atmospheric insights; Erik Petersen (the father-in-law) for linguistic advice in relation to target group; Anders Fogh Jensen (the philosopher) for critique and praise; Kim Bengtsson (AaB) for idiosyncratic, but never unimportant or boring views; Andreas Mark Baden for encouragement and valuable advice; Svend Ploug Johansen for shared experiences at the Lindum stadium; Bo Kampmann Walther (Madridista) for showing the way and for priceless conversations; Sepp Gumbrecht (the melancholiac) for more than words can express (although none of us never seem to be short of words in each other's company); Thomas Rasmussen for editorial sharp eyes and empathy, and, not least, for the Danish title. A special thank to Helge Conradsen, Christian Fahnøe, Casper Heiselberg, Arne Madsen, Michael Nielsen and Jakob Rasmussen for their efforts to spot factual errors in the book's first circulation, and for their positive reception of the Danish version of the book. Finally a big thank you to Kirsty Schaper, Sarah Cole and Bloomsbury Publishing for believing in the book in a global context.

Bibliography

Books

Andrews, David L. (ed.). *Manchester United: A Thematic Study*. Oxfordshire: Routledge, 2004.

Andrews, David L. 'Introduction: situating Manchester United plc'. In David L. Andrews (ed.). *Manchester United: A Thematic Study*. Abingdon: Routledge, 2004.

Barthes, Roland. *Mythologies* (1957). New York: Farrar, Straus & Giroux, 1972.

Blundell, Justin. *Back From the Brink: The Untold Story of Manchester United in the Depression Years 1919–1932*. Manchester: Empire Publications, 2006.

Bohrer, Karl Heinz. *Plötzlichkeit*. Frankfurt am Main: Suhrkamp, 1981.

Bohrer, Karl Heinz. 'Wembley. De smukke taberes eftermæle' (1974). In Peter Christensen & Frederik Stjernfelt (ed.). *Fodbold! Forfattere om fænomenenet fodbold*. Copenhagen: Gyldendal, 2002.

Christensen, Peter & Frederik Stjernfelt (ed.). *Fodbold! Forfattere om fænomenenet fodbold*. Copenhagen: Gyldendal, 2002.

Connor, Jeff. *The Lost Babes: Manchester United and the Forgotten Victims of Munich*. London: HarperSport, 2006.

Crick, Michael & David Smith. *Manchester United: The Betrayal of a Legend*. London: Pelham Books, 1989.

Defoe, Daniel. *A Tour Through the Whole Island of Great Britain* (1724–27). New Haven, Conn.: Yale University Press, 1991.

Delaney, Shelagh. *A Taste of Honey* (1958). London: Eyre Methuen, 1959.

Dunphy, Eamon. *A Strange Kind of Glory: Sir Matt Busby and Manchester United*. London: William Heinemann, 1991.

Ferris, Ken. *Manchester United: Tragedy, Destiny and History*. Edinburgh: Mainstream Publishing, 2001.

Fontenelle, Bernard le Bovier de. *Nouveaux dialogues des morts* (1683). Paris: M. Didier, 1971.

Galeano, Eduardo. *Soccer in Sun and Shadow* (1988). London: Verso, 2003.

Glanville, Rick. *Sir Matt Busby: A Tribute*. London: Virgin Publishing, 1994.

Goldblatt, David. *The Ball is Round: A Global History of Football*. London: Penguin, 2006.

Greenwood, Walter. *Love on the Dole* (1933). Harmondsworth: Penguin, 1986.

Gumbrecht, Hans Ulrich. *In Praise of Athletic Beauty*. Cambridge, Mass.: Harvard University Press, 2006.

Gumbrecht, Hans Ulrich. 'Spiel mit Stil'. In *Cicero: Magazin für politische Kultur*, March 2006.

Hopcraft, Arthur. *The Football Man: People and Passions in Soccer* (1968). London: Aurum, 2006.

Hough, Ian. *Perry Boys: The Casual Gangs of Manchester and Salford*. Preston: Milo Books, 2007.

Kelly, Ned. *Manchester United: The Untold Story*. London: Michael O'Mara Books, 2003.

Kleist, Heinrich von. 'On the Marionette Theatre' (1810). Trans. Thomas Neumiller. *The Drama Review* 16:3 (1972): 22–26.

Liversedge, Stan. *Not Just Another Club*. London: Janus Publishing Company, 1996.

Maconie, Stuart. *Pies and Prejudice: In Search of the North*. London: Ebury Press, 2007.

Marcus, Steven. *Engels, Manchester, and the Working Class*. London: Weidenfeld and Nicolson, 1974.

Mellor, Gavin. 'The rise of the Reds: An historical analysis of Manchester United as a "super-club"'. In *Singer & Friedländer Football Review 1999–00 Season*. London: Singer & Friedländer, 2000.

Mellor, Gavin. '"We hate the Manchester Club like poison": the Munich disaster and the socio-historical development of Manchester United as a loathed football club'. In David L. Andrews (ed.). *Manchester United: A Thematic Study*. Abingdon: Routledge, 2004.

Murphy, Alex. *The Official Illustrated History of Manchester United 1878–2006*. London: Orion Books, 2006.

Nexø, Martin Andersen. *Soldage* (1903). Copenhagen: Borgen, 1995.

O'Neill, Tony. *Red Army General: Leading Britain's Biggest Hooligan Firm*. Preston: Milo Books, 2004.

Osborne, John. *Look Back in Anger* (1956). London: Faber and Faber, 1965.

Roberts, Robert. *The Classic Slum: Salford Life in the First Quarter of the Century* (1971). London: Penguin, 1990.

Rosaaen, Kirsten & John Amis. 'From the Busby Babes to the Theatre of Dreams: image, reputation and the rise of Manchester United'. In David L. Andrews (ed.). *Manchester United: A Thematic Study*. Abingdon: Routledge, 2004.

Schmeichel, Peter. *The Great Peter*. Copenhagen: Børsens Forlag, 1999.

Sebald, W.G. *The Emigrants* (1992). Trans. Michael Hulse. London: Harvill Press, 1996.

Vargas Llosa, Mario. 'The empty pleasure'. In John Turnbull, Thom Satterlee & Alon Raab (eds.). *The Global Game: Writers on Soccer*. Lincoln Neb.: University of Nebraska Press, 2008.

Vialli, Gianluca & Gabriele Marcotti. *The Italian Job: A Journey To the Heart of Two Great Footballing Cultures*. London: Bantam Press, 2006.

Wagg, Stephen. 'The team that wouldn't die: on the mystique of Matt Busby and Manchester United'. In David L. Andrews (ed.). *Manchester United: A Thematic Study*. Abingdon: Routledge, 2004.

Whelan, Tony. *The Birth of the Babes: Manchester United Youth Policy 1950–1957*. Manchester: Empire Publications, 2005.

Web

www.manutd.com (club's official website)

www.stretfordend.co.uk (fansite, statistics)

www.oldtrafford.dk (Danish fansite)

www.thebusbybabes.com (Busby Babes and the Munich disaster)

www.munich58.co.uk (memorial page for the Busby Babes)

www.spartacus.schoolnet.co.uk/FmanchesterU.htm (about Man Utd 1878–1912)

www.arnemadsen.dk (private fansite)

Film

Manchester United Official History 1878–2002, (2002).

Manchester United Season Review, (1992/93–2006/07).

The Busby Babes: End of a Dream, (1998).

Surviving Disaster: Munich Air Crash, (2006).

Music Made in Manchester (2002).

Orfeu Negro (1959) by Marcel Camus.

A Taste of Honey (1961) by Tony Richardson.

Trainspotting (1996) by Danny Boyle.

Look Back in Anger (1958) by Tony Richardson.

Olympia 1: Fest der Völker (1938) by Leni Riefenstahl.

Olympia 2: Fest der Schönheit (1938) by Leni Riefenstahl.

24 Hour Party People (2002) by Michael Winterbottom.

Control (2007) by Anton Corbijn.

Index